ANTITRUST AND THE BOUNDS OF POWER – 25 YEARS ON

This collection of essays addresses the transformations ongoing in the field of competition law by analysing current developments through the prism of Giuliano Amato's *Antitrust and the Bounds of Power* – thereby building an intellectual bridge between past and present.

Giuliano Amato's book, Antitrust and the Bounds of Power: The Dilemma of Liberal Democracy in the History of the Market was published by Hart in 1997. It has predicted, articulated, and explained many of the changes that have taken place in competition law in the last 25 years, and it is referred to by generations of competition lawyers as a key theoretical work.

There are many mutually invigorating reasons and explanations for the paradigmatic transformations that have occurred in competition law, economics, and policy since the 1990s. Some are triggered by the internal evolution of competition law; others are determined by the broader societal context. In this book, leading competition law thinkers reflect on these metamorphoses; they explore the state of affairs in the field, connecting it with and advancing their analyses through the ideas developed by Giuliano Amato in his ground-breaking book.

With a foreword by Frédéric Jenny and an afterword by Giuliano Amato, this book is essential reading for anyone interested in the evolution of competition law.

Antitrust and the Bounds of Power – 25 Years On

Edited by
Oles Andriychuk

•HART•
OXFORD • LONDON • NEW YORK • NEW DELHI • SYDNEY

HART PUBLISHING

Bloomsbury Publishing Plc

Kemp House, Chawley Park, Cumnor Hill, Oxford, OX2 9PH, UK

1385 Broadway, New York, NY 10018, USA

29 Earlsfort Terrace, Dublin 2, Ireland

First published in Great Britain 2023

A catalogue record for this book is available from the British Library.

A catalogue record for this book is available from the Library of Congress.

Library of Congress Control Number: 2022946179

ISBN: HB: 978-1-50996-213-6
ePDF: 978-1-50996-215-0
ePub: 978-1-50996-214-3

Typeset by Compuscript Ltd, Shannon

FOREWORD

Giuliano Amato became President of the Autorita' Garante della Concorrenza e del Mercato in November 1994. His appointment came as a surprise to some. He was known both as a professor of constitutional law and as a very successful Italian politician who had held a number of ministerial positions, and had been President of the Council of Ministers of Italy (the equivalent of prime minister) from 1992 to 1993. This background did not obviously seem to be the most conducive to chairing a still relatively unknown and young institution.

But Giuliano Amato had a long-standing interest in exploring the frontiers between private power and public power in liberal democracies, a topic which he had written about in the early years of his academic career, and he saw competition law as one of these frontiers.

Under his leadership, the Autorita' Garante della Concorrenza e del Mercato became a highly respected institution both nationally and internationally, and Giuliano Amato was soon recognised in the international competition community as one of the most prominent and creative thinkers about the nature, the goals and the development of antitrust and competition law.

Besides his success at anchoring the Autorita' Garante della Concorrenza e del Mercato as a prestigious institution, he had the depth of vision and the wisdom to steer the institution away from a purely legalistic approach to competition law and to promote a more economic approach without falling into the trap of the Chicago school economists, prone to consider that market theory provided the only valid justification of competition law and that economic analysis was the only key needed to implement it.

Elaborating on his perspective and drawing on his scholarship as a Constitutional expert, on his experience as the head of a competition authority and on his knowledge of the US (where he had studied) 25 years ago, Giuliano Amato published *Antitrust and the Bounds of Power*, a deeply penetrating book comparing the way the US and Europe delineate private economic power and public economic power.

The crucial element of his analysis is that the freedom of individuals to trade can lead private power to infringe not only on the economic freedom of others but also on the integrity of public decision and that, consequently, there is a need in a liberal democratic society to protect society both against illegitimate individual power and against illegitimate public power. The function of competition or antitrust law is then to set the economic boundaries for both private and public power.

Whereas, according to Giuliano Amato, both European competition law and US antitrust law are historically based on a concern that private economic power could both infringe on the economic freedom of others and corrupt political power, the solutions used to meet this concern differ through different interpretations of the concept of efficiency.

As he puts it:

> The truth is there is no single concept of economic efficiency: there are at least two, and their antitrust implications are in the main different. For those who understand it solely and exclusively as non-restriction of the output, almost all the 'per se' illegalities, including price-fixing – might confidently be let drop, since it is better to verify from case to case whether the behaviour challenged leads to inefficiency, that is to those restrictions or not; and if it does not, it is needlessly 'intrusive' to prevent it. For those who instead see it as the maximum possible opening of markets, the 'per se' illegalities retain their significance, since they preserve that opening by keeping the likelihood of new access and more intense competitive dynamics higher. (…) The former protect competition and not competitors, consumers and not weaker firms. The second think that to protect competition ignoring existing competitors may destroy competition itself and therefore maintain the old 'right to sell', the right not to be shut down unless justified, under the protection of special responsibilities" upon dominant firms).
>
> As we can see, two different antitrust perspectives emerge from the two versions, and the difference always, and significantly, leads to the same aspect. The first is antitrust law that delays intervention to the last, leaving the market to provide as far as possible by itself for a definition of its own dynamics and its own equilibria: only imminent risk, with no alternatives of output restriction, justifies and permits intervention. The second is antitrust law that seeks to prevent that risk from emerging and inserts itself more frequently and earlier into ongoing market dynamics, seeking to influence their structure. The first in other words sets the boundary of public power as far ahead as possible, accepting the risk of private power; the second does not accept that risk and instead more runs the risk of preventive intrusion by public power.

Twenty-five years after Giuliano Amato's perceptive and enlightened discussion of the relationship between liberal democracy and antitrust, his analysis of the nature of antitrust and competition law has lost none of its strength or its relevance.

The recent neo-Brandeisian criticism of antitrust in the US is based on two main arguments regarding economic power. First, empirically, antitrust has not prevented a dramatic increase in inequality, an increase in concentration and profit margins, and a meteoric increase in the private economic power of large firms notably (but not exclusively) in the digital world where large platforms are able to exert an undue and often hidden influence on the political decision-making process. Second, analytically, the growing reliance of courts and competition authorities in the US on a narrowly construed consumer welfare standard has focused antitrust law enforcement on the consideration of the acquisition and the use of market power rather than on the acquisition and use of economic power, as was the political intention of its fathers.

This questioning of the goals and the substantive standards of antitrust and of its effectiveness, which has become a highly charged political issue in the US and gives rise to a less politically charged but lively technocratic debate in Europe on the respective role of competition law enforcement and ex ante regulations, is all the more striking in that at least until the end of the first decade of the 21st century, there was a consensus among the competition community to disregard the constitutional and political history of antitrust and competition and to converge towards a narrow economic approach in antitrust and competition law enforcement.

The fact that Giuliano Amato's book, written a quarter of a century ago, is key to our reflection on the current debate is a testimony to both the depth of his analysis and to the enduring necessity to periodically reconsider the delicate balance between private and public powers in light of our initial goals, our past experience and the technological and economic evolution of our economies.

Frédéric Jenny

CONTENTS

Foreword v
List of Contributors xi

1. *Introduction: The Dilemma of Liberal Democracy in the History of the Market: A New Look* 1
   Oles Andriychuk

PART I
COMPETITION POLICY: NEW WORLD? NEW MISSION?

2. *Antitrust and the Rebound of Power: Reimagining Antitrust Cosmopolitanism* 25
   Eleanor M Fox

3. *Ensuring Market and State Accountability: The Private–Public Distinction in the EU Internal Market* 33
   Miguel Poiares Maduro

4. *The Boundaries of Antitrust in the European Union* 51
   Giorgio Monti

PART II
COMPETITION LAW ENFORCEMENT

5. *'Consumer Welfare' and the EU Courts: An Unexpected Refuge for a Persecuted Concept?* 73
   Assimakis Komninos

6. *Antitrust and the Golden Thread: Balancing the Presumption of Innocence with the Public Interest in Competition Enforcement* 87
   Niamh Dunne

7. *Procompetitive Effects in EU Competition Law* 117
   Stavros Makris

PART III
THE CONCEPT OF POWER

8. *Preserving the Bounds of Power: The Narrow Path to a Future-Proof Competition Policy*.......167
Ginevra Bruzzone

9. *Digital Antitrust and Private Powers: The (Uneasy) Case of Marketplace Platforms*.......191
Roberto Pardolesi

10. *Revisiting the Concept of Power in the Digital Era*.......209
Anna Gerbrandy

11. *Afterword*.......225
Giuliano Amato

Index.......231

LIST OF CONTRIBUTORS

Giuliano Amato, Professor, President of the Constitutional Court of Italy, Rome, Italy.

Oles Andriychuk, Professor, Newcastle University, UK; Digital Markets Research Hub.

Ginevra Bruzzone, Professor, LUISS School of European Political Economy, Rome, Italy.

Niamh Dunne, Associate Professor, London School of Economics, London, UK

Eleanor M Fox, Professor, New York University School of Law, New York, USA.

Anna Gerbrandy, Professor, Utrecht University, the Netherlands.

Frédéric Jenny, Professor, ESSEC Business School; Chairman, OECD Competition Committee, Paris, France.

Assimakis Komninos, Partner, White & Case LLP, Brussels, Belgium.

Miguel Poiares Maduro, Professor, Católica Global School of Law, Lisbon, Portugal; European University Institute, Florence, Italy.

Stavros Makris, Lecturer, University of Glasgow, UK.

Giorgio Monti, Professor, University of Tilburg School of Law, the Netherlands.

Roberto Pardolesi, Professor, LUISS School of European Political Economy, Rome, Italy.

1

Introduction

The Dilemma of Liberal Democracy in the History of the Market: A New Look

OLES ANDRIYCHUK[1]

The publication of Giuliano Amato's book, *Antitrust and the Bounds of Power: The Dilemma of Liberal Democracy in the History of the Market*,[2] marks one of the most significant milestones in the evolution of the theory and practice of competition law, economics and policy. Focusing substantively on two central antitrust jurisdictions – the EU and the US – the book articulates and answers questions representing the core of the global theoretical discussions on the function of competition law, and its role in the broader constellation of societal values and liberal democratic governance.

The main dilemma of liberal democracy is formulated by Amato as follows:

> How can private power be prevented from becoming a threat to the freedoms of others? But at the same time, how can power conferred on institutions for this purpose be prevented from itself enlarging to the point of destroying the very freedoms it ought to protect?[3]

This volume offers thoughts and reflections of impactful antitrust thinkers, discussing in various ways this conundrum.

The book by Professor Amato was published precisely a quarter of a century ago. This jubilee occasion allows – and indeed invites – us to re-examine these eternal, quintessential elements of the theory of antitrust through the prism of the 1997 text.

Admittedly, the time of writing the book was characterised by the apotheosis (and thus by the beginning of decline) of three concurrent periods: (i) the

[1] Prof Oles Andriychuk, Newcastle University Law School, Digital Markets Research Hub, @oandriychuk1.

[2] G Amato, *Antitrust and the Bounds of Power: The Dilemma of Liberal Democracy in the History of the Market* (Hart Publishing, 1997).

[3] ibid.

professional period of EU antitrust law when the axiomatic and formulaic legalism was challenged by a 'fresh wind' of a more economic approach; (ii) the ideological period of the End of History and (iii) the institutional period of the EU constitutionalism and federalisation.

All three external contexts have predetermined many ideas of the book and, conversely, the book has contributed to shaping all the three existential conditions within which it was written.

As far as the first – professional – antitrust period is concerned, the voice of dissatisfaction with legal formalism in antitrust was already established and robust in the US, and gradually gained momentum in Europe. While acknowledging and explicating the shortcomings of the rule-oriented competition policy, and while being cautiously optimistic about the emerging, more economic approach, the book also makes it clear that the legal and economic arms of antitrust should go hand in hand. The latest developments in the area also demonstrate that without the common denominator of liberal democratic governance, each of the technical hands of antitrust risks mutating into a casuistic, axiomatic self-centred intellectual autarky – be it the autarky of economics or the autarky of law. Starting with observing the increasing technicalisation of antitrust law, the book warns about the similar excessive reliance on economic technicalities. In the 2020s, the discussions about the theoretical foundations of competition policy still attempt to reconfigure the central epistemic elements of antitrust precisely along these very lines.

As to the second period, Amato remarkably notes, back in the 1990s, that the dilemma of liberal democracy can never be solved by simply constraining private power – 'the idea, foreign to liberal society and yet enthusiastically accepted by many throughout this century, of simply eliminating economic freedom so as, a priori, to prevent it degenerating into power'.[4] In the period of the End of History, this was self-evident. Much less so today, when different forms of neo-authoritarianism revive rapidly, exploiting successfully in hybrid proportions various fruits and achievements of liberal democracy, picking selectively the elements which work for them and ignoring others, blending them with the robust non-democratic components of authoritarian governance, undermining thereby the beliefs in universality and linear evolution of liberal democracy. Global antitrust proselytism was seen in the 1990s deterministically, as an unavoidable and only possible way of standardisation and unification. Today, we see how diverse and fragmented the interpretation and enforcement of the same basic antitrust principles could be if applied in jurisdictions with different understandings of the relationship between the public and the private. The façade of common origins of antitrust unites various cultures and civilisations, demonstrating how diverse competition policy could be. This façade however also provides a shelter to various types of authoritarian governments, which use the vocabulary and apparatus of antitrust for continuing their practices

[4] ibid.

in new forms, exploiting selectively and reinterpreting opportunistically the well-known democratic names and terms.

Finally, the third period – the period of apotheosis of the federalist ideas of EU – was also very different to the situation we experience in the 2020s. The spirit of enlargement and the ethos of the European Constitution was gradually overshadowed by the spirit of nationalism, parochialism and populism. New geopolitical realities also raise a number of challenges requiring the EU to shape new, fresh and often very brave narratives and actions.

Despite these and various other tectonic differences, contrasting the 1990s from the 2020s, there are more similarities and continuities between the periods than there are shifts and disconnections. The evolution of antitrust theory is mainly designed and pursuit by policymakers – but then it is always being disciplined and cooled off by the courts. The former can be more flexible and move from one grand vision to the other. The latter will always be more conservative, maintaining the stability and continuity of the system. Remarkably, at times of the emergence of a more economic approach, the jurisprudence of EU Courts was more legalistic and form-oriented – not least precisely due to the stable continuity mission of the courts. These days, when the policy goals, tools and agenda appear to be shifting away from the categorical axiomaticity of the economic analysis of law, the courts again impel the enforcers to be more consistent – but this time more and more with the economics and evidence-focused empiricism. This volume offers a number of deep insights based on the scrupulous analysis of competition case law, demonstrating the paramount importance of the judicial reading, interpretation and adjudication on various elements of antitrust theory and practice.

Professor Amato begins his book by stating 'I am writing these candid pages for young people embarking on an immersion in antitrust law, so that, as they become specialists, they will still remain aware of the general issues they ought always to bear in mind'.[5] Antitrust is a unique field, known not only for the deepest interpenetration of legal and economic discourses and reasoning. It also combines inextricably the professional technicalities of economics and law with first-order political thinking about the institutional structure of liberal democracy, its normative goals and principles, its challenges and dilemmas. The book captures and formulates these links, making policymakers aware of the important systemic features of the legal and economic sides of profession, while keeping the experts mindful of the broader task of antitrust, thereby preventing the mechanistic application of legal rules and economic models, not letting them to mutate into a canonical dogmatism of technocracy, and allowing them to 'continue to find their roots in the great political and philosophical options with which antitrust law still remains bound up'.[6]

[5] ibid.
[6] ibid.

The dilemmatic nature of the evolution of antitrust thinking implies concurrent existence of various methodological approaches. They are not mutually exclusive – but are often incommensurable. Amato notes in this regard that the

> certainty of the technicians, especially the economists, that the side they take is determined exclusively by the superior validity of the economic analysis … is bound to break against the conscious candour of those in institutional roles who openly take their side … the underlying motives for a choice … spring not from the clash of opposing economic doctrines but from the whole set of values and complex reasons that lead each of us to take this side or that in the dilemma of liberal democracy.[7]

In terms of its substantive content, Amato's book offers a thoughtful excursion into the history of antitrust law in the US and EU. It begins with providing an explication of two concurrent discourses of competition and restraints on trade: the economic discourse focused on the negative implications on supply and demand; and the common law discourse focused of freedom of contract. The latter also inadvertently represents the gist of the dilemma as the freedom of contract can be simultaneously seen as freedom *to restrain* and freedom *from restraints*.

Then Amato offers a retrospective analysis of selected legislation and case law, explored through the prism of the overarching narrative of the book. This part is divided into two chapters, analysing the Harvard and Chicago periods respectively, noting that it is 'always hard to reconstruct the channels, if they really exist, that link the formation of new doctrines, especially those with a high theoretical content, with the evolution of the circumstances they can be applied to'.[8] He further observes that the US antitrust mechanism is becoming increasingly subtle and nuanced, requiring more analytical support.

The next part deals with EU competition policy, starting with a chapter on Europe's industrial culture and an opening observation that the European antitrust history has a radically different development. The main explanation of the difference is that unlike the US, Europe consists of substantially different nations with fundamentally different regulatory cultures (indeed, civilisations), philosophies, ideologies and backgrounds. The chapter traces the Ordoliberal roots of EU antitrust law, economics and policy, demonstrating that the key formal and substantive elements of EU competition policy are based on the ideas developed in Ordoliberal circles. The book shows that the Ordoliberal postulates were not consensually welcomed, explaining the elements and stakes of the discussions taking place on the eve of the adoption of EU competition rules. Additionally, the EU antitrust was also circumscribed by the elements of inter-state competition (hence, the emergence of the mechanism of State aid control and limitation of services of general economic interest, exclusive and special rights, public or 'inherited' monopolies and similar hybrid public-private elements of market economy).

[7] ibid.
[8] ibid.

A significant proportion of Amato's book is dedicated to a comparative analysis of unilateral conduct, regulation of the power of public monopolies as well as merger control. In discussing the latter Amato inter alia stresses the importance of the elements of the participatory antitrust – the concept so commonly used these days.

The last part of the book puts together the threads shaped in the previous chapters. One of the main conclusions of the book is that despite numerous substantive and procedural differences, 'over the decades, the border marked in antitrust law to prevent transgression on economic freedom has been undoubtedly shifting forward'.[9] The chapters of this book make it clear that the trend continues.

Remarkably, Amato concludes that it would be wrong to expect that the purified vision of antitrust would eliminate uncertainties and disagreements – warning that 'some, from a comprehensible optical illusion, are beginning to expect it'.[10] He further notes that it would be very myopic to expect that by abandoning the vagueness and all-inclusiveness of political choice and balancing, the antitrust would evolve into a kind of natural science, offering with axiomatic syllogistic accuracy 'only the single, true solution required in each case by antitrust rules finally cleansed of all the rest'.[11] This idea underpins the core of studies on the epistemic foundations of antitrust reasoning.[12]

Amato's book is hard to categorise into a specific normative or methodological school and tradition. It reflects the then emerging trend of a more economic approach, demonstrating the shortcomings of the formulaic period of competition law, but also acknowledging its numerous contributions in pursuing EU competition agenda. It acknowledges the importance of a more societal account of competition policy while also discussing numerous advantages and the inevitability of a narrower economics-based approach. Also, as one of the contributors to this volume notes, 'Amato's book was prescient, among many reasons, for foreshadowing a switch from more "regulatory" to "decisional" enforcement practice in Europe'.[13] Even with the introduction of an independent EU antitrust authority the purification would not touch the core of the dilemma of liberal democracy. It would refine partially the discussion, but would never reduce it to a single-metric calculation. 'What will not go are those ones inherent in the very principles of competition, deriving from the crucial dilemma as to the boundary between the risk of market power and the risk of intrusive antitrust measures'.[14]

[9] ibid.

[10] ibid.

[11] ibid.

[12] See eg, A Ezrachi, 'Sponge' (2016) 5 *Journal of Antitrust Enforcement* 49; I Lianos, 'Polycentric Competition Law' (2018) 71 *Current Legal Problems* 161; S Makris, 'Openness and Integrity in Antitrust' (2021) *17 Journal of Competition Law & Economics* 1; O Andriychuk 'Between Microeconomics and Geopolitics: On the Reasonable Application of Competition Law' (2022) 85 *Modern Law Review* 598.

[13] Dunne, ch 6 of this volume.

[14] ibid.

Although 25 years later we live in a very different world, many of the historic differences merely create a new constellation of the foundational principles of antitrust. This does not change the matrix of the dilemma addressed by Amato, but there are clear benefits to looking at it afresh: hence, the idea to publish this volume.

In discussing the possibility of publishing this book, we were motivated by the feeling of a need to categorise the vivid memory of the late 1990s into a holistic historic period, to revise its key ideas and findings, and to explore how these have evolved. The book by Giuliano Amato is a representative intellectual artefact, allowing us to engage in this endeavour. It is subjective – as any monograph – with strong personal voice of the author, yet accurate, representative and symbolic.

With this in mind, we have invited this remarkable cohort of antitrust thinkers, commissioning them with an engaging task to reflect on how the ideas seeded by Amato's book 25 years ago are developing today, in the very different world, and also to project their further evolution. While the primary purpose of this volume is to analyse *retrospectively* the ways in which Amato's ideas have been integrated into the current state of affairs in competition policy, this has inevitably led to the secondary goal of projecting the *future* development of these ideas. Some of the authors refine and update the central messages of the book. Others further invigorate them. There are of course instances where the contributors develop some theses which allow us to look at the issues in a different light or from different perspectives. All these elements of healthy multilogue are indispensable for keeping the discussions engaged and up to date.

The calibre of the authors and the substantive depth of their texts leave us with hope and confidence that the readers will find this book appealing in its own right. The original piece contains clear elements of polemic. It was important for us when shaping the contours of this project to produce a book which would reflect this spirit of the curiosity-driven discussion, open-mindedness and healthy disagreement, rather than confining ourselves to an easier endeavour of putting together a collection of well-deserved superlatives reflecting in a *liber amicorum* fashion the glorious professional life of this remarkable author and actor.

Most of the contributors to this volume are also united by another important common denominator. In one way or the other their research and practice has been shaped by – but also contributed to shaping of – an amazing and unique academic institution: the European University Institute in Fiesole, Florence. Everyone who had a privilege to be a part of this genuinely European intellectual community knows how important the role of Professor Amato is in it. I personally found participating in his interdisciplinary classes in Competition Law the most intellectually rewarding experience of my professional life, giving me an understanding of the real nature of peripatetic learning, discussion and discovery. It was common practice for the EUI PhD researchers to register for Amato's classes two and more years in a row, and for many Professor Amato will always remain the most inspirational teacher.

As to the substantive part of the volume, it opens with a contribution by ***Eleanor Fox*** 'Antitrust and the Rebound of Power: Re-Imagining Antitrust Cosmopolitanism'.[15] The chapter begins by noting that Amato's book 'frames the dilemma of the crisis of democracy that we face today'.[16] The core of the matter for Fox is in rapidly increasing influence of private power – the influence which so far has been confined neither by market nor government forces.

Fox notes how remarkable it is that so many important phenomena, predetermining the functioning of competition policy today, were absent back in the 1990s. Among the most decisive, she lists Big Tech and Big Data, populism and autocratic governments, the demise of the competition agenda in the WTO, the ICN, the pandemic, the decline of neoliberal vision of antitrust and the emergence of new powerful schools and approaches.

One matter which was relevant then and remains relevant now is the excessive technicalisation of the discipline, the reliance on the omnipotence and infallibility of laissez faire ideology of non-interventionism 'wrapped in a label of neutrality'.[17]

Fox focuses on the key elements of the development of antitrust theory and practice since 1997 – the year (or rather, the period) manifesting a culmination of the global competition agenda. Perhaps, the focus on mastering technicalities and on creating a universal antitrust agenda have distracted our attention from two concurrent developments, which define the contemporary functioning of the field. The first is the rocket-speed penetration of digital technologies into all spheres of our life, triggering the exponential growth of Big Tech industry and an autonomous functioning of the digital economy. The second concerns the rapid increase of nationalistic and authoritarian governments. Both features embody the post-End of History chapter of the evolution of liberal democracy. More factors have started determining antitrust enforcement. Less trust would exist in the magical ability of neoclassical economics to comprehend – let alone steer – the totality of omnipresent complexities and hybridity of different market symbioses.

The chapter elaborates further on the emergence of the global competition order, tracing the paradigmatic historical moment of the evolution of the main institutions, highlighting the key normative and ideological concerns and motives of various stakeholders, and explaining the focal conflicting points of the new antitrust order.

Simultaneous to this trend of uniformisation has been the trend of hybridisation. Fox observes in this regard that the astonishingly high level of market power and control of the emerging Big Tech players has a systemic nature and is based in particular on the remarkable ability to combine an economic toolkit with the possibilities which usually go far beyond antitrust – such as 'surveillance, the spread of disinformation, and psychological capture, holding our attention for as long as

[15] Fox, ch 2 of this volume.
[16] ibid.
[17] ibid.

possible, thus addicting people and selling more ads'.[18] Being essentially borderless and exploiting the consumeristic excitement about the enormous possibilities opened by the digital technologies, the Big Tech companies have scaled up exponentially. Alone, these features exemplify the relative nature of the popular claims and beliefs in the universal ability of neoliberal economics to capture the whole spectrum of economic relationships in its mathematically advanced modelling.

The next important element in the emergence of the new antitrust reality was the rapid increase in nationalistic and authoritarian governments. Alongside many obvious failures to adopt to the new digital circumstances, some governments have succeeded in embedding themselves into the new digital world. Being free from the self-evident constraints imposed by constitutional principles of liberal democracy, they have cherry-picked the most suitable elements of both ideological worlds, creating the new conceptions of the efficient markets. These parallel models exist and develop alongside the traditional ones. Hybridisations and mutations are pervasive, leaving less room for refined purified models of governance.

This has further undermined the expectations for antitrust to develop a comprehensive apparatus for shaping the world economy in the consensually shared spirit of global partnership, cooperation and convergence. Fox not only articulates new challenges, but also offers some appealing conceptual solutions to many of them, concluding that '25 years later, [Amato's] call to democracy of markets and democracy of political governance, and appreciation of their intertwining, is all the more clarion'.[19]

The next chapter is ***Miguel Poiares Maduro's*** 'Ensuring Market and State Accountability: The Private/Public Distinction in the EU Internal Market',[20] which offers a nuanced investigation of the evolution of the complex relationship between the private and the public in the market. Maduro begins by noting that, indeed,

> Very few legal scholars have had Giuliano Amato's capacity to put the analysis of the relevant constitutional and economic legal rules and cases in the context of a broader understanding of how the relationship between markets and the State has changed.[21]

He also acknowledges the sophistication of Amato's legal scholarship and explains that his contribution aims to continue on the discovery of the proper categorisation of the private and the public in the market, and on exploring various channels of their mutual influence on each other.

Maduro's thesis is that the elements of the private and the public are present in different proportions and combinations as a continuum in *all* economies in *all*

[18] ibid.
[19] ibid.
[20] Maduro, ch 3 of this volume.
[21] ibid.

historical periods. These two elements are unavoidable even in situations where some political regimes declare explicitly either absolute libertarianism (ie, the apotheosis of the private) or on the contrary – totalitarian control by the public, manifesting thereby their ideological intentions to rely exclusively on any of the two market's hands. The 'one-handed' model of the market is conceptually impossible. Clearly, markets are inherently two-handed, and the invisible hand of the entrepreneurial discovery is always accompanied by the visible hand of regulator. The matter is about proportions and mutual impact, not about a juxtaposition and mutual exclusion[22] – or in Maduro's words:

> There is no such thing as a totally free market economy as there is no such thing as a fully state-controlled economy. Even the most liberalised economies have some minimum forms of market regulation in the same way that even the most controlled state economies need to rely on some minimal forms of private economic activity.[23]

This statement and its justification allow us to make a number of far-reaching hypotheses. While, for regulation-focused societies, these hypotheses would mainly concern the increasing role of the private, for societies embedded more strongly in the market-centred imperatives, they may concern a more favourable attitude to a proactive regulatory modality. It becomes clear that both ideal-type models are currently in the process of some convergence or hybridisation. Of course, this process is far from linear, and will never become a mechanistic Babel towel-style fusion. Maduro concludes this point with an observation that 'the public and private spheres can no longer be distinguished institutionally',[24] which leads him to define the precise scope of the chapter. Its central argument is that such systemic interdependence can give rise to, among other things, problems with accountability and participation. More specifically, in the EU context, the challenge concerns an increasing blurring of the conceptual borders which were decisive for designing EU law.

Maduro elaborates further by submitting that such a convergence poses significant risks as EU Member States 'may use this conceptual flexibility in such a way as to create forms of evasion from the application of some EU rules',[25] illustrating this 'temptation' with a number of examples. Thus, the substantive part of the chapter consists of the analysis of the case law of the EU Courts, focusing on three different fields, which illustrate the articulated convergence concern. Maduro asks if there is – and if there could be – a coherent approach and judicial conceptualisation to this systemic trend. He ultimately answers this question positively, providing a substantiation of this hypothesis.

[22] O Andriychuk, '"Competition Overdose:" Curing Markets from Themselves? Ten Points for Discussion' (2021) 41 *Legal Studies* 519.

[23] Maduro, ch 3 of this volume.

[24] ibid.

[25] ibid.

The areas scrutinised by Maduro are: (i) the concept of undertaking, and in particular the component of economic activity; (ii) the application of competition law to the state; and (iii) 'golden share' cases. He notes that the list could be further extrapolated to other spheres – such as eg, the concept of State aid.

In relation to the first issue, Maduro focuses on explicating the evolution of the concept of undertaking, addressing the issue that is central to his overall discussion: the notion of economic activity, tracing the key steps of its proper (and ongoing) calibration by the EU Courts. The conclusion could be made that 'When the court referred to activity which can be pursued by private entities, it therefore referred to activity, which is carried out under market conditions'.[26] Clearly, establishing that the activity has an economic characteristic does not imply its unequivocal subsumption to pure antitrust rules, as its specific public-private nature could be taken into account via the proxy of Art 106 TFEU.

The second element of the discussion concerns the principle of loyal cooperation, which envisages that some activities by private market participants could be designated by the state a special quasi-public status. Such a designation thus has to be properly reflected and taken into consideration when enforcing competition rules. Maduro traces the intellectual background of the problem, highlighting a remarkable dispute between Pierre Pescatore and Giuliano Marenco on the very purpose of the rules regulating internal market and economic constitution. Pescatore's proposition was that the rationale of loyal cooperation should be interpreted rather broadly, capturing inter alia the overall impact of state measures on competition. For Marenco, this approach is too expansive. Evidently, the matrix of this debate remains relevant, and Maduro submits that in the current context such tensions will continue to grow. Maduro further elucidates the case law framing these discussions, introducing among other things an elegant formula that helps to evaluate under what circumstances the formal public constraints may indeed be seen as exempting the conduct from antitrust liability, offering a test, which envisages 'from courts a certain factual analysis of the decision-making process of the public authorities involved to assess that there is, in fact, an effective state supervision'.[27] Such an approach is contrasted with the one requiring an assessment of the anticompetitive elements of state measures with their subsequent balancing against other legitimate public interests. The key normative element of this approach is that 'state measures should only be excluded from Articles 101 and 102 if they correspond to a genuine state intervention in the market, formulated in light of the public interest in a decision-making process which is not controlled by the private entities which are supposed to be in competition in that market'.[28]

The last aspect of the chapter concerns the issue of 'golden shares' – ie, shares in privatised companies which still belong to the state. Maduro summarises the

[26] ibid.
[27] ibid.
[28] ibid.

existing case law on this issue and emphasises an important specificity of these cases, as they are often covered by the logic of free movement provisions, not only by competition law. The dilemma is presented as follows: the 'state should not be able to "use" a private form to escape public accountability (including under free movement rules) while, at the same time, not being subject to market accountability either'.[29]

As explained in the conclusion of the chapter, the discussed situations are only examples, and the hybrid private-public nature of the relevant economic activities are becoming more ubiquitous and more intricate. As an example, Maduro refers to the mechanism of State aid control, emphasising that despite increasing difficulty in dealing with various forms of private-public relationships, consistency remains the paramount parameter for the effective functioning of the system – and particularly its legal aspects.

The chapter by ***Giorgio Monti***, 'The Boundaries of Antitrust in the European Union' concludes the first part of the volume. It identifies and discusses one of the central propositions of Amato's book – the thesis that the area should be refined and liberated from its multi-purposiveness.

Monti begins his 'impressionistic sketch' by exploring the evolution of the normative dimension of competition policy before and after publication of Amato's book. Then he focuses on where the antitrust purity/liberation movement went perhaps too far, allowing thereby various relevant incarnations of market power passing below the radars of the policy. After discussing the fields with an insufficient level of antitrust attention and coverage, Monti scrutinises instances where the liberation did not go far enough. His chapter concludes by addressing the question of proper separation, asking 'how do we decide when it should resist and when it should yield?'.[30] As antitrust is simultaneously over- and underinclusive, this dialectical tension raises a number of questions about (the very feasibility of) establishing protocols and algorithms of selecting, prioritising, reconciling and synchronising various strategic societal goals with competition policy.

A significant proportion of Monti's chapter is dedicated to tracing the latest developments in EU competition law, analysing them through the prism of the ideas articulated in Amato's book. He discusses inter alia the questions of proper definition of the goals of antitrust policy, analysing and comparing various proactive and protective antitrust modalities, summing up that 'antitrust prohibits conduct that harms economic welfare, but the criteria which we use to address this notion may vary as society or technology evolves'.[31]

Monti further engages in an intriguing discussion, analysing situations of antitrust *permeability* by looking at the uneasy relationship of competition with industrial policy *sensu lato*. He scrutinises them through the prism of one of Amato's arguments about the requirement of the reformed TEC/TFEU rationale,

[29] ibid.
[30] Monti, ch 4 of this volume.
[31] ibid.

which while mandating for the Commission and Member States to develop their policies in coordination with each other for ensuring the competitiveness of European economy, stipulates that this communication should take place in accordance with a system of open and competitive markets and undistorted competition. For Amato this clearly manifests a legal basis of a thin and pure antitrust, not influenced directly by different – and otherwise fully legitimate – societal interests. Such a scenario would be much more plausible *before* and much less so *after* the Maastricht revision of the Treaty.

After exploring at the beginning of his chapter the situation as seen by Amato in 1997, the next, *prospective*, part of Monti's contribution looks at the post-1997 development, asking if the issues, which appeared to be settled – at least as a matter of primary law – then remain as open and amorphous 25 years on. There was a relatively short period when the ideas of a more economic approach reached their apogee, allowing observers to conclude that the conundrum is either solved or at least is approaching to its logical and rational resolution. In the 2020s many of these conceptual puzzles have been reignited. In the remainder of his chapter Monti offers a number of illuminating reflections on the new challenges for antitrust, raised by the cascade of newly developing external and internal factors.

Monti further scrutinises the increased instances of reliance on non-economic factors, exploring in the last section of his chapter various approaches to the delicate issue of rebalancing exemption provisions. He looks in particular at two recent emblematic discussions: the blocked Siemens/Alstom merger; and sustainability-minded horizontal cooperation. Both have been fiercely and pervasively debated in the literature, and both demonstrate how many challenges are emerging for the economics-centred approach of antitrust. Clearly, the very structure of the EU decision-making institutions, and in particular the Commission, makes the purified approach to competition policy very implausible. Monti's chapter deals with these issues of institutional design. The latest significant regulatory challenges have direct repercussions on the discussion around the architecture of competition law enforcement mechanisms and the potential room for an independent antitrust authority.

Finally, Monti puts forward an argument that a purified approach to antitrust is not necessarily equal to the more economic approach. The ultimate criterion of 'incompatibility with the internal market' allows, after all, for alternative or additional benchmarks. Changing the metrics does not necessarily lead to changing the adherence to the narrow competition-focused theory of antitrust. The purity, in other words, does not always imply uniformity and monosemy. This leads to an intriguing discussion on interpretive theory of open-textured competition law. Monti concludes in King Solomon's way submitting that 'the boundaries of antitrust are to be found inside the legal texts, which limit the scope antitrust intervention and non-intervention'.[32]

[32] ibid.

Part II opens with a contribution by ***Assimakis Komninos***, '"Consumer Welfare" and the EU Courts: An Unexpected Refuge for a Persecuted Concept?'. The key purpose of this chapter is to scrutinise recent trends and highlight the key stages of evolution of the concept of consumer (*qua* end users and intermediaries) welfare, discussing the role it plays in the jurisprudence of EU Courts. It begins with a note that in the US the concept of consumer welfare has been matured and shaped to a 'quasi-religious' status by its protagonists in recent decades, contrasting this with the EU, where it is much less clear-cut.

Komninos describes vividly the feeling with which the recent tensions about the notion of consumer welfare in the US are perceived by many in the EU: 'Are we embracing a wrong dogma that has fallen out of favour in its birthplace?'.[33] His contribution develops three main theses. The first concerns the specificity of EU case law, which was never focused exclusively on price as the only parameter of assessing economic conduct. Competition as a process was always present in judicial practice of EU Courts. From this, the second thesis derives. It explains the increased instances of reference to consumer welfare by the momentum of a more economic approach and reformatting of EU competition law from a form-orientated rationale to a result-oriented one. In this regard consumer welfare is more an embodiment of the methodological shift to economic analysis rather than a clear-cut normative postulate. The third point develops and concretises the second one, noting that

> the EU case law has seen consumer welfare as more of an abstract objective or principle, as opposed to an operational standard or test. It serves only to distinguish the mere exclusion of rivals (which may be pro-competitive) from distortion of competition that leads to consumer harm.[34]

For Komninos, the EU notion of consumer welfare is more a logical and objective step of the intellectual evolution of competition law than embodiment of certain normative position – the position which would always have its ideological opponents. While for the former vision an abandoning of consumer welfare would be seen as a pendulous movement to its substantive opponents, in the latter paradigm any eventual change of the Treaty would be seen as a *retrogression*.

The author further explains that while in the US the reference to welfare was seen as a standard to guide decision-makers in specific cases, in the EU the phenomenon of economic competition is seen in a functionalist way, aiming at protecting values and principles embedded in the EU economic constitution. The latter has Ordoliberal roots, and Komninos links it with the 'rational commercial conduct consistent with the profit-maximising strategy of a non-dominant company, based on superior efficiency',[35] linking it further with strong single market imperative,

[33] Komninos, ch 5 of this volume.
[34] ibid.
[35] ibid.

which pays particular attention on those practices which additionally harm EU market integration objectives. The EU incarnation of the concept of consumer welfare is broader and not open to other important non-price parameters.

In the substantive section of his chapter Komninos outlines the legal evolution of the idea of consumer welfare in the EU, starting with the first documents that referred to the concept in a more or less explicit way – the Commission's 1996 Green Paper on vertical restraints, and then the Commission's 2004 Article 101(3) TFEU Guidelines. The concept has been refined in various other subsequent Commission's documents.

Important in this regard is the 2009 Guidance Paper on exclusionary abuses, which projects into the EU antitrust reasoning the logic of pro- and anticompetitive foreclosure of competitors. While this logic offers further flexibility to formalistically applied rules, the pro- or anti-competitive model equates the need for exemption/non-application of Article 102 to its overall procompetitiveness.

In his retrospective analysis of how the notion of consumer welfare has transposed from the policy documents of the Commission to the matrix of case law, Komninos observes the conservative nature of courts, and how, specifically in the EU, they have been designed to be less political and more controlling. This explains why the transposition has not happened quickly, and it has been done with some degree of inertia. Over 40 years, the EU Courts have not invoked the concept of consumer welfare in their judicial reasoning, being anchored mainly in the market integration narrative. Komninos offers an informative chronological overview of how the concept has gradually been adopted into the vocabulary of the EU Courts, illustrating this uneasy transition with numerous examples, and observing the leading role in this process of various Advocate Generals, categorising it in different stages, and discussing each of them in detail. Komninos includes in his analysis the latest paradigmatic cases, projecting thereby continuity of the problems discussed in Amato's book to the future.

Part II continues with the chapter by ***Niamh Dunne***, 'Antitrust and the Golden Thread: Balancing the Presumption of Innocence with the Public Interest in Competition Enforcement'. The author focuses on a discussion of the fundamental dilemma of developing a model of antitrust enforcement, which on one hand would not allow private power to go beyond the bounds of legitimacy, and on the other not let public power to pursue this control in a way that might also cross the legitimacy line.

Clearly, these relationships have a pendulous nature, and in the present circumstances the societal demand is moving in the pro-enforcement direction. Yet precisely due to the dilemmatic nature of both fundamental tensions, and also due to their inherently dialectical mutual dependence, the current mood will eventually change its path, with the counterpressure coming from the underprioritised normative choice. This is the immune system and the very raison d'être of liberal democracy.

Dunne begins her chapter by tracing the evolution of the regulatory desire to shape competition policy in a more effective way. She mentions many factors, including steeper penalties, greater decentralisation of public enforcement to national authorities, facilitation of private enforcement or adoption of a 'more economic approach'. The author also notes in this regard that 'Missing from this raft of innovations, however, is one of the most straightforward and sensible suggestions in Amato's book: namely, to entrust EU-level action to an independent authority rather than the politically controlled Commission'.[36]

The author continues by offering a detailed analysis of the structure of contemporary EU antitrust enforcement, discussing a number of links to and reflecting upon Amato's book, observing inter alia that 'the key development, from this perspective, was abandonment of the centralised notification system for potentially anticompetitive agreements, which had been the focus of much of Amato's frustration with existing enforcement structures'.[37]

Similar to Amato, Dunne also engages in the philosophical discussion about the very phenomenon of economic competition and its regulation – with the quintessential Janus-faced dilemma of its self-distortion. On one hand, the instances of completely unregulated competition would eventually lead to well-known mutations, and some restriction is inevitable. On the other hand, by interfering into the spontaneous order of things, regulators apply 'coercive … public power … to restrain and direct and occasionally punish the profit-making activities of private market actors',[38] and thus conceptually – at least in the liberal democratic spirit – the normative burden of proof remains on the side of the enforcer.

With this in mind, the author engages in an appealing and well-structured investigation into the legal theoretical nature of the very phenomenon of legitimacy, identifying and scrutinising its several dimensions in the area of competition law. One issue resonates in particular: giving the inherently dilemmatic nature of both competition and its regulation, most – if not all – antitrust infringements are much less about intentions and moral faults, and much more about objective consequences. This rationale may in fact be reversed with regard to the new *ex ante* sector-specific rules regulating competition in the digital economy. In the author's view this may become a problem, particular from the human rights dimension of enforcement, especially if all the stages of the decision-making mechanism would remain in hands of a single authority. Dunne substantiates further this line of reasoning by exploring the mechanism of judicial review in EU competition cases, offering a nuanced analysis of the relevant Articles 101 and 102 TFEU cases.

In the conclusion to her chapter the author inter alia notes that the '"magic box" quality of the competition rules, coupled with the Commission's combined prosecutorial and adjudicatory functions, raise the spectre of amorphous and expanding liability',[39] which – as is discussed in the chapter – should be counterbalanced

[36] Dunne, ch 6 of this volume.
[37] ibid.
[38] ibid.
[39] ibid.

with a robust mechanism of judicial review as the quintessence of legitimacy of the system. In Dunne's view, such a balance is not necessarily achieved, and the problems articulated in Amato's book and discussed further in this chapter, will continue to be relevant in the future.

Dunne ends her chapter by noting that the divides in antitrust are not reduceable to the left/right dimension of political discussion and that 'Amato's dilemma remains as compelling and challenging today as it was 25 years ago, or indeed back in 1957 when the Treaty of Rome was first enacted'.[40] The author also cautions the community of antitrust thinkers against 'an almost pathological hostility to economics as a perceived obstacle to the untrammelled regulatory power of the competition rules'.[41]

The chapter by ***Stavros Makris***, 'Procompetitive Effects in EU Competition Law' closes Part II of the book. It systematises various instances of establishing procompetitive effects in cases of anticompetitive agreements, abusive practices and mergers. Makris aims to answer a set of intriguing questions as to which practices could be identified as procompetitive; whether there is consistency between them; what role they call to play; and how they could be demonstrated.[42] The author identifies four proxies for identification of anticompetitive effects: (i) dealing with market failure; (ii) intensification of competitive pressure; (iii) the total welfare-enhancing element; and (iv) the distributional element of consumer welfare.

Clearly, from a purely semantic perspective, these effects may not necessarily be *verbatim* procompetitive, and clearly not all possible competition-enhancing implications of a practice are relevant to this special definition. As the author indicates, the role of the concept is akin to an analytical shortcut, with its primary function being avoidance of balancing and overenforcement. The author's analysis of the recent cases convincingly demonstrates that the EU Courts 'are frontloading procompetitive effects in all three key regimes rather than leaving them to the assessment of Article 101(3) TFEU, Article's 102 TFEU and merger control's efficiency defence'.[43] Makris scrutinises the implications of this change in the sequencing.

It is hard to disagree with the author that despite the clear-cut appearance of all the four proxies (*qua* analytical shortcuts), the notion of procompetitive effect remains open-textured. Not all may necessarily agree that such openness to interpretation has always positive role. For some, eg labelling an effect procompetitive if it merely enhances welfare, would remain questionable, but the contribution offers a thorough and detailed analysis of existing case law, which underpins the taxonomy.

[40] ibid.
[41] ibid.
[42] Makris, ch 7 of this volume.
[43] ibid.

The substantive part of Makris' chapter engages with the four proxies. He begins with discussing in detail situations when 'the practice or agreement in question deals with a market failure in a non-anticompetitive manner (ie without diminishing rivals ability and willingness to compete)',[44] followed by cases where 'a practice or an arrangement affects positively rivals' ability and incentives to compete',[45] with the compensatory relationship of the clash between inter- and intra-brand competition in vertical agreements being the most illustrative instance (the history of the emergence and evolution of the concept of inter- and intra-platform competition in both jurisdictions is addressed in detail in Amato's book). The third category deals with the instances of economic efficiency, and the last with net consumer gains. Makris further emphasises that no cumulative application of these four criteria is usually expected. Each would conceptually suffice for exempting otherwise anticompetitive practice – or more categorically, for not seeing the practice as being anticompetitive as such. The author further discusses substantively both of the modalities.

Makris concludes his chapter by noting that the discussed concept of procompetitive effect remains open, and submits that the 'category of procompetitive effects is not exhaustive and it could be maintained that new economic insights can reveal new types of procompetitive effects'.[46] He further observes that typically courts deal with the issues of procompetitive effects before engaging with Article 101(3) TFEU (and *mutatis mutandis* analogous defences in cases of unilateral conduct and merger control). This implies further flexibility and openness to interpretation of the bounds of EU competition law. Finally, Makris notes that 'procompetitive effects as counterindicators of a restriction of competition play an increasingly prominent role than as justifications of an established restriction',[47] and offers a number of explanations of this trend, linking his chapter with the normative insights of Amato's book.

Part III begins with a chapter by ***Ginevra Bruzzone***, 'Preserving the Bounds of Power: The Narrow Path to a Future-Proof Competition Policy'. The author begins by noting an important feature of the period when the book was written: the widespread enthusiasm with which the area of antitrust was being transposed to the vocabulary of neoclassical economics. Any attempt to map a discussion about the political nature of competition policy and its direct link with liberal democracy would usually be seen as nothing more than 'merely an enlightening intellectual perspective, with no direct relevance for the concrete policy issues'.[48] In this regard the book did not sit comfortably within the overarching zeitgeist.

The first trigger for revising the holistic beliefs in the monosemic nature of the theory of economic competition was the financial crisis of 2008, casting

[44] ibid.
[45] ibid.
[46] ibid.
[47] ibid.
[48] Bruzzone, ch 8 of this volume.

well-substantiated doubts on the ability of the models to comprehend the reality in its entirety.[49] This coincided with comprehensive – and still ongoing – digital transformation, social and environmental challenges. All these and various other factors trigger the appetite for a more interventionist antitrust policies and further synchronisation of competition law with the variety of other public policies.

Against this background Bruzzone raises three central questions requiring substantive discussion: (i) reconciling the objective demand for broader policy goals with concerns about structural weaking of the mechanisms of competition and return to centralised governance; (ii) confining the omnipotence of private power – especially, but not only – in the digital economy, so that it does not undermine the pillars of liberal democracy; and (iii) developing the system of checks and balances preventing the new – especially, but not only – *ex ante* tools from going too far and compromising the rule of law. The chapter addresses all three issues.

As to the first challenge, Bruzzone expresses a well-coined concern that the development of a more accommodative antitrust may weaken it. This would clearly be the case if the communication process between various societal values and interests were seen as a one-way street with only the interests of undistorted competition being compromised to the benefits of other societal goals. She sees this danger as being most plausible in relation to Article 101 TFEU and merger control. The crucial question remains of whether it is still feasible to design a polycentric interaction within the constellation of various public interests in the way allowing a more robust presence of the discourse of the competitive process in pursuing these non-competition policies. While the need for establishing such regulatory multilogue is being recognised and has led to some material changes (eg, the UK Digital Regulation Cooperation Forum, and a greater interaction between competition and privacy professional clusters), the format and the tangible features of the multilogue are still at an embryonic stage.

Bruzzone submits that such modality is likely to be more dependent on the context and as such transform competition policy into a case-by-case administrative enterprise with an excessively high level of regulatory discretion and overreliance on interpretive flexibility of law, noting that this shift is equally susceptible to various influences of private power, just as the excessive reliance on purified economics in the previous period was. The author abandons the binary public interests v economics-centred configuration of antitrust policy, demonstrating with several detailed examples that reducing the discussions to such categoricalness is both harmful and incorrect, and concluding that 'The ordoliberal design of EU competition rules [while not being focused exclusively on economic efficiency], with little room for administrative balancing of different

[49] For a legal theoretical discussion on this issue see Andriychuk, 'Between Microeconomics and Geopolitics' (2022).

interests in the application of competition rules, is extremely important in this respect'.[50]

After articulating her position on the issue of enforcement discretion and compensatory activism, Bruzzone reverts to the problem of designing an effective mechanism of constraining private economic power by means other than a mechanistic delegation of more discretion to public authorities.

Bruzzone notes that the susceptibility of a more economic approach of transforming itself into a technocratic rather than broader political and philosophical exercise was well foreseen in Amato's book. Such susceptibility, however, has not been seen – for the right reasons – as a sufficient reason for treating the approach sceptically. Rather cautiously, Bruzzone submits in this regard that quarter of a century later,

> although both the legal and the economic assessment of cases have become so technical that sometimes even for experts it is not easy to find a soul in the matter, it would be clearly misleading to blame the impact-based approach for weakening antitrust enforcement.[51]

The author further articulates an important and often ignored feature of the phenomenon of economic competition: its inherently multifaceted nature. Even in the single-metric format of price, the competitive spirit evolves in various ways, having many measurable and even more immeasurable implications on the markets and their participants. Such plurality increases exponentially with the introduction of various goals and factors as new variables in the equation as well as additional temporal, regional or sectoral flexibility. Clearly, not all of these factors should or could become relevant for antitrust analysis. Claiming otherwise would be as grotesque as claiming the omnipotence of price theory to encapsulate all the intricacies of the societal phenomenon of economic competition.

The question of the proper calibration of the path between *Scylla* of over-inclusiveness and *Charybdis* of under-inclusiveness of antitrust is discussed in the second sectionof Bruzzone's chapter. The author focuses on analysing the design of the formats of an effective administrability of the impact-based approach in various areas of competition law, engaging pervasively with cases and theories illustrating the main propositions of her thesis.

In the final section of her chapter the author explores the imminent question if the established ex post competition rules should be complemented by the new (predominantly) *ex ante* proactive mechanisms. In comparing the more bespoke nature of the UK and German reforms with the supposedly more general system of the EU Digital Markets Act, Bruzzone favours the former. Evidently, an increased enforcement discretion should be accompanied with, and counterbalanced by, not only a tailored selection of addressees of the rules, but also of the scope of their obligations, remedies and the situations in which the application of the rules could be necessary.

[50] Bruzzone, ch 8 of this volume.
[51] ibid.

The concluding section of the chapter discusses a range of issues related to institutional design. Bruzzone observes that in

> his seminal book of 1997 Giuliano Amato wrote that his aim was to remind both young students and specialists that, below technical profiles, competition law has a deep political and philosophical dimension: antitrust is meant to address the fundamental dilemma of the liberal democracy, ie how to set proper boundaries for both private economic power and public power.[52]

Bruzzone concludes in this respect that the agenda articulated in Amato's book is a 'permanent agenda'.

The chapter by ***Roberto Pardolesi***, 'Digital Antitrust and Private Powers: the (Uneasy) Case of Marketplace Platforms', continues the discussion on the application of the ideas of Amato's book to the digital economy, focusing on an important segment of digital markets – marketplace platforms.

Pardolesi begins by articulating one of the central dilemmas of liberal democracy discussed in Amato's book. In some sense, competition policy is akin to *Ouroboros* as it also targets its main objective – competitive process – constraining its ruinous ability to cannibalise itself. The author portrays colourfully the period when *Antitrust and the Bounds of Power: The Dilemma of Liberal Democracy in the History of the Market* was written as a 'deliberately eccentric' ideological confrontation of two populist rhetorics.

In different periods both over- and under-enforcement antagonists gain their specific momentum, requiring a redesign of most of the ongoing antitrust discussions and challenges into the newly dominant discourse. He perceives this process with a philosophical irony and distance.

Pardolesi also offers his understanding of the specificities of the 'digital tsunami',[53] focusing particularly on those which are usually seen as requiring the readjustment of various antitrust policies and principles. Similar to other contributors, he notes a remarkable increase of private market power among the few biggest digital companies.

After acknowledging the similarities between various digital giants, Pardolesi reverts to the important differences between them. The conclusion in this regard is that with a reasonable factual calibration one can trace many systemic similarities between the elements of markets power 25 years ago and today.

A noticeable portion of Pardolesi's contribution is dedicated to the ongoing German Facebook saga and the resulting questions of contractual (over-)power, and information asymmetry in B2C as well as P2B relationships.

The chapter ends with the discussion of how the ideas developed in Amato's book could be used to address some of the challenges raised.

A significant part of the final chapter – 'Revisiting the Concept of Power in the Digital Era' by ***Anna Gerbrandy*** – is also dedicated to the digital changes reviving

[52] ibid.
[53] Pardolesi, ch 9 of this volume.

discussions around the role of antitrust in liberal democratic governance. The author begins with an engaging personal introduction outlining her engagement with Amato's book, noting that usually, 'where one draws the balance between them is dependent on socio-cultural and political contexts; that where one draws that line is ultimately also a personal, normative, preference'.[54]

The author is in the midst of a major research project exploring the concept of modern bigness, and her analysis of the role of public and private economic powers in competition law offered through the prism of Amato's book is relevant both for this volume and the project.

Gerbrandy begins her substantive discussion with an exposition of the key changes to the concept of economic power over the last 25 years. The main trend is the digitisation and datafication of the economy. Their corporate power is at the core of the concept of modern bigness.

Gerbrandy offers a taxonomy distinguishing 'between the *foundations* of power, the *dimensions* of power and the *domains* across which the power can manifest'.[55] The overarching conclusion of this submission is that 'in a democratic society, based on the rule of law, too much power needs to be bound',[56] and that the mechanism of democracy cannot function without an inherent system of checks and balances, implying that the modern bigness type of private power goes far beyond the established canons of democratic governance. The issue of designing specific model of balancing is for Gerbrandy ultimately a political matter and 'a lasting legacy of Amato's *Antitrust and the Bounds of Power*'.[57]

The book ends with an Afterword by Professor Amato, reflecting upon the evolution of competition law, economics and policy over the last 25 years through the prism of this volume's contributions.

Working on this book was a pleasure and honour. I should like to express my gratitude to Professor Amato for helping to shape my understanding of the phenomenon of economic competition and its interactions with the political and cultural incarnations of competition during my PhD years at the EUI and further on. I am also grateful to all the astonishing authors for offering their remarkable analysis, helping to position Amato's book into the overall intellectual landscape of the evolution and functioning of competition law, economics and policy. The appreciation of all of the authors go to the publisher – and in particular to Roberta Bassi, Rosemarie Mearns, Linda Goss and Vicki Hillyard – for their effective and expedient management of the project as well as to the anonymous reviewers. The 1997 book was published by Hart, and it is symbolic and essential that this volume is being published by under the same name.

[54] Gerbrandy, ch 10 of this volume.
[55] ibid.
[56] ibid.
[57] ibid.

Finally, in the current circumstances it is my moral duty to manifest explicitly the things we usually do not express in public: I send the warmest gratitude and love to my Motherland – Ukraine – defending itself bravely, flourishing again soon.

All the authors wish the readers an exciting time with the book. Please remember to note your ideas for a comparison with the new antitrust reality of the next quarter-century cycle. 2047 is approaching.

PART I

Competition Policy: New World? New Mission?

2

Antitrust and the Rebound of Power: Reimagining Antitrust Cosmopolitanism

ELEANOR M FOX[1]

I. Introduction

Giuliano Amato's *Antitrust and the Bounds of Power*[2] has not only weathered well; it frames the dilemma of the crisis of democracy that we face today. Private power is global and has not been significantly contained by either the forces of competition or antitrust law. Public power has been unmoored from the checks and balances of the institutions of governance and is flourishing without pushback from robust winds of competition.

Professor Amato is exactly right that there are bounds beyond which private power must not go lest it trample on our freedoms and autonomy, and there are bounds beyond which public power must not go lest it trample on our freedoms and autonomy. And very unfortunately, both have exceeded their bounds.

Professor Amato wrote his book in the late 1990s.[3] This was before Big Tech/Big Data, before the new wave of populism and autocratic governments, before the demise of the competition agenda in the World Trade Organization (WTO) and the later crippling of the WTO, before the creation of the International Competition Network (ICN), before the COVID-19 pandemic, and before the rise in the US of the Neo-Brandeisian school to counter neoliberalism. He wrote elegantly of the growing capture of antitrust law by big business and laissez-faire

[1] Eleanor Fox is the Walter J Derenberg Professor of Trade Regulation at New York University School of Law. She thanks Alexandre de Streel for his helpful comments.

[2] G Amato, *Antitrust and the Bounds of Power: The Dilemma of Liberal Democracy in the History of the Market* (Hart Publishing, 1997).

[3] Professor Amato wrote the book at the end of a seminar we co-taught at New York University School of Law, which was an exciting and productive collaboration. As he writes in the preface, 'The text is thus an unwinding of the guiding thread of that seminar' (ibid vii). It is a pleasure to reflect on the seminar and revisit the book.

philosophy, the increasing over-technicalisation of antitrust analysis, and the threat that this technocratic form of antitrust built (as it often is) on assumptions that markets work well, will replace a vision of markets backed by antitrust that yield a fair distribution of gains. He wrote of the need for a global competition framework to contain firms bigger than governments, and of the symbiosis of antitrust and democracy.

This chapter will fill out the history since 1997. It will explain the undermining of the project for a world competition framework, the formation of the ICN as a roots-up alternative, the growth of Big Tech and its abuses, the increasing technicalisation of the antitrust law wrapped in a label of neutrality, the constant shrinking of US antitrust through Supreme Court doctrine, the increasing disconnect between the public's conception of how antitrust should contain power and the reality, and the suspense at the moment of this writing as to whether the US Congress will revamp US antitrust to recognise new forms of power and abuses that need to be caught if we are to legitimate the market system.

The chapter ends with a suggestion for approaching the problem of power and markets, and for an examination of how to reimagine the path towards antitrust coherence in the world.

II. A Brief History of Antitrust, Power and the World Economy Since 1997

This section reviews developments of economic power and its control through antitrust since the publication of the Amato book. The description is not reassuring. It underscores the importance of Professor Amato's analysis.

1997 was a year that should have induced serious thinking about the need for vision higher than the nation state. This was the year in which the US flagship Boeing, the world's leading producer of big jet aircraft, proposed to buy McDonnell Douglas, a distant third to Airbus's number 2. The US cleared the merger as not anticompetitive on grounds that McDonnell Douglas had lost its edge and was in decline, while the EU came close to enjoining the merger and settled for a thick set of behavioural injunctions.[4] Also, 1997 was a year in the midst of vibrant discussions within the WTO and among the antitrust family of nations addressing the proposition that the global character of so many transactions and so much conduct evoked the need for global antitrust.

The EU led the way, fleshing out a proposal for a world competition framework. It would begin with building blocks of capacity building, technical assistance and WTO values of nondiscrimination and transparency, and work

[4] See E Fox, 'Antitrust Regulation Across National Borders: The United States of Boeing versus the European Union of Airbus' (1998) *Brookings*.

up to a competition law against cartels and abuse of dominance with national enforcement and WTO dispute resolution.[5]

But the vision was not to be realised, at least not so soon. It was attacked by the United States, which feared loss of sovereignty, rules protecting competitors rather than competition and efficiency, and faceless bureaucratic decision-makers it could not trust to carry out the analytic-heavy rules of law. There was scepticism also from developing countries, which feared that the rules that emerged would grease the path for multinationals taking over their markets and a loss of policy space for their own economic development.[6] Into the breach came the ICN, formed in 2001. Whereas a WTO solution would have been top-down and mandatory, and would have involved the trade representatives of the nations, the ICN solution would be bottom-up and voluntary, and involve only the antitrust authorities of the nations. It would be a forum for sharing perspectives on principles of law and procedures, and, by cross-fertilisation, working towards convergence, thus helping to make competition agencies more effective and smoothing the playing field for business by softening systems' conflicts. The Organisation for Economic Co-operation and Development (OECD) would continue as a research and sharing platform, also cross-fertilising and inducing convergence, and the United Nations Conference on Trade and Development (UNCTAD) would continue as a forum catering to the needs of the developing world. And so it has gone, with ICN providing a vibrant forum for agency-sharing, and OECD and UNCTAD continuing on their paths, reinvigorated by the new competition from ICN. But no global law, global framework, or global institution has emerged.

Meanwhile, two phenomena have appeared: the growth of Big Tech; and an exponential increase in nationalistic and authoritarian governments. Big Tech emerged in the 2010s. The category includes Google (Alphabet), Apple, Facebook (Meta), and Amazon (collectively, the GAFA), and sometimes Microsoft, Netflix, and one or two others. The five biggest tech firms have a market capitalisation of about US $9 trillion[7] – bigger than most nations. Their markets are distinguished by enormous network effects, which produce both value for users and barriers to entry; they accumulate vast amounts of data and sit astride functionally related markets. Their power presents itself differently for different business models, but it includes power that is not usually associated with antitrust such as surveillance, the spread of disinformation and psychological capture, holding our attention for as long as possible, thus addicting people and selling more ads. They typically charge some users a zero price (and take users' data, which they cull and sell). Being Internet-based, they transcend national borders; they are global. Being data-driven and computer-focused, their super-profitability does not depend on the

[5] See E Fox, 'Linked-In: Antitrust and the Virtues of a Virtual Network – Looking Back and Forward' in P Lugard and D Anderson (eds), The International Competition Network at Twenty: Origins, Accomplishments and Aspirations (Intersentia, 2022).

[6] ibid.

[7] See 'Largest Tech Companies by Market Cap', available at companiesmarketcap.com/tech/largest-tech-companies-by-market-cap.

usual monopolist's behaviour of cutting back market output and thus does not fit the economic casebook model for identifying a monopolist. They have become indispensable trading partners for a large cadre of small businesses and emerging entrepreneurs.

The COVID-19 pandemic, which started in 2020, has increased the footprint of Big Tech, for pandemic mandates closed offices and schools and shifted billions of dollars of commerce from brick and mortar locations to the Internet. Access to the Big Tech platforms became even more critical for businesses to reach their customers.

While the Big Tech firms have made important innovations, it is now well documented that they use their power to forestall competition, abuse and exploit. They dampen competition with other platforms and preempt the competition of the firms they invite to do business on their platforms.[8] Frustrated businesses, a concerned public and politicians campaigning for a more equal society depict Big Tech as the epitome of business and markets that work for the elite and not for the masses, and describe the growth of their power as skewing wealth distribution in favour of elites and undermining democracy.[9]

While private power grows, illiberal government power has seen a rebirth. Much of the new illiberalism is attributed to the rise of populism, as documented by Maciej Bernatt in *Populism and Antitrust: The Illiberal Influence of Populist Government on the Competition Law System*.[10] Bernatt locates the phenomenon as arising in the last 10 years (coincidentally corresponding with the rise of Big Tech) marked by the election of charismatic and divisive populist leaders who promise a better life for their tens of million followers who feel left out of a society that is working for elites, not for them. Bernatt identifies Greece, Hungary, Poland, the Czech Republi, and India as countries in which such divisive leaders have stayed in power often for more than one term. He identifies Brazil and the United States as countries in which populist politicians have won presidential elections 'and reshaped the political and economic scene'.[11] He mentions Austria, France, Germany, Italy and the UK as countries in which populist politicians and parties have gained strength and become important political players.[12]

Bernatt concentrates on Hungary and Poland, and describes their transition to illiberal democracy. He documents the interference by the government of each with the country's judicial system, undermining the rule of law and weaponising

[8] See, eg, Subcommittee on Antitrust, Commercial and Administrative Law of the Committee on the Judiciary, United States House of Representatives, 'Investigation of Competition in Digital Markets, Majority Staff Report and Recommendations' (2020).

[9] eg A Klobuchar, *Antitrust: Taking on Monopoly Power from the Gilded Age to the Digital Age* (Alfred A Knopf, 2021); T Wu, *The Curse of Bigness: Antitrust in the New Gilded Age* (Columbia Global Reports, 2018); Z Teachout, *Break 'Em Up: Recovering Our Freedom from Big Ag, Big Tech, and Big Money* (All Points Books, 2020).

[10] CUP, 2022.

[11] ibid 4.

[12] ibid.

antitrust. For example, the Government of Hungary consolidated the whole domestic press and appropriated it as its own mouthpiece, creating a special exemption from antitrust.[13] Bernatt proposes as (partial) solutions, when possible: bolstering the independence of the competition agency; strengthening the institutions to withstand onslaughts on the rule of law; using antitrust more aggressively to preserve competitive markets so they can play their role as a check against the illiberal state; and putting teeth into the oversight by the EU of the democracy backsliding by Member States.[14]

III. The Perfect Storm: What Role for Antitrust, and is it Up to it?

Are we in the grip of the perfect storm? Private power has (many believe) gone too far and is trampling on our freedoms and our autonomy. Public power has gone too far (although not in the vein worked by Professor Amato in his book, who then had reference to libertarian fear of overly aggressive antitrust), trampling on our freedoms and our autonomy. Indeed, this poisonous combination of excessive private power and authoritarian governance can lead an illiberal government to use the powerful private players to do its bidding (as per Hitler), and it can also lead to private firms' facilitating political abuses, as in Facebook enabling the Cambridge Analytica scandal, facilitating a foreign government's interference in a Presidential election.[15]

Antitrust is not the answer to abuses of power by illiberal government. Robust markets (with abuses capped by antitrust and robustness preserved by antitrust) is an important check in the Ordoliberal sense,[16] but it is not a sufficient check, especially in a world where large firm size is often dictated by economies of scale and accepted by the people, frustrating the vision of the many diverse firms competing. Fighting for agency independence, rule of law, transparency and due process in antitrust is unquestionably worth it, but success in that fight does not substantially dent authoritarian government power. The potential of the EU to discipline its own illiberal Member States is a better hope than good antitrust norms for saving democracy; but even the dedicated weapon in the EU's arsenal has proved too weak in view of unanimous voting rules and the unfortunate non-uniqueness of illiberal European states.[17] The answer is deeply political.

[13] ibid 161.
[14] ibid ch 6.
[15] See N Confessore, 'Cambridge Analytica and Facebook: The Scandal and the Fallout So Far' *New York Times* (4 April 2018), available at www.nytimes.com/2018/04/04/us/politics/cambridge-analytica-scandal-fallout.html.
[16] See DJ Gerber, 'Constitutionalizing the Economy: German Neo-Liberalism, Competition Law and the "New" Europe' (Winter 1994) 42 *American Journal of Comparative Law* 25.
[17] Bernatt, *Populism and Antitrust* (2022) 221–22.

We turn, then, to antitrust proper and to the charge that Big Tech (as symbolic of all big business) has gotten too big and abusive, and the claim that antitrust should cut it down to size or at least stop its abuses. Is antitrust up to the task? We concentrate here on reining in conduct of Big Tech that could comfortably fall into the discipline of antitrust (thus excluding, but not forgetting, brainwashing by disinformation, preying on galvanising attention, invasions of privacy, misappropriation of data, and other extensions of power that negatively complement and feed economic market power).[18]

There are two basic categories that cause difficulty in applying antitrust to call Big Tech power to account. The first is whether the challenged Big Tech firm qualifies as a dominant firm under EU law, or as a monopoly under US law. The second is whether the challenged conduct is anticompetitive and illegal, or whether it is not proscribed because, for example, it does not sufficiently and provably harm consumers or is thought to be justified by the firm's efficiencies. These two inquiries pose big barriers to efficient, timely and successful antitrust enforcement against apparently abusive and anticompetitive conduct. For example (all of which are charged and some verified): sabotage on the platform – Facebook cuts off Vine's access to data when Vine launches an invention that is just too good. Or: Facebook and Google snatch up all start-ups that, they predict, would otherwise become competitive thorns-in-the-side. Amazon appropriates ideas from rivals on its platform whenever the rival's data show the popularity of its innovations. Apple blocks game developers from informing its gamers that they can use the developer's payment system to avoid Apple's 30 per cent surcharge. Facebook obstructs users from porting their data to another platform, and undermines interoperability.[19]

How does the EU handle these obstacles to successful litigation? How does the US?

The power question. The EU, as well as several other jurisdictions, recognises that Big Tech has new forms of power. The firm may not qualify as 'dominant' under traditional standards, and yet it may have significant market power and engage in abusive conduct that the law should control. 'Dominance' is a screen, simply limiting the scope of single firm acts that can be challenged as abusive. It can be an arbitrary screen. Several jurisdictions have expanded the net as applied to the biggest Big Tech platforms. The EU is poised to adopt a special regulation,

[18] See JE Cohen, *Between Truth and Power: The Legal Constructions of Informational Capitalism* (OUP, 2019) noting profound societal shifts brought about by big data, network-based platforms, and how their operations reflect 'complex and mutually interpenetrating sets of relationships and practices that involve a heterogeneous array of public, private, and public-private actors and associations' (204), implying the shallowness of any silo-focused discipline that does not account for power across boundaries.

[19] These examples appear in the House of Representatives staff report and recommendations (n 8), and are alleged in numerous investigations and complaints.

the Digital Markets Act,[20] applicable to the largest 'gatekeepers' – platforms that are keepers of critical gateways to the Internet and that create dependencies within their ecosystems. The UK's Competition and Markets Authority has formed a Digital Markets Unit, and the country is considering a statute that, if adopted, would subject digital platforms with 'strategic market status' based on 'substantial entrenched market power' to a bespoke Code of Conduct.[21] An amendment in Germany extends its antitrust law to unilateral conduct of firms of 'Paramount Significance for Competition Across Markets'.[22]

The US requires proof of monopoly. This element is not easy to satisfy,[23] and jurists' insistence on technocrats' definition of monopoly could mean that antitrust challenges to GAFA simply do not pass the first screen, and the firm may be free to do as it likes with antitrust impunity. Pending legislation would change the standard for a specific range of acts.

The conduct question. Proof that alleged abuses are anticompetitive and illegal is equally challenging. The EU has handled the problem through its Digital Markets Act (DMA), proscribing certain conduct with no chance for an efficiency justification. The UK appears en route to designating certain conduct as questionable, but would tailor the proscriptions to the particular firm's business model. Under the DMA, conduct that is proscribed may or may not amount to abuse of dominance; it doesn't matter.

For the US, the conduct question is especially difficult. US case law decrees that firms, even monopoly firms, have no duty to deal. Exclusionary acts are subsumed in the category of refusals to deal.[24] Pending legislation would forbid the biggest platforms from preferencing their own products.

In sum, there is a crisis of power. Public power has gone too far. Private power has gone too far. Firms are global and antitrust systems are national. The truly global firms know no borders. Several jurisdictions are poised to reprehend specific exercises of private power, each in their own way. In the US, control of private power is especially weak. What is the future of the regulation of global private power?

[20] See European Parliament, 'Deal on Digital Markets Act: EU rules to ensure fair competition and more choice for users' (European Parliament News, 24 March 2022), available at www.europarl.europa.eu/news/en/press-room/20220315. See www.europarl.europa.eu/news/en/press-room/20220315IPR25504/deal-on-digital-markets-act-ensuring-fair-competition-and-more-choice-for-users.

[21] See United Kingdom Competition & Markets Authority, 'Corporate report, Annual plan 2022 to 2023' (2022), available at www.gov.uk/government/publications/competition-and-markets-authority-annual-plan-2022-to-2023/annual-plan-2022-to-2023.

[22] German Act Against Restraints of Competition, s 19a, added by amendment of 2021.

[23] See *FTC v Facebook, Inc*, __ F Supp 3d __ (DDC 29 June 2021), dismissing a complaint for failure to plead enough facts to show that Facebook is a monopoly. An amended complaint survived Facebook's motion to dismiss but the court commented that, although the FTC had now 'cleared the pleading bar', 'the agency may well face a tall task down the road in proving its allegations'. __ F Supp3d __ (DDC 11 January 2022).

[24] *Verizon Communications v Law Offices of Curtis V Trinko*, 540 US 398 (2004). Exceptions from the rule of no duties to deal, even by monopoly firms, is very limited. See E Fox, 'The Decline and Fall and Renewal of US Leadership in Antitrust Law and Policy' (2022) *Competition Policy International Antitrust Chronicle*, available at www.competitionpolicyinternational.com/category/antitrust-chronicle.

IV. The Future of Control of Global Private Power

Business is increasingly global, which means that exercise of market power is increasingly global. Antitrust actions and regulations are springing up in different jurisdictions, in different forms. Is this diversity of rules and regulations the future of antitrust, or is antitrust coherence in our future? Professor Amato asked the same questions 25 years ago.[25]

Most of the more sophisticated antitrust jurisdictions of the world are on a track to recognise new forms of private power and to reprehend it. US is an outlier. The answer to the question of coherence might depend on the adoption or not of legislation in the US. Legislation could change the center of gravity of US antitrust and move it to a model more reflective of business realities. If significant legislation is adopted in the US, there is room for productive conversations among the world leaders in antitrust, who might agree in principle on what is market power and what are abuses that should be controlled. If it is not, still, we need fora and conversations among the competition authorities of the world on power and its abuse, and a search for the best possible common norms.

V. Conclusion

Professor Amato's dream of 'a shared antitrust code in a multinational context'[26] is all the more needed in the context of global private power that exceeds its bounds, and all the more difficult to achieve in the context of growing nationalism in which public power exceeds the bounds of liberal democracy.

Professor Amato presciently wrote *Antitrust and the Bounds of Power: The Dilemma of Liberal Democracy in the History of the Market.* Twenty-five years later, his call to democracy of markets and democracy of political governance, and appreciation of their intertwining, is all the more clarion.

[25] Amato, *Antitrust and the Bounds of Power* (1997) ch 8.
[26] ibid 129.

3

Ensuring Market and State Accountability

The Private–Public Distinction in the EU Internal Market

MIGUEL POIARES MADURO[1]

Very few legal scholars have had Giuliano Amato's capacity to put the analysis of the relevant constitutional and economic legal rules and cases in the context of a broader understanding of how the relationship between markets and the state has changed. This chapter is a tribute to the sophistication of his legal scholarship by attempting to target, in the context of EU law, one of the most changing and elusive distinctions, that between public and private actions in a market.

There is no such thing as a totally free market economy as there is no such thing as a fully state-controlled economy. Even the most liberalised economies have some minimum forms of market regulation in the same way that even the most controlled state economies need to rely on some minimal forms of private economic activity. There is a continuum of hybrid economic models that, in some cases, involve a substantial degree of market freedom and, in others, state planning and control. As a consequence, the divide between the state and private action has never been absolute. It has, however, become increasingly hard to define as those hybrid models become increasingly complex and seem to get closer together. State capitalism, for example, involves both significant degrees of state planning and control and a widespread use of the free market. At the same time, free market regimes have also seen the rethinking of the traditional role of the state in the

[1] Dean, Católica Global School of Law and Part-time Professor, School of Transnational Governance, European University Institute. This chapter is based on the ideas of a paper published as 'The Chameleon State: EU Law and the Blurring of the Private/Public Distinction in the Market' in R Nickel (ed) *Conflict of Laws and Laws of Conflict in Europe and Beyond – Patterns of Supranational and Transnational Juridification* (Intersentia, 2010). This was, in turn, strongly influenced by my Opinions as Advocate General on cases involving these topics. The current chapter develops and updates those ideas.

market, bringing in a variety of new forms of exercise of public power that further blur the private–public distinction in the market.

States increasingly make use of private regimes to pursue public interests either by assuming private forms or by delegating into private entities the pursuit of public interests. This means that the public and private spheres can no longer be distinguished institutionally.[2] It is now common for states to intervene in the market, not through the traditional mechanisms of regulation or public ownership but in a private legal form, as another market participant. In some instances it is the state that grants private operators the shield of a public legal form. There are also instances where the state imposes on private entities the pursuit of actions that it itself may not be legally authorised to undertake. In all these cases, it becomes increasingly difficult to distinguish between private and public participations in the market and between the pursuit of traditional public goals and the pursuit of private interests whose protection the state deems in the public interest.

This difficulty does not simply represent a conceptual challenge for the law. It also blurs the traditional distinction between the market and the state as alternative modes of decision-making subject to different mechanisms of accountability. In the state, transparency, participation mechanisms and separation of powers are all legal and political instruments aimed at making sure that, as much as possible, public decisions do correspond to the public interest by taking into account all affected interests and making sure that no particular interest captures those public decisions. Competition is the market's equivalent to separation of powers, in the same way that consumer information is its equivalent to transparency. They constrain and limit abuses of economic power and maximise welfare through the free and informed choices of consumers. State and markets are different decision-making processes whose maximisation of public welfare is deeply dependent on the functioning of their respective mechanisms of accountability and participation. As it is well known, state and market failures are recurring. They are linked to the institutional malfunctions in those mechanisms of accountability ad participation in different life settings. One of the most important functions of rules and courts is to identify, limit and correct such failures.

My argument in this chapter is that the blurring of the private–public distinction creates increased challenges to the application and operation of the different mechanisms of accountability and participation of the market and the state. In the EU realm, this phenomenon presents additional challenges as the increased difficulty of distinguishing between forms of private and public action threatens to undermine the conceptual borders according to which the scope of some EU rules has been conceived. Furthermore, there is a risk that states may use this conceptual flexibility in such a way as to create forms of evasion from the application of some EU rules. In some areas, like free movement or State aid, for example, the

[2] A Ibrahim, 'A re-evaluation of the concept of economic activity for the purpose of EU competition rules: the need for modersination' (2015) 15 *European Competition Law Journal* 265, 267.

state may feel tempted to assume a 'private form' to evade the application of those rules, since, in principle, they are not applicable to private actors. In other areas, by contrast, regarding certain EU rules which are only applicable to private activity the state may give a 'public form' to private behaviour in order to exempt it from those rules.

My analysis of the case law of the European Court of Justice will focus on three different areas where this challenge emerges. I will try to identify how the Court has dealt with it in these different areas and, finally, try to determine if there is (and, indeed, whether there can be) a coherent approach to this issue in its different manifestations. I would argue that such a coherent approach is emerging, and that it is founded on a general requirement of consistency and coherence in state intervention in the market; this requirement aims to protect, in turn, the proper functioning of the mechanisms of accountability of the market and the state processes of decision-making.

The areas of the case law I have identified for this purpose are the following: (i) the concept of an undertaking and its link to economic activity; (ii) the application of competition rules to the state (ie the coordinated application of Articles 4 and 101 EC); and (iii) the so called 'golden shares' cases. Other areas could have been included, including different dimensions of the concept of State aid.[3]

I. The Concept of an Undertaking

Articles 101 to 106 of the Treaty on the Functioning of the European Union (TFEU) are only applicable to undertakings. They are, in principle, not aimed at controlling state regulation of the market which is susceptible of restricting free competition but are, instead, addressed at the anticompetitive behaviour of undertakings (including, however, public undertakings and undertakings to which the state has granted special or exclusive rights). The concept of undertaking is therefore essential to the definition of the scope of application of these competition rules. It is well established that an entity engaged in an economic activity constitutes an undertaking for the purposes of EU competition rules. In light of this, the prima facie application of competition rules to the state or state entities is based on one fundamental criterion: whether a certain activity of the state or public body is considered 'economic activity'.

The Court has had the opportunity to clarify the concept of economic activity, as applied to the state, in multiple judgments. The starting point for the Court's inquiry into the notion of economic activity was the *Höfner and Elser* judgment. There, the Court held that a public monopoly on employment procurement could be qualified as pursuing an economic activity since 'employment procurement has

[3] Such an analysis could include matters such as its granting through private resources or the criteria of private creditor and private investor.

not always been, and is not necessarily, carried out by public entities'.[4] In itself, this might lead us to think that any activity susceptible of being performed by a private entity (or a profit-making entity in the more restrictive sense mentioned in the Opinion of Advocate General Jacobs[5]) would have to be included in the concept of economic activity. This, however, would be too broad since, potentially, any activity (including defence) is susceptible of being carried out by private entities. It is for this reason, I would argue, that the Court has in subsequent decisions introduced some limits and refined this broad definition.

In fact, the broad reference in *Höfner and Elser* to activities susceptible of being carried out by private entities has to be contextualised by the circumstance that, in that case, the state de facto accepted the competition of some private operators to the public monopoly. What was relevant was that such activity took place in a market context as demonstrated by competition with private operators. When the Court referred to activity which can be pursued by private entities, it therefore referred to activity which is carried out under market conditions. This effectively comports with the criteria developed by the Court in all its subsequent decisions.

It is in this light too that one should also read the reference in former Advocate General Jacobs' Opinions to whether these activities could, at least in principle, be carried out by a private undertaking in order to make profits.[6] The comparison with potential private operators is not relevant in all cases where these could perform a certain activity, but only where they either already actually exercise that activity in competition with the state, or could do it under conditions similar to how it is exercised by the state. It is in this instance that the comparison criterion helps us to determine whether the state activity takes place in a market or under market conditions.

What is relevant is to ascertain whether the state excludes a certain activity from the market (in which case it would be a non-economic activity), or whether the state, either in competition or under a monopoly regime, pursues that activity as a market activity (in which case it must be considered an economic activity). This inquiry can be carried out by using two concurrent criteria highlighted in the *AOK* case,[7] that summarised well the developments in the case law post-*Höfner and Elser*.

In the *AOK* case, the Court had to assess the lawfulness of the German 'sickness funds' practice of setting maximum reimbursement sums for medical drugs, a practice that was challenged by pharmaceutical companies. In order to

[4] Case C-41/90 *Höfner and Elser* [1991] ECR I-1979 [22]; see PJ Slot (1991) 28 *Common Market Law Review* 964.

[5] AG Jacobs' Opinion in case *AOK*, cited, delivered 22 May 2003.

[6] See [27] of the Opinion in the *AOK* case and case C-222/04, *Cassa di Risparmio*, [2006] ECR I-289, Opinion of the Advocate General Jacobs [78].

[7] Joined cases C-264/01, C-306/01, C-354/01 and C-355/01, *AOK* Bundesverband et al, [2004] ECR I-2493; see BJ Drijber (2005) 42 *Common Market Law Review* 523.

determine whether the conduct of the German federal associations of sickness funds ('fund associations') violated competition rules, the Court first had to establish whether these could be considered undertakings for the purposes of Articles 101 to 106. The fund associations, supported by the observations of the Commission, argued that their activities were not economic activities since they exclusively pursued a social function, were deprived of any profitable goal and were organised under a principle of solidarity. In turn, the pharmaceutical companies argued that since the sickness funds were competing between themselves regarding the amount of the contributions to be paid by the insureds, the services provided and the management and organisation of their services, their activity was an economic activity, and that, consequently, they ought to be considered as undertakings, subject to the application of competition rules.

The judgment of the Court started by recalling, at [46], that 'The concept of an undertaking in competition law covers any entity engaged in economic activity, regardless of the legal status of the entity or the way in which it is financed'.[8]

The Court then analysed the nature of the activity in question. The Court recalled that, in the social security domain, it has developed a series of criteria allowing the exclusion of certain activities from the concept of economic activity. That is notably the case of entities that pursue an exclusively social goal, and whose activity is founded on a principle of solidarity, is devoid of a profit purpose, and where the contributions paid do not correspond to the services provided.[9] However, the Court also recognised that even entities that partly fulfil those criteria may still be considered as undertakings.[10] In other words, if the activity in question takes place in competition with other economic operators and/or if, even when pursuing goals of solidarity, it is, in effect, dominated by a principle of capitalisation, it must be qualified as economic activity.

In the case at hand, the sickness funds exercised an activity with an exclusive social function, devoid of any profit purpose and founded on the principle of solidarity. Moreover, the competition which was possible between them was restricted to a very limited set of circumstances and was also subject to a principle of solidarity (through the existence of a mechanism for redistribution between the different sickness funds). The Court concluded that this limited competition was not sufficient to attribute to their activity the nature of economic activity: 'The sickness funds are therefore not in competition with one another or with private institutions as regards grant of the obligatory statutory benefits in respect of treatment or medicinal products which constitutes their main function'.[11]

Furthermore, the fact that the Court has consistently remarked that the nature of an economic activity must be established per se and not in light of the overall activity of the entity in question (in other words, a certain entity can perform

[8] *AOK* (ibid) [46].
[9] ibid [47].
[10] ibid [49] and [50].
[11] ibid [54].

both economic and non-economic activities for the purposes of the application of competition rules) did not affect the outcome of this case, since the Court considered that by simply determining the precise maximum amounts to be reimbursed for medical drugs as imposed by the law: 'the associations of sickness funds did not pursue a self-interest that could be distinguished from the purely social goals of the sickness funds'.[12]

Thus, the judgment in *AOK* further clarified the notion of economic activity and can help us shed light on the underlying normative criterion that determines when state activity ought to be considered economic activity subject to competition rules.

First, if the activity is pursued in the same market by competing private and public bodies, the public bodies must also be subject to competition rules in order to avoid situations where, while competing with private entities, the public bodies simultaneously claim immunity from competition law. The existence of private operators is in itself sufficient evidence that a market exists with regard to that activity which requires the applications of competition rules. This was the purpose of the inquiry undertaken by the Court in *AOK* on the nature of the competition with respect to the activity undertaken by the sickness funds. A follow-up case, *Cassa di Risparmio*,[13] dealt with the concept of undertaking in the context of State aids and concerned whether banking foundations could be considered undertakings for the purposes of receiving State aid. There, the Court made an even clearer reference to this test by determining that there would be no economic activity if the activity had an exclusive social character and was not exercised in a market in competition with other operators. In a recent judgment, *Dovera*, the Court stated, however, that such competition will not always automatically lead to classify a public body, operating under a principle of solidarity, as an undertaking. It appears that the body will be classified as such, even if non-profit, only with respect to the activities which can be said to have an economic nature.[14]

Second, even where the state has created a statutory monopoly for pursuing a certain activity, it is possible for its own activity to be carried out under market conditions; in that case, it still ought to be subject to competition rules. This is the focus of the inquiry undertaken in many of the Court's decisions on whether the activity in question is carried out with an exclusive social function and under a principle of solidarity or under a principle of capitalisation. To determine which of these principles dominates the activity in question, the Court has developed a set of balancing criteria which depend on the area at stake, and which include the

[12] ibid [62] and [63].

[13] Case C-222/04, *Cassa di Risparmio di Firenze* [2006] ECR I-289.

[14] Judgment of the Court in Joined Cases C-262/18 P and C-271/18 P, 11 June 2020, particularly [49]-[50]. See also the Opinion of Advocate General Pikamäe, [110] ff.

services provided, how contributions are determined, its mandatory nature, the forms of solidarity embodied in the scheme, etc.[15]

To sum up, one could say that what determines whether a certain public activity amounts to an economic activity depends on whether such activity constitutes state participation in a market (as distinct from state intervention in the market). Modifying and refining the initial *Hofner and Elsner* definition, there is economic activity when the activity in question is carried out by the state in the same way that a private operator in the market would pursue it (under a principle of capitalisation and/or to compete with private operators).

It must be recalled that this test serves only to determine whether the activity in question falls within the scope of application of competition rules. It is still possible for the state to combine market and non-market conditions in a certain activity sector, including imposing restrictions of competition. However, in that case the activity would have to be assessed under the conditions put forth in Article 106(2). They will be undertakings entrusted with the operation of services of general economic interest whose pursuit of the tasks attributed to them has to be balanced with the goals of the competition rules under the criteria put in Article 106(2).

The case law is therefore based on determining the true nature of the state action and imposes a requirement of consistency upon the state. If the state decides to undertake a certain activity under market conditions or to delegate it in part to the market, it must be subject to competition rules. Instead, if the state fully maintains a certain activity outside the market, precluding any competition and carrying it out under the principle of solidarity and not capitalisation, the activity is not subject to EU competition rules. A similar argument of consistency has also been put forward by Advocate General Pikamãe in the *Dovera* case. He understands such requirement of consistency as determining that states 'are free to exclude certain activities from the application of competition rules only on condition that they actually implement the principle of solidarity'.[16]

It is obvious that by limiting the application of Articles 101 to 106 to undertakings, the TFEU did not intend to subject all state activity to competition rules. However, Article 106 also makes clear that certain forms of state activity are covered by those rules. The need for consistency or coherence means that if a sate conducts itself as an economic operator, Articles 101 to 106 have to apply. The same principles guide the application of competition rules to the state whenever it ratifies, implements or reinforces decisions taken by undertakings, as we will see in the next section.

[15] *AOK* (n 7).

[16] Opinion of Advocate General Pikamãe [112] citing in a similar sense my own Opinion in Case C-205/03 P, EU:C:2005:666 [27]).

II. The Principle of Loyal Cooperation and Competition Rules: Granting Public Form to Private Behaviour

As stated before, Articles 101 and 102 are only applicable to undertakings. But another hard question has emerged as a consequence of the possibility that certain forms of state action may lead to the same anticompetitive results as those which such provisions aim to prevent. It is well known that the Court has interpreted these provisions together with the principle of loyal cooperation of Article 4 TFEU to establish that

> while it is true that Article 86 [now Article 102 EC] is directed at undertakings, none the less it is also true that the Treaty imposes a duty on Member States not to adopt or maintain in force any measure which could deprive that provision of its effectiveness.[17]

A long and intense debate has emerged on how to interpret the scope of state action that ought to be prohibited in light of the need to maintain the effectiveness of competition rules. The debate was initiated by a famous dispute between Pierre Pescatore and Giuliano Marenco[18] that exposed two very different conceptions of the purpose of internal market rules and the economic constitution they embody. The first argued that the coordinated approach of the principle of loyal cooperation with competition rules should extend as far as to reviewing the impact of state measures on free competition, while the second strongly opposed it. To some extent, these opposing views have framed a long-lasting debate. Some have argued that this general statement of the Court ought to constitute the basis for an extensive application of competition rules, leading to its application to state rules whenever the latter could be said to threaten the objectives of the former. However, some favour a more literal reading of the Treaty provisions and argue that state legislation ought to be excluded from the scope of application of competition rules independent of its impact on the values protected by the EU competition rules. While the first thesis emphasises the values of free competition embodied in the EU economic constitution, the second thesis is based on the assumption that the EU rules ought not to interfere with the economic model of the state, and that is reflected in the Treaty exclusive application of competition rules to undertakings. This debate may also partly explain some of the tensions in the case law.

Moreover, as the blurring of the distinction between private and public actions accentuates itself, such tensions will tend to grow. In my view, the Court has gradually developed, also in this respect, an institutional approach that focuses on protecting the distinct forms of state and market accountability. Instead of itself

[17] Case 13/77, *GB-Inno-BM*, [1977] ECR I-2115 [31].

[18] P Pescatore, 'Public and Private Aspects of European Community Competition Law' (1986–87) 10 *Fordham International Law Journal* 373; G Marenco, 'Competition between National Economies and Competition between Businesses – A Response to Judge Pescatore' (1986–87) 10 *Fordham International Law Journal* 420.

blurring the distinction between how it approaches state and private actions in the market, the Court is primarily concerned with protecting how public and private actions are made accountable even if, paradoxically, that may lead to the application to state action of competition rule. In fact, the predominant fear is that state measures may, in effect, be captured by private anticompetitive behaviour. The overall aim is the same as that guiding the case law described in the previous section but, in this case, it is not public authority that assumes a private form but, rather, private interests which may be disguised under the cover of state authority.

Since the broader statement of the *GB-Inno* decision, the Court has taken a more careful but, in my view, substantially well-founded path in controlling state measures under these provisions. As we will see below, the underlying normative approach is similar to that which guides the Court's case law on the concepts of economic activity and undertaking. According to a well-known line of cases, Articles 101 and 102 are only infringed by state measures in two scenarios: where a Member State requires or favours the adoption of agreements, decisions or concerted practices contrary to Article 101 TFEU or reinforces their effects;[19] or where that state divests its own rules of the character of legislation by delegating to private economic operators responsibility for taking decisions affecting the economic sphere.[20] In the first scenario, the agreement between private undertakings is external to the state, although it is required, favoured or has its effects reinforced by the latter. In the second case, the state delegates its decision-making authority to the private entities.

In two well-known Opinions, Advocates General Jacobs and Léger have, however, expressed some concerns about the limits inherent in this approach which they perceive as being too dependent on establishing the previously anticompetitive behaviour of the private parties themselves.[21] They have consequently proposed somewhat revised criteria to determine the application of Articles 101 and 102 to state measures. For these Advocates General, the measure in question does not constitute an infringement of Articles 4 and 101 TFEU, if (i) its adoption is justified by the pursuit of a legitimate public interest; and (ii) if Member States actively supervise the involvement of private operators in the decision-making process. However, in *Arduino*,[22] the Court apparently remained faithful to its traditional approach. The case concerned Italian legislation fixing maximum and minimum honorariums for lawyers. While the final decision belonged to the Italian Minister, the Italian Bar association played an important role in the setting of the fees, subject to final governmental approval.

[19] Case C-198/01, *CIF*, [2003] ECR I-8055 [46]; see P Nebbia (200) 41 *Common Market Law Review* 839.

[20] Case 136/86, *Aubert* [1987] ECR 4789 [23]; case C-35/96, *Commission v Italy* [1998] ECR I-3851; case C-35/99, *Arduino* [2002] ECR I-1529 [35], and Order of 17 February 2005 in case C-250/03 *Mauri* [2005] ECR I-1267 [30].

[21] Opinion of Advocate General Jacobs, Joined cases C-180/98 to C-184/98, *Pavlov* [2000] ECR I-6451 [160]-[163].

[22] *Arduino* (n 20); see AJ Vossestein (2002) 39 *Common Market Law Review* 841.

I do believe, however, that the Court's traditional approach, if properly developed and understood, contains, in itself, sufficient elements to take into account the concerns of Advocates General Jacobs and Léger and may not be as restrictive as they feared. Instead, while rightly highlighting some possible risks in the case law, their proposal also entails a substantial risk. In their proposal, the conditions imposed on the State were cumulative, which meant that any measure liable of affecting competition would always have to be assessed in terms of the pursuit of a legitimate public interest. This might be too broad, risking overloading the Court and attributing to Articles 101 and 102 a role in reviewing most of the state's economic legislation. Instead, the second criterion suggested by Advocates General Jacobs and Léger can, and, in my view, ought to, be understood as being compatible with the criteria developed in the case law of the Court in this area.

These criteria appear to be dominated by the need to assess the true nature of state intervention in the market. The inquiry is whether the state's legislative process is dominated by a concern to protect the public interest, or, conversely, whether the degree to which private interests intervene in the decision-making process is likely to interfere with the public interest allegedly pursued by the state measure. The capture of the public decision-making process by private interests would, at least, raise the suspicion that the state measure may protect those private interests instead of pursuing the public interest. This requires an institutional understanding of the test of delegation on private actors. That fits well with Advocates General Jacobs and Léger's requirement of effective state supervision. This interpretation guarantees that the application of competition rules is excluded only where it is due to a real submission to the public interest and not where there is a serious risk of capture of the political process by private actors. The purpose of the application of competition rules to state measures 'is not to challenge the anti-competitive effects of State actions, but instead to ensure that the decision-making process is not determined by private interests'.[23]

This institutional approach requires an assessment of the degree of involvement of the private entities in the legislative process, in order to guarantee that their participation at the stage at which a rule is proposed or their presence within a body responsible for drafting that rule does not have a determining influence on the content of the rule and outweighs the taking into consideration of other interests. The purpose is to prevent the control of the public decision-making process by the private entities whose competition is at stake, leading to a legislative provision whose sole or predominant purpose might be the protection of certain private entities from the elements of competition, to the detriment of the public interest. As such, such test serves to protect the integrity of the accountability processes of both the State and the market.

[23] Ibrahim, 'A re-evaluation of the concept of economic activity' (2015) 276, citing M Thunstrom, J Carle and S Pervan Lindeborg, 'State Liability Under the EC Treaty Arising from Anticompetitive State Measures' (2002) 25 *World Competition* 515, 518 and O Odudu, 'The public/private distinction in EU Internal Market Law' (2010) 4 *Revue Trimestrielle de Droit Européen* 823.

Such a test requires from courts a certain factual analysis of the decision-making process of the public authorities involved to assess that there is, in fact, an effective state supervision. It is also not uncommon for courts to focus, on the contrary, on the procedural dimensions involved in the adoption of the challenged measure. It is, in any case, a more feasible and normatively defensible task than that of having to assess the anticompetitive effects of state measures and balancing them with other public interests. It is, in any case, a more feasible and normatively defensible task than that of having to assess the anticompetitive effects of state measures and balancing them with other public interests.

I believe that this approach also fits the Court's judgment in *Arduino*. There, the Court stressed that it considered there to be real supervision by the state, and maintained that 'it does not appear that the Italian State has waived its power to make decisions of last resort or to review implementations of the tariff'.[24] The Court's disagreement with the Advocate General, which argued for the measure to fall within the scope of review under competition rules, seems to be based on different factual assessments of the degree to which the state had maintained effective supervision of the process rather than on a different understating of the normative criteria that ought to guide the application of competition rules to state measures.

That the Court did not intend to further restrict the application of competition rules to the state was made clear in a subsequent case which appeared to even open the door for a broader interpretation of the application of competition rules by stating that

> since the Treaty of Maastricht entered into force, the EC Treaty has expressly provided that in the context of their economic policy the activities of the Member States must observe the principle of an open market economy with free competition.[25]

I would argue, however, that the best way for the Court to protect this principle is by protecting the integrity of the processes of accountability of both the state and the market and not by getting itself into defining, in the absence of clear demarcation lines in the Treaties, what ought to be the realm of the market and the realm of the state.

While the case law reviewed in the previous section deals with cases where a state may take a private form and, in so doing, no longer be subject to the processes of accountability inherent in state action (and evade the application of certain EU rules based on such forms of accountability of state actions), the cases reviewed in this section deal instead with the risk inherent in having private interests effectively controlling state decision-making. When that is so, such private interests could use the cover of the state to escape the accountability inherent in being subject to competition rules. The state may end up serving as an instrument to protect the

[24] *Arduino* (n 20) [40].
[25] Case C-198/01, *CIF* [2003] I-8055 [47].

anticompetitive behaviour of private actors. To prevent this, state measures should only be excluded from Articles 101 and 102 if they correspond to a genuine state intervention in the market, formulated in light of the public interest in a decision-making process which is not controlled by the private entities which are supposed to be in competition in that market. In both lines of cases, however, a requirement of consistency is imposed on state action precisely to guarantee that any form of action in the market, public or private, is subject to their respective instruments of accountability.

A recent decision helps make this general approach clearer by, to a certain extent, merging both areas of the case law. It confirms that the focus of the task undertaken by the Court remains in distinguishing genuine state action from private action in a market and making sure that they are subject to their respective forms of accountability. In *Ordem dos Técnicos Oficiais de Contas (OTOC)*, the Court had to assess if a professional association to which the state entrusted certain regulatory powers could still be, in this respect, subject to competition rules.[26] The Court was clear in stating that it remained subject to competition rules (in the case, Article 101) and that a regulation adopted by the professional association, under the regulatory power invested in it by the state, was a private action. The Court stated that OTOC, even if regulated by public law and exercising a power invested on it by the state, was 'acting rather as a regulatory body of a profession of which constitutes, moreover, an economic activity'.[27] In its assessment, the Court highlights the fact that the decision-making bodies of OTOC are only composed by its members and that public authorities play no role in their appointment or that the regulatory power of OTOC benefits from a large discretion and it is not subject to any conditions and criteria by the state.[28] The Court also stresses the inherent conflict of interest in having the professional association regulating a market in which itself is competing.[29] Such conflict of interest is a clear example of the risk of the integrity of the accountability and participation processes inherent in market competition that the Court needs to protect.

III. Golden Shares

Another area of case law confirms the overall approach highlighted in the two previous sections. This is the area of the case law addressing the so called 'golden shares'. These are shares retained by the state in privatised companies and which are granted special rights with respect to certain decisions of those companies and their business activities. In a series of infringement actions brought against several

[26] Case C-1/12, *Ordem dos Técnicos Oficiais de Contas*, ECLI:EU:C:2013:127.
[27] ibid [46].
[28] ibid [47]-[50].
[29] ibid, eg [45].

Member States by the European Commission, these measures were challenged on the grounds that they violated the free movement of capital and the right of establishment. The cases where the Court initially developed its approach date from the end of 2002.[30] But this approach was even more fully articulated in subsequent judgments.[31] This line of cases regarding free movement rules helps to make clear that there is a broader approach in the case law, with respect to the protection of the distinctive forms of accountability of markets and states, that goes beyond the domain of competition law. In fact, I would claim we can also find it in areas such as State aids or the application of free movement rules to certain forms of private action. Here, I focus only on three examples, the latter involving this application of free movement rules to 'golden shares'.

As in other areas of community law, the Court is called in to define the limits that the EU legal order imposes on forms of state intervention in the market which, instead of constituting classic exercises of state intervention in the market (either by regulating the market or by public ownership of certain economic activities) make use of private instruments or market mechanisms while attempting to retain some form of public control over the latter. The question arises, in these instances, on the limits and control imposed on the forms of state action once the state chooses the pursuit a certain function through traditional market mechanisms.

Advocate General Damaso Ruiz-Jarabo Colomer has argued that since the state could, in principle, retain full control over certain companies though public ownership (which is, notably, protected by Article 345 TFEU), it should also be possible for the state to retain a more limited form of control by retaining certain special rights in privatised companies.[32] Stated in even broader terms:

> It is almost unthinkable that the Treaty should be intended to allow the Member States to retain the full shareholding in any undertaking, with the maximum restriction on the freedoms of establishment and movement of capital which that implies, and, at the same time, to stand in the way of a liberalised system subject to limited administrative conditions which are non-discriminatory and, therefore, more in keeping with the aim of integration. To put it another way: if withdrawing financial activities from the private sector, by allocating them to publicly owned bodies (nationalisation or socialisation, pure and simple), creates a special system of ownership, as opposed to the ordinary system of ownership, there is no reason why a system of private ownership subject to special powers should not be viewed in the same way or should be treated less favourably.[33]

[30] Case C-367/98, *Commission v Portugal* [2002] ECR I-4731; case C-483/99, *Commission v France* [2002] ECR I-4781; case C-503/99, *Commission v Belgium* [2002] ECR I-4809; case C-98/01, *Commission v United Kingdom* [2003] ECR I-4641; see H Fleischer (2003) 40 *Common Market Law Review* 493.

[31] See, for example, Case C-463/00, *Commission v Spain* [2003] ECR I-4581; Case C-174/04, *Commission v Italy* [2005] ECR I-4933.

[32] *Commission v Spain* (ibid), and *Commission v United Kingdom* (n 30).

[33] *Commission v Portugal*; *Commission v France*; and *Commission v Belgium* (n 30) [66].

The Court did not follow this reasoning and took the view that Member States could not

> plead their own systems of property, referred to in Article (354) of the Treaty, by way of justification for obstacles, resulting from privileges attaching to their position as shareholder in a privatised undertaking, to the exercise of the freedoms provided for by the Treaty.[34]

In my view, this position of the Court is in line with its case law in the two previous areas I have reviewed, notably that related to the definition of economic activity where the state acts as a market participant. There is an obligation of coherence that is imposed upon the state once it decides to open a certain sector to the market.

This requirement is particularly important in the case of the privatisation of former state companies. In effect, while the state is entitled to maintain public ownership of certain companies by the Treaty, it is not entitled to be selective in the access it grants to certain economic sectors once these are open to the market. If the state were entitled to maintain special forms of market control over privatised companies, it could easily frustrate the application of free movement rules by granting only selective and potentially discriminatory access to substantial parts of the national market. It is for this reason that once a state decides to privatise a certain company, the protection of the free movement of capital demands that the economic autonomy of this company be protected, except where it is necessary to safeguard certain fundamental public interests recognised by EU law. The intervention of the state can no longer be determined by the purpose of securing an economic and managerial control over the company in a manner contrary to the normal operation of the market while, paradoxically, making use of the market. If that was authorised the state could use, on the one hand, the private nature of the company to evade the forms of accountability to which state action is subject to and, on the other hand, claim its public nature to evade the accountability resulting from market mechanisms. It is for this reason, that such special rights have to be subject to particular scrutiny and need to be justified by the pursuit of a possible general economic interest associated with that company.

The later also demonstrates that the purpose of the Court is not that of favouring a particular model of corporate law, based on proportionality between ownership and control, or, even less, to favour economic liberalisation.[35] The purpose is that of protecting the integrity of the different mechanisms of accountability inherent in state and market decision-making. The state should not be able to 'use' a private form to escape public accountability (including under free movement rules) while, at the same time, not being subject to market accountability either. It is this that

[34] *Commission v Spain* (n 31) [67].

[35] For a critique of this type of case law, I Antonaki, 'Keck in Capital? Redefining "Restrictions" in the Golden Shares' Case Law' (2016) 9 *Erasmus Law Review* 177, 185–86.

justifies submitting to enhanced judicial scrutiny the cases where a state grants itself special rights in a company.

This enhanced scrutiny does not mean that the state cannot institute such special rights. The Court has recognised that 'certain concerns may justify retention by Member States of a degree of influence within undertakings that were initially public and subsequently privatised'.[36] However, from the case law of the Court, it is clear that such influence must not be aimed simply at retaining economic or market control over the company and must be limited to the objective of guaranteeing the fulfilment of certain public interest obligations. Once the state has taken the decision that is in the public interest to privatise a certain company or sector of activity, it cannot attempt to artificially retain economic control over the company by restricting, in effect, market access to that company. While the state may choose to maintain a certain company under public ownership, once it decides to privatise it, it must not set in place rules which can restrict access to that company by certain market operators, to the advantage of others or of the state itself. Restrictions are therefore only acceptable if necessary for the pursuit of certain public interests attributed to those companies and not to guarantee the maintenance of a state economic control over those companies. It is for this reason that the Court has stressed the 'principle of respect for the decision-making autonomy of the undertaking concerned'.[37] The special nature of the regime that the state creates for itself increases the risk that the state may be trying to maintain control over the government of such companies in such a way as to try to elude both the mechanisms of accountability and control to which state action is usually subject and those to which companies would be subject to in that state. It is such institutional risk that triggers the need for stricter judicial control.

As a consequence, if on the one hand the Court accepts that derogations to the fundamental principle of the free movement of capital may be accepted 'if there is a genuine and sufficiently serious threat to a fundamental interest of society',[38] on the other hand these derogations are limited to what is necessary to guarantee that 'the performance, under economically acceptable conditions, of the tasks of general economic interest which it has entrusted to an undertaking' would not be jeopardized.[39] It is also for these reasons that the state must identify the specific public interest worth of protection and that the rules granting special rights to the state should be based on objective and precise criteria that do not go beyond what is necessary for pursuing that public interest and guaranteeing the possibility of effective review by the Courts.

As in other areas, one can identify a requirement of consistency or coherence that is imposed on Member States. Once a decision is taken to subject a certain

[36] *Commission v Belgium* (n 30) [43].
[37] ibid [49].
[38] ibid [47].
[39] *Commission v Spain* (n 31) [82].

company to the market, the state can no longer use its authority to create a special regime that will give it particular control over that company unless it can justify such special regime as being necessary to pursue a particular public interest.

IV. Conclusion

The areas reviewed are only examples of the increased challenges that are arising for applying EU rules to the new forms of state participation or intervention in the market and the difficulty of distinguishing between private and public legal forms of action. As stated, this analysis could be extended to other areas. In the area of State aid, for example, it is foreseeable that this issue will gain importance as new legal forms are adopted by the state and by private operators, or as the state comes up with new instruments for intervention which will make it more difficult to determine what constitutes State aid and what does not.[40] At the same time, in the private domain, the multiplication of private actors with regulatory powers similar to those of the states will continue to push for an extension of the scope of application of EU rules.

So far, the Court has answered these challenges by developing a case law that is both flexible and built upon solid normative foundations. The criterion underlying these different areas of case law appears to be that a requirement of coherence or consistency is imposed on the state in its relationship with the market. This criterion can be said to make sense not only as a necessary tool for allowing the scope of EU rules to adapt to the changing faces of the state but also, in broader terms, for guaranteeing the different mechanisms of accountability inherent in the market and the state.

The power the state exercises in the political sphere is subject to democratic control and the rule of law. Particular sets of rules impose certain forms of accountability on different forms of state action. The market, by contrast, provides a different form of accountability dominated by competition which is, itself, protected by competition rules. When the exercise of state power takes a public form and occurs outside the market, it is subject to certain mechanisms of accountability which, in the EU context, are reflected in rules such as free movement and non-discrimination. Such public exercises of power are also assumed to take place under a decision-making logic which differs from that of the actors in a market (though both can, at times, pursue the same goals). Instead, the use of a private legal form and the substitution of state intervention in the market by state participation in that market often entails the exclusion of these forms of state activity from those traditional mechanisms of public accountability. It is therefore essential, both in terms of proper accountability of the state and of control of

[40] See the recent case *Cassa di Risparmio di Firenze* (n 13).

any form of power, to identify the exact character of the activity in question and subject it to the corresponding accountability mechanisms, be they those of the market (if the private form is genuine) or reinstate those of the state (when it is not). A principle of consistency serves to distinguish one from the other. In addition, a consistency requirement is also important for the purposes of guaranteeing the transparency necessary for the functioning of the mechanisms of political accountability existent in the state's political process. This accountability will only be effective if the state is required to make the nature and purpose of its decision-making correspond to what it proclaims to be that nature.

This requirement of consistency also operates at the level of the market in two ways. First, by guaranteeing that when the state acquires a private form and is no longer subject to the classic mechanisms of public accountability it becomes subject to the alternative mechanism of accountability inherent in the market (mainly competition). Second, by guaranteeing that the state is not allowed to intervene to protect certain private operators from the mechanisms of accountability inherent in market competition. In other words, that private actors can also not make use of hybrid private–public forms to pursue private interests while excluding them from market accountability either by capturing a public decision-making process or by being given by the state a regulatory power similar to public power.

4

The Boundaries of Antitrust in the European Union

GIORGIO MONTI[1]

I. Introduction

At the time Giuliano Amato's *Antitrust and the Bounds of Power* was published, there were very few works about European competition law which discussed it in its wider context, and few comparative works in that vein.[2] Most of the scholarship was doctrinal and much was produced by practitioners. While practical analysis matters, technical antitrust doctrines, Amato showed, 'find their roots in the great political and philosophical options with which antitrust law still remains bound up'.[3] Matching doctrinal development with the story of ideas about markets is the major achievement of his book.[4] Of the many reflections found in it, the one which is the focus of this chapter is Amato's claim that the transformation of EU antitrust law from a system that focused on economic freedom to one that focused on economic efficiency meant that there should be 'a liberation of antitrust law from the multiple purposes it has served in the past enabling it to be … antitrust law pure and simple'.[5]

In this chapter I discuss whether antitrust has been liberated and if such liberation is desirable. It is structured in the following way. In section II, I trace the normative perspective which Amato used to reach this recommendation and its implications. Then, I take each implication in turn and discuss it in light of the evolution of EU antitrust in the last 25 years. In section III, I argue that

[1] Professor Amato and I both taught at the European University Institute (EUI). During my stint there, I learned a considerable amount from my 31 PhD students, and I have used some of their contributions to antitrust scholarship to develop this chapter.

[2] An exception was AD Neale and DJ Goyder, *The Antitrust Laws of the United States of America: A Study of Competition Enforced by Law*, 3rd edn (CUP, 1981). A year later DJ Gerber, *Law and Competition in Twentieth Century Europe* (OUP, 1998) brought even more insights.

[3] G Amato, *Antitrust and the Bounds of Power: The Dilemma of Liberal Democracy in the History of the Market* (Hart, 1997) 2.

[4] I have tried to emulate this in my work, see G Monti, *EC Competition Law* (2007).

[5] Amato, *Antitrust and the Bounds of Power* 116.

the transformation of antitrust which had just begun in 1997 now threatens the ability of antitrust to contain all manifestations of market power. Here, liberation has gone too far. At the same time, those calling for a re-strengthening of antitrust to prohibit more forms of conduct are advancing claims that push the boundaries of antitrust outwards again: are they going outside antitrust boundaries? In section IV, I argue that the liberation of antitrust from multiple purposes has occurred by reference to the Commission's enforcement track record, but competition law suffers repeated challenges to open itself up to exempting practices for strategic or other policy reasons which it appears to both accept and resist.[6] Here, liberation is under pressure: how do we decide when antitrust should resist and when it should yield?

The purpose of this discussion is to try and answer the two questions above by articulating a set of principles to help us understand when a change in antitrust perspective is legitimate, thereby establishing criteria to spell out the boundaries of antitrust.[7] Section V brings the discussion to a close by defending a vision of antitrust that is, from Amato's perspective, impure, but by showing that lack of purity is in the very nature of the antitrust enterprise. Space precludes detailed consideration of every development of antitrust during the past 25 years, but hopefully this impressionistic sketch covers key developments that justify the claims made here.

II. Antitrust Pure and Simple

While antitrust has always been a law to control economic power, Amato claimed that the scope of its application has changed. First, in its original incarnation, antitrust was capable of controlling big firms for their impact on the economy as well as on national politics. However, with the opening of markets to trade, the capacity of antitrust to control the political manifestations of private power waned.[8] 'A big firm that does not have economic power over a market that has expanded beyond national limits may nonetheless have in the domestic political process that abusive power it was the antitrust objective to contain.'[9] Thus, it became more tricky to check political power absent market power. Second, developments in economics led to a narrowing of the scope of antitrust by observing the economic efficiencies of forms of conduct that were once forbidden, a phenomenon that is particularly clear when considering vertical integration and vertical restraints. This does not mean that enforcement ends, but that it focuses on instances where

[6] On this, see also S Makris, 'EU Competition Law as Responsive Law' (2021) 23 *Cambridge Yearbook of European Legal Studies* 228.

[7] This tries to build on the important contributions of Ioannis Lianos. See in particular, I Lianos 'Polycentric Competition Law' (2018) 71 *Current Legal Problems* 161.

[8] On this theme see also A Daly, *Private Power, Online Information Flows and EU Law – Mind the Gap* (Hart, 2016) observing the private power of digital firms.

[9] Amato (n 3) 104.

market power causes inefficiency. Amato recognised that there remain debates about what efficiency means, suggesting at least two concepts; one focuses solely as 'non-restriction of output', which is the position taken by those who propose light touch antitrust intervention; and the other sees efficiency as 'the maximum possible opening of markets', which is probably close to a contemporary Ordoliberal understanding of competition law enforcement.[10]

In the context of this refocusing of antitrust only towards the economic effects of market power, EU and US antitrust retain fundamental differences, notably the EU's emphasis on the single market imperative and the special responsibility held by dominant undertakings. In Amato's view these aspects of EU competition law will 'remain in the antitrust picture'.[11] However, what Amato felt the Europeans could jettison is 'interference in the antitrust area from policies of other types that have so far influenced it'.[12] The justification offered for this view is that the Maastricht Treaty signed in 1992, in particular the new Article 130 EC (now Article 173 TFEU), required that the European Community (now Union) and the Member States develop a set of policies in coordination with each other to 'ensure that the conditions necessary for the competitiveness of the Community's industry exist'. What mattered for antitrust law is that this industrial policy shall be carried out 'in accordance with a system of open and competitive markets' and that the legislator specified that this provision 'shall not provide a basis for the introduction by the Community of any measure which could lead to a distortion of competition'.[13] Thus, an anticompetitive agreement cannot be justified because it creates an EU champion. Generalising from this, according to Amato, 'The EC Treaty imposes the avoidance of any confusion and requires antitrust to be antitrust alone'.[14]

These changes would yield three consequences. First the regulatory stance of EU competition law would wane because one would no longer balance competition and non-competition considerations. Second, there would be greater emphasis in applying competition law by reference to economic yardsticks, which would in particular affect the interpretation of Article 101(1) TFEU. Third, this would call into question the role of the Commission as an antitrust enforcer. If the rules are antitrust pure and simple, then an EU competition authority would be better placed to make such technocratic choices, and the Commission might be limited to absolving restrictive agreements in the name of a public interest.[15] Having sketched Amato's argument for a transformation, we now take stock of developments since 1997 and discuss how far this transformation has occurred and what reactions there have been to it.

[10] ibid 115. E Deutscher and S Makris, 'Exploring the Ordoliberal Paradigm: The Competition-Democracy Nexus' (2016) 11 *Competition Law Review* 181.

[11] Amato (n 3) 116.

[12] ibid.

[13] Article 130(3) EC.

[14] Amato (n 3) 119.

[15] ibid 122. The text is sketchy on the role of the Commission and on the grounds that might be invoked to authorise agreements.

III. The More Economic Approach to Antitrust

A. The Evolution of the More Economic Approach

Just a year after the publication of Amato's book, the Commission published a follow-up report on its review of vertical restraints. This is a remarkable document because it is one of the few times the Commission has openly admitted 'shortcomings in current policy'.[16] Its self-assessment reflected criticisms in the literature: straight-jacketing effects of block exemption regulations, under-enforcement as firms with market power could benefit from block exemptions, over-enforcement resulting from a lack of coverage of the block exemptions. The conclusion was that 'a more economics-based approach is required'.[17] Here began a major transformation of EU competition law.[18] The consequence of this approach, according to the Commission would be that fewer agreements would be covered by Article 101(1) TFEU.[19] The result of this Green Paper are well known: the Commission produced a new-look Block Exemption Regulation, which exempted agreements only of undertakings below a given market share threshold and allowed these undertakings to enter into whatever contract they wished, provided that a small set of blacklisted contractual arrangements were not present.[20] This led to a much more liberal system, allowing undertakings without market power to design distribution agreements in the way they wished without fear of regulatory intervention. At the time of writing, this new-look Block Exemption Regulation is undergoing its second revision and its fundamental structure remains intact. The main focus of the reform is to secure acceptable rules in a market where online sales are of increasing importance.[21] This more economic approach clashes with the Commission's enforcement against vertical restraints that segment the internal market, but as Amato had recognised, this European idiosyncracy is well-embedded in the EU system.[22]

Having said that, there is a risk of the more economics-based approach going too far and reducing the capacity to enforce the law. This has occurred in the context of Article 102 TFEU, although the developments in this field

[16] Communication from the Commission on the application of the Community competition rules to vertical restraints – Follow-up to the Green Paper on vertical restraints [1998] OJ C365/3, S 1.

[17] ibid S 2.

[18] AC Witt, *The More Economic Approach to EU Antitrust Law* (Hart, 2016) for critical assessment.

[19] Amato (n 3) 50–54, where he observes that the ECJ had already been moving in this direction in its case law and regretting the regulatory approach of the block exemptions of the time.

[20] Regulation 2790/99 on the application of Article 81(3) of the Treaty to categories of vertical agreements and concerted practices [1999] OJ L336/21.

[21] MJ Schmidt-Kessen 'Selective Distribution Systems in EU competition and EU trademark law: resolving the tension' (2018) 9 *Journal of European Competition Law and Practice* 304.

[22] G Monti, 'Keeping Geo-Blocking Practices in Check: Competition Law and Regulation' (19 February 2021), available at ssrn.com/abstract=3789176. Economists have recommended a less interventionist stance, see EAGCP (Economic Advisory Group on Competition Policy), 'Hardcore restrictions under the Block Exemption Regulation on vertical agreements: An economic view' (September 2009).

remain patchy.[23] Much as with vertical restraints, commentators considered the Commission's approach to Article 102 TFEU to be form-based and overly aggressive.[24] As with vertical restraints, the Commission consulted economic experts and stakeholders to assess whether to recalibrate its policy.[25] Unlike verticals, the Commission's official documents did not acknowledge errors in its previous policy, but the resulting soft law document took a narrower view on the application of Article 102 TFEU.[26] Of particular importance for the purposes of this discussion is that the Commission rethought its approach to dominant firms. In particular, the Commission took the view that an abuse would only be found if the conduct causes anticompetitive foreclosure:

> '[A] situation where effective access of actual or potential competitors to supplies or markets is hampered or eliminated as a result of the conduct of the dominant undertaking whereby the dominant undertaking is likely to be in a position to profitably increase prices to the detriment of consumers.[27]

This is a much narrower view than that explained by the Court in its earlier case law, where the emphasis was on the extent to which dominant firms harmed the competitive process more generally. For example, in assessing discounts offered by a dominant firm to its customers, the Court took the view that there could be four reasons for condemning rebates offered by a dominant undertaking to its customers. They could: (i) remove or restrict the buyers' freedom to choose their sources of supply; (ii) bar competitors from access to the market; (iii) apply dissimilar conditions to equivalent transactions with other trading partners; or (iv) strengthen the dominant position by distorting competition.[28] The new approach that focuses on anticompetitive foreclosure does not require proof of direct consumer harm, however. It merely asks the Commission to establish that the conduct in question is capable of causing anticompetitive foreclosure. Nevertheless, establishing this capability requires a greater investment of resources on the part of the Commission, as can be seen in the *Intel* decision.[29]

Having narrowed down the interests protected under Article 102 TFEU, the Commission also indicated that anticompetitive foreclosure is a concern when the rival is as efficient as the dominant undertaking. Thus, excluding inefficient rivals, appears authorised under the new approach.[30] The problem with this emphasis

[23] G Monti, 'Abuse of a dominant position: A post-intel calm?' (2019) 3 *CPI Antitrust Chronicle*.

[24] DA Crane and G Mirailles Murciego, 'Toward a Unified Theory of Exclusionary Vertical Restraints' (2011) 84 *Southern California Law Review* 605.

[25] Report by the EAGCP, 'An economic approach to Article 82' (July 2005).

[26] Guidance on the Commission's enforcement priorities in applying Article 82 of the EC Treaty to abusive exclusionary conduct by dominant undertakings [2009] OJ C45/7.

[27] ibid para 19.

[28] Case 322/81, *Nederlandsche Banden-Industrie-Michelin v Commission* EU:C:1983:313 [73]. See also, to the same effect, *Hoffmann-La Roche & Co. AG v Commission*, Case 85/76, EU:C:1979:36 [90].

[29] Case COMP/C-3/37.990 – Intel (decision of 13 May 2009), which is still subject to judicial proceedings.

[30] Case C-209/10, *Post Danmark A/S v Konkurrencerådet* EU:C:2012:172 [22].

on efficient rivals is that it is often unknown what a new rival might bring to the market but for the exclusionary conduct of the dominant undertaking. From this perspective, the scope of application of Article 102 TFEU is further reduced. It is not yet entirely clear whether the as efficient competitor standard, which has been applied in the context of price-based exclusionary conduct such as discounts and predatory pricing, applies to other forms of unilateral conduct.

The effect of these two moves is to raise the agency's costs in applying competition law. Even economists who support an aggressive antitrust stance against dominant undertakings require fairly sophisticated methods before conduct is condemned. Of particular interest in this context is the approach to rebates. In the Guidance Paper the Commission suggested a fairly complex test for identifying rebates likely to exclude as-efficient rivals, but even this degree of sophistication did not satisfy economists who support the application of antitrust against rebates, who maintained that the Commission 'could have done a better job in formulating the theory of harm in a more coherent way'.[31]

Even if critics think that the Commission has not yet fully digested modern industrial economics in its Article 102 TFEU case law, the concern remains that the Commission has swallowed more economics than is necessary, because Article 102 TFEU

> is not designed only or primarily to protect the immediate interests of individual competitors or consumers, but to protect *the structure of the market* and thus *competition as such (as an institution)*, which has already been weakened by the presence of the dominant undertaking on the market.[32]

This foundational stone of the application of abuse of dominance is being speedily eroded.

B. Widening the Concerns of Antitrust again

An even more radical critique of the economic approach is that it leads to significant under-enforcement by its adoption of a consumer welfare standard which leads to unnecessarily lenient treatment of business conduct. This critique originates in US scholarship where the past 25 years have seen an even more significant retreat in the public enforcement of antitrust law by US agencies than that which was noted by Amato.[33] It is not clear whether the retrenchment in the US is the result of the consumer welfare standard or of courts raising the standard of proof

[31] C Fumagalli, M Motta and C Calcagno, *Exclusionary Practices: The Economics of Monopolisation and Abuse of Dominance* (CUP, 2018) 217.

[32] Case C-95/04P, *British Airways plc v Commission* EU:C:2006:133, Opinion of AG Kokott [68] (emphasis in the original).

[33] R Pitofsky (ed), *How the Chicago School Overshot the Mark: The Effect of Conservative Economic Analysis on U.S. Antitrust* (OUP, 2008).

for plaintiffs, but the current debate in the US has not led to a convincing alternative antitrust standard.[34] This so-called Neo-Brandeisian critique of antitrust has much less traction in the EU where public antitrust enforcement by the Commission and some national competition authorities has remained vigorous and serves as a benchmark for some US reformers.[35]

In the EU, the most radical challenge to the economics-based approach in the case law is found in the *Bayer/Monsanto* decision.[36] The Commission was faced with arguments for a more aggressive antitrust stance when considering the effect of a merger in the markets for seeds and pesticides. A number of organisations were concerned that the Commission's analytical framework was too narrow. In addition to assessing the effects of the merger on prices, innovation incentives and the reduction in product variety, they claimed that one should look at the merger 'also in terms of loss of biodiversity as a harm to the environment'. Moreover, when considering innovation, one should not just focus on whether the merger would reduce incentives to innovate, but also whether the right kind of innovation would occur post-merger. They claimed that one should assess the risk of misuse of innovation. On the facts, it was claimed that 'the merged entity would have very little, if any incentive, to innovate towards the use of less chemical products or towards healthier farming products'.[37]

The Commission's response was that while the TFEU requires the Commission to have regard to multiple objectives, including the protection of human health and environmental protection requirements, these objectives formed no part of its assessment under the Merger Regulation because the legislator did not confer upon it the competence to address these effects. However, this reading is simplistic, for two reasons. The first is that the Commission labels the arguments of the opponents of the merger as non-competition concerns. This assumes a particular vision of what competitive markets should be like and thus requires a deeper justification as to why it is that the likely reduction in innovation is relevant for competition law, but the risk of less innovation in more sustainable products is not a competition parameter. A normative choice has been made to include within 'competition' a set of considerations and exclude others, but the justification is not apparent.[38] This is not least because there is evidence, in this specific merger, that innovation

[34] AD Melamed and N Petit, 'The Misguided Assault on the Consumer Welfare Standard in the Age of Platform Markets'(2019) 54 *Review of Industrial Organization* 741, G Monti, 'The American antitrust counter-revolutionaries: A European perspective' in N Charbit and S Gachot (eds) *Eleanor M. Fox: Antitrust ambassador to the world – Liber Amicorum* (Concurrences, 2021).

[35] see eg LM Khan and S Vaheesan, 'Market Power and Inequality: The Antitrust Counterrevolution and Its Discontents' (2017) 11 *Harvard Law & Policy Review* 235, 283, noting that US 'antitrust agencies and courts should look to European Union abuse of dominance law for a model to emulate'.

[36] Case M.8084, *Bayer/Monsanto* (20 December 2018).

[37] ibid [3007].

[38] In the healthcare field, it has been argued that the focus on choice as a parameter of competition can be at the expense of considering the quality of healthcare. T Stavroulaki, 'Connecting the Dots: Antitrust, Quality and Medicine' (2019) 31 *Loyola Consumer Law Review* 175.

by the larger players is skewed to maximising revenue.[39] The second is that if we say that the considerations above are not competition-related, then Recital 23 of the Merger Regulation requires that the competition appraisal is carried out 'within the general framework of the achievement of the fundamental objectives' expressed in the Treaties.[40] The Commission fails to explain how merger analysis can be carried out with respect to this requirement. It is not enough to state that there are other EU policies that regulate agricultural markets and that therefore there are other means of addressing non-competition market failures. Recital 23 requires an integrated approach, for example by asking in detail how far existing regulations addresses concerns raised by opponents to the merger, say biodiversity. Where there is existing legislation, the non-competition concerns can be set aside because there is a regulatory safeguard. However, where there is no legislation protecting society from a particular negative effect such as a reduction in biodiversity, it is arguable that the Commission can step in and block the merger on that ground if it is shown that the market power of the merged entity leads to a reduction in biodiversity. Obviously, this recommendation requires an even more complex merger analysis than what is being carried out.

This discussion raises a key question about the boundaries of antitrust. Supporters of the consumer welfare standard suggest that antitrust applies only when conduct harms economic welfare.[41] Even under this optic (and so without accepting calls for a wider reading of the scope of antitrust law) the risk of innovation being poorly directed can count as a parameter of economic welfare. If consumers demand research in more sustainable farming methods but the merged entity has enough market power to refuse to respond to such demand and continue only less sustainable lines of innovation, then this is an economic harm to which merger law should respond. The Commission's characterisation of the complaint as a non-competition concern looks insufficiently robust and a better conceptual framework is required to distinguish between harms that are protected by competition law and those harms that are not within its purview. Four principles are suggested here. These apply in particular to the EU and US systems because in both the legislative text is open-textured and scant legislative guidance is provided to determine its scope.

The first is that the boundaries of antitrust are drawn with reference to the interest the law is designed to protect. Amato, along with most commentators, considers that economics helps interpret the laws, hence a standard based on economic welfare is established. The history of EU antitrust suggests a further

[39] ME Stucke and AP Grunes, 'An Updated Antitrust Review of the Bayer-Monsanto Merger', The Konkurrenz Group (6 March 2018) 14–15.

[40] Regulation 139/2004 on the control of concentrations between undertakings [2004] OJ L/24/1, recital 23. Now these are found in Art 3 TEU.

[41] The discussion between total and consumer welfare is not relevant for the purposes of this chapter. See R Pittman, 'Consumer Surplus as the Appropriate Standard for Antitrust Enforcement' EAG 07-9 June 2007.

interest – keeping markets open. The pursuit of these two interests normally converge, but the latter is more aggressive when it comes to dominant firm conduct. Applying these two approaches allows the development of an innovation theory of harm upon proof that the merger reduces incentives to innovate. But neither would allow intervention if the merger does not reduce incentives to innovate as a whole but there is evidence that the 'wrong' kind of innovation is carried out. As we said above, the economic welfare standard could prohibit a merger leading to the wrong kind of innovation only upon proof that that kind of innovation is desired by consumers. The open market approach to antitrust would be agnostic about the direction of innovation. Both approaches would condemn innovation efforts designed to exclude rivals, but here the reason for condemning bad innovation in this context is because it harms consumer welfare or the competitive process.[42]

The second principle is that the conduct has to fulfil the other requirements of the statute. Thus, unilateral conduct by a non-dominant firm which causes pollution is excluded from the scope of antitrust because there is no dominance for Article 102 TFEU to apply nor an agreement to build up a case under Article 101 TFEU. Each antitrust case is composed of conduct falling within the statute plus the undesired effect that the law is designed to protect.

The third, which follows from the above, is that the application of competition law should always achieve the objective of safeguarding the interests the law protects. For example, every time Article 101 TFEU is applied to cartels one is preventing a practice that harms consumer welfare or the competitive process.[43] If we apply this principle to a dominant undertaking polluting the environment, we can see that there might be the odd case that a competition authority will take that achieves this, but that this is not a harm that is generally addressed by applying antitrust. In fact, it might well be that by opening markets to competition there is more pollution. For example, consider the opening up of the market for postal services: the incumbent attempts to foreclose market access to competing firms who would deliver mail. By facilitating entry, we duplicate the number of vans delivering post, increasing emissions. This approach helps explain why the impact of a merger on sustainability is not a direct concern under the analysis of mergers, whether as part of the competition assessment or as a concern that should be integrated in the assessment of the merger under Recital 23.

It might be argued that this third principle does not solve the following puzzle: if a dominant company pollutes because it faces no competition and has no incentive to improve its practices while at the same time consumers express their distaste at the firm's ecological insensitivity, is this not a form of exploitative abuse which EU antitrust law protects under Article 102(b) TFEU? After

[42] JA Ordover and RD Willig, 'An Economic Definition of Predation: Pricing and Product Innovation' (1981) 91 *Yale Law Journal* 8.

[43] There are gaps in antitrust coverage, of course. See eg S Stroux, *US and EC Oligopoly Control* (Kluwer, 2004).

all, there is case law suggesting that sloth is an abuse of a dominant position. In *Höfner v Macrotron*, for example, the European Court of Justice (ECJ) held that if a Member State confers a monopoly over the provision of a service to an undertaking in such a way that the undertaking 'is manifestly not in a position to satisfy the demand prevailing on the market for activities of that kind'[44] then there is an infringement of competition law which may be imputed to the state of the undertaking. However, observe that in this judgment emphasis was also placed on the exclusionary effects of the legislation: nobody else could offer the service in competition with the public body entrusted with providing the service. The harm thus was to the competitive process, and so this case law falls within the first principle.

The fourth and final principle is that antitrust law need not apply if the interest protected by antitrust is already safeguarded by another more specific regulatory instrument. An example is the application of Article 102 TFEU to excessive prices of pharmaceuticals. Insofar as there is effective price regulation, there is no need to apply Article 102 TFEU, but as soon as a medicine's price falls outside of the regulatory framework, one may check excessive prices using antitrust. Other commentators (and the Commission in the *Bayer/Monsanto* case) have suggested that this fourth principle should be wider. They state that antitrust should not apply if another regulatory intervention would address the harm better than competition law. This is incorrect because antitrust's broad reach is precisely what allows one to apply it in instances where there is a regulatory gap. In particular when considering EU competition law, we can find examples of antitrust cases that have identified a regulatory gap which is then filled by the legislator.[45] Furthermore, there can always be better ways of addressing harm to competition or to consumer welfare than the application of competition law, but we apply competition law when we are confident that enforcement serves as a systematic means of protecting a given interest.

Armed with these four principles we can discuss one recent addition to the tasks of competition law which some are calling for: addressing inequality. This is based on the observation that increased concentration caused by lax antitrust

[44] Case C-41/90, *Höfner and Elser v Macrotron GmbH*, EU:C:1991:161 [31].

[45] One refusal to deal settlement in the field of computer reservation systems for airlines led to a regulation that addressed the sector as a whole; Regulation (EC) 80/2009 on a Code of Conduct for Computerised Reservation Systems [2009] OJ L35/47; an attempted Art 102 case against roaming led to the roaming regulation applicable to all operators; Regulation (EU) No 531/2012 of the European Parliament and of the Council of 13 June 2012 on roaming on public mobile communications networks within the Union (recast) [2012] OJ L172/10; a spate of cases against multilateral interchange fees led to the incomplete regulation of these fees Regulation (EU) 2015/751 of the European Parliament and of the Council of 29 April 2015 on interchange fees for card-based payment transactions [2015] OJ L123/1; and litigation in national courts regarding collecting societies led to legislation to try to ensure more competition in this sector Directive 2014/26/EU on collective management of copyright and related rights and multi-territorial licensing of rights in musical works for online use in the internal market [2014] OJ L84/72.

enforcement has contributed to growing asymmetries of wealth. Antitrust is called to 'say its piece'.[46]

To a certain extent, EU antitrust law addresses economic inequality indirectly in two ways.[47] First, by keeping markets open it tries to create a level playing field among entrepreneurs. According to the ECJ, 'a system of undistorted competition can be guaranteed only if equality of opportunity is secured as between the various economic operators'.[48] Second, some national competition authorities applying Article 102 TFEU to challenge excessive prices charged by pharmaceutical companies have observed how bringing the prices of a drug down reduces the cost to the public health system, benefiting all patients and taxpayers.[49] Here the exercise of prosecutorial discretion can be used to address conduct that has an adverse effect on the poorest segments of society. This can be developed further, for example by prosecuting cartels among supermarkets rather than looking for collusion among auction houses. However, neither of these approaches requires a radical rethinking of EU competition law. The emphasis remains on keeping markets open or protecting consumers.

A more radical approach would entail an aggressive merger policy to prevent higher concentration or breaking up dominant firms with the sole purpose of ensuring less inequality. Would this be consistent with competition law's boundaries? If we apply the four principles above, we can suggest that while today the protective scope of competition law focuses on a certain vision of well-performing markets (affording opportunities for new entry and satisfying consumer demand), there might be a further transformation of EU competition law such as that we saw with the more economics-based approach. EU competition law's core values are not set in legislative stones. However, even if one were to agree to transform EU competition law into a legal system where mergers are prohibited if they risk augmenting inequality among citizens, it is not clear how the third principle would be satisfied. Would less concentration necessarily lead to less inequality whenever we review mergers? If not, then there is no space for inequality as an antitrust standard.

Some might argue that the fourth principle militates against the application of competition law because taxation serves to save the citizens from inequality. To this claim there are two responses. The first, as suggested above, asks whether

[46] Amato (n 3) 108, referring to the oligopoly problem.

[47] See also the important contribution of I Lianos, 'Competition Law as a Form of Social Regulation' (2020) *Antitrust Bulletin* 3.

[48] This was set out first in Case C-202/88, *France v Commission* EU:C:1991:120 [51]. In this case France challenged one of the early Directives opening up the telecommunications market. This dictum has been applied in a number of cases where the dominant undertaking was a former state monopoly.

[49] Italian Competition Authority, 'Annual Report 2019' 19. For the Competition and Markets Authority (CMA) see the latest press release on the Pfizer/Flynn saga: www.gov.uk/government/news/cma-accuses-pharma-firms-of-illegal-pricing. These efforts are hampered by a very high standard of proof. See L Hancher and G Monti, 'Excessive Pricing in Pharmaceuticals: Perspectives from EU Antitrust and Regulation' (forthcoming).

existing levels of taxation solve the inequality problem. It may be that they do not and further intervention is needed. The second is that even if taxation addresses the inequality problem by transferring more resources to citizens, it does not empower them, while blocking a merger addresses the structural inequality between consumers and firms in a different way to taxation.[50]

In sum, antitrust prohibits conduct that harms economic welfare, but the criteria which we use to address the notion of economic welfare may vary as society or technology evolves. The meta-principle of antitrust is that the first principle discussed above is variable and determined exogenously. However, the second, third and fourth principles place some limits as to how far competition law can prohibit conduct that harms certain interests, such inequality among citizens or environmental damage. While we may see sustainability and equality as attributes constituting well-functioning markets, antitrust enforcement might not be well placed to address them consistently because competitive markets are not necessarily likely to yield equality or sustainability. This discussion leaves one question open, which is when is it legitimate for antitrust to change direction and move from protecting one set of interests to another. We pick this up in section V.

IV. Antitrust, Alone?

A. Growing Impermeability

Since the 1970s, there have been Commission decisions that authorised restrictive practices in the name of industrial policy and other non-competition considerations.[51] Amato selected one of these decisions – *Ford/Volkswagen* – as an illustration of the 'permeability of the antitrust principles, which are hybridized and weakened by the joint presence of industrial policy and social cohesion objectives'.[52] In this decision, the Commission allowed the establishment of a joint venture to manufacture a multipurpose vehicle in a deprived area of Portugal. The parties would both contribute to this project, but each would then compete in the retail market by customising the vehicles produced by the plant. The agreement was authorised under Article 101(3) because the plant would use the most advanced production

[50] Both points draw on Lianos, 'Competition Law' (2020).

[51] The place of these decisions in antitrust has been a favourite among PhD candidates at the EUI; see RB Bouterse, *Competition and Integration: What Goals Count?* (Kluwer, 1994); W Sauter, *Competition Law and Industrial Policy in the EU* (OUP, 1998); C Townley, *Article 81 EC and Public Policy* (Hart, 2009); C Talbot, *Competition law in times of crisis: case studies of the European passenger airline sector and the Irish beef industry* (EUI, 2016); J Mulder, *Social Legitimacy in the Internal Market: A Dialogue of Mutual Responsiveness* (Hart, 2018).

[52] Amato (n 3) 62. This decision is also interesting having regard to the first section of the paper because judged with the more economics-based approach it is unlikely that one would find a restriction of competition. Indeed, many joint ventures among car-makers exist today, none of which have attracted the attention of competition agencies. For the business motivation, see A Brandenburger and B Nalebuff, 'The Rules of Co-opetition' (2021) 99 *Harvard Business Review* 48.

technology, the vehicle would include several technical features and would have low emissions and fuel consumption. In addition, the Commission observed that the joint venture would create jobs in Portugal, contributing to the reduction of regional disparities. What was the relevance of these considerations? According to the decision: 'This would not be enough to make an exemption possible unless the conditions of Article 85 (3) were fulfilled, but it is an element which the Commission has taken into account'.[53] This ambiguous statement is as unhelpful as the Commission's rejection of non-competition factors in the *Bayer/Monsanto* decision discussed in section III. Here too the Commission fails to make clear the role that these factors should play in tolerating a restriction of competition. As we explained in section II, Amato considered that this approach should be a thing of the past because the revision of the Treaty emphasised that industrial policy could not be pursued at the expense of competition.

Are these days of generous antitrust exemptions behind us? In 2004 the Commission clearly thought so. It issued a soft law document to interpret Article 101(3) where it took two positions in relation to this provision that indicate an attempt to align it to the more economics-based approach that it had developed for Article 101(1) TFEU. The first condition (that the agreement must contribute 'to improving the production or distribution of goods or to promoting technical or economic progress') was said to only include efficiency gains.[54] The fact that the agreement could also contribute to securing other Treaty goals would only be considered if those goals could be 'subsumed under the four conditions' of Article 101(3).[55] This ambiguous phrase, coupled with the Commission's statement that 'the objective of Article [101] is to protect competition on the market as a means of enhancing consumer welfare and of ensuring an efficient allocation of resources',[56] served as a clear indication that *Ford/VW* was not going to be followed. The emphasis on consumer welfare also shaped the Commission's interpretation of the second condition (that the consumers must receive a fair share of the resulting benefit). The Commission took the view that this means that 'the pass-on of benefits must at least compensate consumers for any actual or likely negative impact caused to them by the restriction of competition found under Article [101(1)]'.[57] However, this is not faithful to the letter of the Treaty and means that the Commission instead weighs up the overall impact of the agreement on consumer welfare. This is in line with the more economics-based approach but out of sync with the Treaty, requiring a wider analysis of the positive effects of an agreement.

Further confirmation of the more economics-based approach is the Commission's and the courts' more attentive assessment of the efficiency claims

[53] Case IV/33.814, *Ford/Volkswagen* [1993] OJ L20/14 [36].
[54] Guidelines on the application of Article 81(3) of the Treaty [2004] OJ C101/97 [50].
[55] ibid [42].
[56] ibid [13].
[57] ibid [85].

brought by firms. In nearly all the analyses of the application of Article 101(3) post-modernisation the Commission has found that the claimed positive effects were not demonstrated or that the agreement was not indispensable to achieve the stated positive effects.[58] Finally, the efficiency defence as redesigned in the Guidelines is now also the same defence that applies in Article 102 TFEU and under the EU Merger Regulation. This brings coherence to the EU's antitrust enterprise: harm is shown when conduct reduces economic welfare, but defendants may disprove this by revealing how the practice in question improves welfare instead.

B. Calls for a Rebalancing

However, there are calls for a widening of the exemption provisions. These calls are justified because the approach by which justifications for anticompetitive conduct are narrowed is not in line with the case law of the ECJ. While the courts have not always been clear about the role of other factors in competition law analysis, reference in the case law has been made to the benefits from securing stable employment, the impact of conduct on media pluralism, the avoidance of over-indebtedness and facilitating future innovation efforts.[59] Of these calls to sideline competition law two are particularly notable and discussed here.

The first is the political pressure that the Commission found itself in when it blocked the merger between Siemens and Alstom, which would have created a global powerhouse in high-speed trains because it considered the merger would harm competition. Some Member States have launched a campaign to facilitate the integration of industrial policy considerations in merger control to reverse this approach, allowing industrial policy to trump competition considerations.[60] Likewise, the European Parliament 'encourages the Commission, on a case-by-case basis, to take into account a longer-term vision encompassing the global dimension and potential future competition in its competitive assessments' and to revise merger guidelines 'to take into account efficiency gains linked to mergers, including the challenge of EU industrial competitiveness'.[61] This appears to be a step back into the kind of industrial policy that the Commission fought against by the use of the economic approach. The Commission's more recent clearance of

[58] See eg Case C-382/12 P, *Mastercard v Commission* EU:C:2014:2201; T-491/07 RENV, *Groupement des cartes bancaires (CB) v Commission* EU:T:2016:379.

[59] The case law is reviewed in G Monti and J Mulder 'Escaping the Clutches of EU Competition Law: Pathways to Assess Private Sustainability Initiatives' (2017) 42 *European Law Review* 635. See also O Brook 'Struggling With Article 101(3) TFEU: Diverging Approaches Of The Commission, EU Courts, And Five Competition Authorities' (2019) 56 *Common Market Law Review* 121, and the works at n 51 above.

[60] 'Manifesto for a European industrial policy fit for the 21st century', available at www.gouvernement.fr/sites/default/files/locale/piece-jointe/2019/02/1043_-_a_franco-german_manifesto_for_a_european_industrial_policy_fit_for_the_21st_century.pdf

[61] European Parliament resolution of 9 June 2021 on competition policy – annual report 2020 (2020/2223(INI)) paras 68 and 69.

a merger between Fiat and Peugeot might be read as the Commission caving to such pressure: Bruno Le Maire, the French economics and finance minister, and Stefano Patuanelli, his Italian counterpart, said that they 'warmly welcome' the merger, which will create a 'new European champion'.[62] However, on the facts, the merger was allowed subject to commitments to ensure that there was no distortion of competition.[63] In other words, the Commission's favourable view means that industrial policy may be pursued by states or firms provided that the actions do not distort competition. As Amato suggested, the EU Treaties themselves place a limit on this: not only is the EU's industrial policy premised on the existence of competitive markets, but Member States too are obliged, on the basis of Article 120 TFEU, to pursue their economic policies 'with a view to contributing to the achievement of the objectives of the Union'. This includes 'the principle of an open market economy with free competition, favouring an efficient allocation of resources'.

The second is pressure brought to bear largely by industry, which takes the view that there is insufficient guidance to allow firms to understand what kinds of horizontal cooperation might be authorised when parties seek to collaborate to contribute to achieve sustainability objectives. Some national competition authorities have also taken the view that some forms of industry cooperation should be authorised when a restriction of competition is compensated by reduced harms to the environment.[64] At a technical level this discussion raises the following questions: if rivals agree to switch to a mode of production which pollutes less but increases the prices of the products they sell, can this restriction of competition be authorised? Given the Commission's current interpretation of Article 101(3) TFEU it is not clear how far reduced pollution could qualify as an efficiency and since consumers pay more for the resulting product the second requirement for exemption is not met either.

At the time of writing the Commission is proposing a revision of its Guidelines on horizontal agreements which accommodate the need to facilitate this kind of cooperation. In particular, the Commission takes a wide view of the notion of efficiencies, including 'the use of cleaner production or distribution technologies, less pollution'.[65] It also suggests a slight widening of the notion of consumer benefits. The Commission suggests that consumers may secure a gain from efficiencies in three ways: (i) by individual use-value (eg, there is better choice of products consumers desire); (ii) by individual non-use value (ie, consumers pay more but they are willing to do so knowing that their choice of buying a product produced

[62] J Ewing, 'Fiat Chrysler and Peugeot Approve a Merger They Need to Survive' *New York Times* (4 January 2021).

[63] Case M.9730 – *FCA/PSA* (21 December 2020).

[64] Hellenic Competition Commission, 'Staff Discussion Paper on Sustainability Issues and Competition Law' (2020), Authority for Consumers and Markets (Netherlands), 'Draft Guidelines on Sustainability Agreements' (2021).

[65] European Commission, 'Draft Guidelines on the applicability of Article 101 of the Treaty on the Functioning of the European Union to horizontal co-operation agreements' (2022), para 578.

in a sustainable way has a desirable impact on society); (iii) by obtaining a collective benefit (eg, society as a whole benefits from the reduced pollution and if some of the persons buying the products are likely to me members of that society then these collective benefits can count).[66]

To give this some flesh: suppose all toothbrush makers agree to switch from plastic to biodegradable materials with the result that prices rise. On the Commission's view there could be a gain to consumers in three ways: some consumers may benefit individually by having more choice of biodegradable toothbrush; others may agree to the higher price knowing that society is made better off; and society as a whole (which includes those who buy toothbrushes) gains because of reduced pollution and reduced plastic waste that needs to be disposed. In taking this approach, the Commission seeks to utilise existing economic tools to better measure the impact of conduct on markets. This approach thus seeks to fit sustainability into the economic paradigm that has been developed during the past 25 years.

There are two concerns with this policy stance. The first is the risk of type 2 errors: will the Commission exempt cartels that yield no benefits to society?[67] In this respect the Hellenic Competition Commission's idea of developing a sustainability sandbox by which one can select certain initiatives and monitor the extent to which they yield the positive effects they promise can serve as a mechanism to avoid these risks.[68] The second is that since tolerating antitrust exemptions because sustainability constitutes an economic gain for society could be taken further and additional economic gains could be brought in to justify restrictions of competition. Here, boundaries have to be established.

V. Finding the Boundaries of Antitrust

Recall that one of Amato's key points was that once antitrust is stripped of its extraneous policy baggage, its enforcement should be in the hands of an independent authority and not a political body like the Commission.[69] With the ECN+ Directive imposing clear independence criteria for NCAs, the Commission's continued role in antitrust appears increasingly hard to justify. As we have suggested, the Commission's substantive reorientation of competition law through the use of economics has been its means of asserting a de facto independent role. Its adjustment of procedures to ensure that these are fair is also an effort to establish its

[66] ibid, paras 588–609.

[67] MP Schinkel and L Teuren, 'Green Antitrust: (More) Friendly Fire in the Fight against Climate Change' in SJ Holmes, D Middelschute and M Snoep (eds) *Competition Law, Climate Chance and Environmental Sustainability* (Concurrences, 2021).

[68] Hellenic Competition Commission, 'Public consultation: Proposal for the creation of a sandbox for sustainability and competition in the Greek market', available at www.epant.gr/en/enimerosi/sandbox.html

[69] See also G Amato, 'A European Cartel Office?' in *Collected Courses of the Academy of European Law* Volume VIII, Book 1 (Kluwer, 1997).

legitimacy.[70] The Commission's ability to resist relaxing competition law in light of the financial crisis and the pandemic are further indications of the independence of the Commission.[71] Whether this institutional design is sustainable in the long run remains to be seen. In particular, with banking union and the Digital Markets Act, the regulation of significant players is being centralised in EU institutions and this might push the development of independent enforcement authorities.[72]

Whatever new institutional design arises, patterns discussed in this chapter suggest that the contours of antitrust are contested, both when determining what conduct constitutes an antitrust offence (section III) and in determining whether anticompetitive conduct should be tolerated in the name of other interests (section IV). Professor Amato foresaw the arrival of a coherent approach to antitrust, and if we take his approach there seem to be three forces that allow for a legitimate change in antitrust policy: changes in the economy which make antitrust more or less suited for protecting certain interests (eg, globalisation makes it harder to contain political power); changes in our understanding of economics;[73] and constitutional changes (eg, Treaty reforms). This leads to the current consensus, which has rightly been described as a monocentric approach to antitrust.[74] In contrast to this, others have drawn on social contract theories to suggest that changes in this social contract could be the driving force for a recalibration of antitrust prohibitions and exemptions.[75] I hesitate to agree with the use of the social contract because it seems to me that this is a grand bargain among members of society which calls for an overall assessment of all state policies to determine how each is best calibrated to achieve justice. It seems invidious to just reset competition policy on the basis of changes in the social contract. Furthermore, changes in the social contract have to be signalled by a strong consensus. Just because more scholars and politicians express concerns about inequality or the environment may not be sufficient to rethink antitrust.

And yet, as Amato showed, antitrust changes emphasis across time, but it is reasonable to demand some limits. The EU's constitutional texts can be used to find some: there is enough in the EU Treaties to suggest that industrial policy considerations cannot serve to authorise anticompetitive conduct. But there is not much else in the Treaties that constrains the interpretation of competition policy, because it is expected to operate within the wider framework of the social market

[70] HL Karlsson, *Conceptualising Procedural Fairness in EU competition Law* (Hart, 2020).

[71] D Chalmers, G Davies and G Monti, *European Union Law: Text and Materials*, 4th edn (CUP, 2019) 878–79; G Monti, 'Business cooperation in times of emergency: The role of competition law' Competition Policy International – EU News (May 2020).

[72] G Monti and A de Streel, 'Improving Institutional Design to Better Supervise Digital Platforms' (CERRE, 2022).

[73] It has been shown that economic analysis serves as a more powerful constraint on the Commission than do judgments of the ECJ. P Ibáñez Colomo, *The Shaping of EU Competition Law* (CUP, 2018) 328.

[74] Lianos, 'Polycentric Competition Law' (2018).

[75] See in particular Lianos (n 47).

economy that the EU seeks to establish and sustain.[76] Likewise, economics is not a science that constrains antitrust. The current monocentric consensus appeals to a specific reading of economics, but nothing prevents the use of alternative economic frameworks to address markets.[77] As one economist has shown, 'different economic theories have different views on how markets work or fail to work'.[78] In his view policy should be shaped by a richer reflection taking into account all economic theories.

But economics is not an obligatory methodology that competition authorities must use to determine whether conduct harms competition or whether competition harms should be tolerated in the name of other benefits. It has gained this pre-eminence because by choosing a narrow set of economic parameters, competition agencies can claim to treat all infringements in a coherent manner. It has now become institutionalised as the dominant discourse which serves to challenge the legitimacy of those arguing for antitrust from a different perspective. Insofar as economics is the legally required mechanism to prove harm, it even requires that those advocating another approach should first make a case for changing the law, raising the barriers to alternative discourses.[79] Nothing however prevents the Commission from stating, for example, that exclusionary conduct by a dominant firm is an abuse when it denies the capacity of rivals to compete, without making reference to any school of economic thought, but just by reference to the risk that exclusion makes to the internal market. After all, the test of illegality for all antitrust prohibitions is whether the conduct is 'incompatible with the internal market'. It follows that few real boundaries exist to help us determine what conduct constitutes an antitrust infringement. Given an appropriately sophisticated economic construction restrictions on innovation, reductions in privacy, harm to media pluralism, increases in inequality and harm to the environment could all fall within antitrust law's prohibition.

Alternatively, a political reading of competition law can allow one to make similar findings without the need for complex expertise by simply referring to desired outcomes one expects from markets. As suggested above, in the EU and legal systems where competition laws are open textured, limits are not established by reliance on economics but by four interpretative principles. First, the relevant interests protected by the competition rules are identified; second, the conduct

[76] eg Art 11 TFEU, requiring that environmental protection requirements be integrated in Union policies; Art 9 TFEU, indicating that Union policies take into account inter alia the promotion of a high level of employment, social protection, and the protection of human health.

[77] K Bania, *The Role of Media Pluralism in the Enforcement of EU Competition Law* (Concurrences, 2019); E Deutscher, 'How to measure privacy-related consumer harm in merger analysis?' in B Lundqvist and MS Gal (eds), *Competition Law for the Digital Economy* (Edward Elgar, 2019).

[78] HJ Chang, *Economics: The User's Guide* (Pelican, 2014) 387.

[79] E Popp Berman, *Thinking Like an Economist: How Efficiency Replaced Equality in U.S. Public Policy* (Princeton, 2022) 86–88 (tracing the introduction of the economic style at the antitrust agencies in the 1960s) and 189–92 for how this style prevented the emergence of more aggressive antitrust. Chs 9 and 10 for its continued institutionalisation and resilience irrespective of the executive's political orientation.

must fall within the four corners of the legal text; third, an interest is not to be protected by competition law if there is another existing set of rules that takes care of this; and fourth, competition law should not apply if it is shown that it is unable to protect the interest at stake in a systematic manner.

What about antitrust exemptions? It seems clear that the Commission's reinterpretation of Article 101(3) TFEU as an efficiency defence and the transposition of this defence to Article 102 TFEU and mergers is deeply problematic. First, there is good reason why Article 102 TFEU does not have the equivalent of Article 101(3) TFEU: dominant firms damage competition by their very existence, so one should hesitate before allowing conduct in the name of efficiency or the pursuit of any other policy goal. Second, Article 101(3) TFEU creates a lexical ordering.[80] It states that two interests have priority over others: agreements eliminating competition and agreements that do not confer a fair share of benefits on 'consumers' ('users' in other Treaty language versions) cannot be exempted, irrespective of the degree of positive effects they yield. This lexical ordering that gives primacy to competition is strengthened by the proportionality requirement as a result of which an exemption is not available if less restrictive alternatives are possible. As with antitrust prohibitions, the claim here is that parties can seek exemption for agreements that provide a wide range of positive benefits provided these are recognised as such in the Treaty. Creating an industrial champion is included. However, these positive effects are not tolerated if values superior to these (competition and a fair return on users) would be trumped.

In sum, the scope of possible interests protected by the application of competition law as well as the scope of the possible interests that may be considered when allowing some restrictions of competition know no bounds other than that these interests must fit within the economic constitution. Here there is a space for legitimate debate and contestation over what antitrust should do. As we have seen the Treaty provides few restraints save for the lexical primacy of competition over other interests, but this term is itself contested. However, some boundaries of antitrust are to be found inside the legal texts, which limit the scope antitrust intervention and non-intervention.

[80] Along these lines, see also G Ghidini, 'Comment: A short note on the generation of efficiencies in the context of the 'constitutional' principles of European Competition Law' in H Ullrich, *The Evolution of European Competition Law* (Edward Elgar, 2006).

PART II

Competition Law Enforcement

5

'Consumer Welfare' and the EU Courts: An Unexpected Refuge for a Persecuted Concept?

ASSIMAKIS KOMNINOS[1]

I. Main Theses

Consumer welfare is the talk of the day. In the US, the country where the concept was born and dominated antitrust enforcement for more than 40 years, it is currently under attack by the 'New Brandeisians'. The 'barbarians' are already within Rome (the enforcement agencies). On the other hand, the European approach towards the concept remains somewhat awkward. Although it never really acquired in Europe the quasi-religious status it has had in the US, it was nevertheless embraced – not without some resistance and incidents, initially by the Commission and subsequently by the EU Courts, as a form of discipling principle that goes hand in hand with the so-called 'new economic approach' that was introduced in the late 1990s in response to the criticisms against the overly formalistic approach of EU competition law enforcement. It is now with some bemusement that the Europeans observe the heated discussions in the US. Are we embracing a wrong dogma that has fallen out of favour in its birthplace? And is the latest embracement of consumer welfare by the EU Courts, and its 'ideological refugee status' in EU case law, an anachronism?

In this chapter to mark the 25-year anniversary of the publication of Professor Giuliano Amato's seminal book, *Antitrust and the Bounds of Power: The Dilemma of Liberal Democracy in the History of the Market*, I develop three main theses: First, the EU case law has historically given more emphasis to competition as process rather than to competition as outcome and EU competition law has never been about just short-term price effects. The mantra has been the safeguarding of

[1] Partner, White & Case LLP; Visiting Professor (2020–22), Université Catholique de Louvain. The views expressed here are strictly personal. The author had the good fortune to be a European University Institute researcher taught by Professor Amato in 1998–99.

an 'effective competitive structure'. Second, the increasing references to consumer welfare, which is a relatively recent phenomenon, have to be seen in the context of the EU case law becoming less formalistic and more attuned to economics, and to developing clear theories of harm which are based on effects as opposed to form. This cannot be but a positive development. Third, the EU case law has seen consumer welfare as more of an abstract objective or principle, as opposed to an operational standard or test. It serves only to distinguish the mere exclusion of rivals (which may be procompetitive) from distortion of competition that leads to consumer harm. At the same time, the term 'consumer' encompasses not only end users but also intermediaries.

Having discussed these three theses, I conclude that, in Europe, there has never been a 'tyranny' of the consumer welfare concept. On the contrary, consumer welfare has been a very welcome over-arching principle that has brought discipline and intellectual rigour to competition enforcement. Even if it were possible for the European Commission and the EU Courts to somehow 'abandon' consumer welfare, which it is not, since EU competition law as interpreted by the EU Courts amounts to primary law that can be changed only through an amendment of the Treaty, it would be a retrogression to disavow it and would not be to the benefit of the quality of enforcement in Europe.

II. Consumer Welfare Coming to the EU

It is not the purpose of this chapter to explain the concept of the consumer welfare standard.[2] In the US, it is seen as a 'standard', in the sense that it can guide the application of the antitrust laws to specific cases. The consumer welfare standard gives emphasis to consumers' surplus and focuses on the buyers' side. Total welfare, on the other hand, encompasses the sum of producers' and consumers' surplus and focuses on deadweight loss and on the effects of the conduct in question on the volume of sales rather than on prices. Traditionally, a total welfare approach has been considered as possibly generating under-enforcement risks. Other standards or objectives have also been proposed, such as consumer sovereignty, freedom of choice, protection of 'smallness' from 'bigness', etc.

[2] The US literature is voluminous. For a few introductory works from a European angle, see S Albæk, 'Consumer Welfare in EU Competition Policy' in C Heide-Jorgensen et al (eds) *Aims and Values in Competition Law* (DJØF Publishing, 2013) 67ff; O Andriychuk, 'Rediscovering the Spirit of Competition: On the Normative Value of the Competition Process' (2010) 6 *European Competition Journal* 575; DR Biggar and A Heimler, 'Is Protecting Sunk Investments an Economic Rationale for Antitrust Law?', 4 September 2019, available at ssrn.com/abstract=3935776; V Daskalova, 'Consumer Welfare in EU Competition Law: What Is It (Not) About?' (2015) 11 *Competition Law Review* 133; F Marty, 'Is the Consumer Welfare Obsolete? A European Union Competition Law Perspective' GREDEG Working Paper No 2020-13; H Schweitzer, 'The Role of Consumer Welfare in EU Competition Law' in Drexl (ed), *Technology and Competition, Contributions in Honour of Hanns Ullrich* (Larcier, 2009).

In Europe, on the other hand, the competition rules have traditionally been seen in a functionalist way, as part of the EU economic constitution designed to protect economic freedom and the competitive process. The Ordoliberalism theories of the Freiburg School have been particularly influential, and the focus is on economic efficiency and 'performance competition' (*Leistungswettbewerb*), which the EU Courts refer to as 'normal competition' or 'competition on the merits'. Under this approach, the competition rules protect rational commercial conduct consistent with the profit-maximising strategy of a non-dominant company, based on superior efficiency.[3] In addition, the EU competition rules have historically been seen through their single market imperative and this explains the long line of cases on parallel trade and market-partitioning, which has always been considered as a European oddity by US antitrust experts.

It was only at the end of the 1990s that consumer welfare started to be mentioned in EU competition policy papers and guidelines. There is no doubt that the European Commission played an important role in spear-heading this development. The Commission was responding to criticism – usually waged by influential US-trained lawyers – that its competition law enforcement was too formalistic.[4]

The first reference to the concept of consumer welfare can be traced back to the Commission's 1996 Green Paper on vertical restraints,[5] which is generally considered the policy document that introduced the 'new economic approach' drive in EU competition law. The first references are rather timid and mention consumer welfare together with 'the structure of competition'.[6] In para 180, the Commission also stated:

> In assessing possible restrictive practices, the notion that the competitive structure of markets must not suffer should always be the foremost consideration. In its decisions, the Commission has consistently demonstrated a willingness to consider economic factors such as efficiency and consumer welfare.

Consumer welfare had a more central role in the Commission's Article 101(3) TFEU Guidelines, a centerpiece in its modernisation package of 2004.[7] In paras 13 and 33, the Commission stressed that the objective of the competition rules and of Article 101 in particular is 'to protect competition on the market as a means of enhancing consumer welfare and of ensuring an efficient allocation of resources'. The same approach was followed in the Commission's 2004 Horizontal Merger

[3] See eg R Nazzini, *The Foundations of European Union Competition Law, The Objective and Principles of Article 102* (OUP, 2011) 171.
[4] See eg the seminal article by BE Hawk, 'System Failure: Vertical Restraints and EC Competition Law' (1995) 32 *Common Market Law Review* 973.
[5] European Commission, Green Paper on Vertical Restraints in EC Competition Policy COM(96), Brussels (22 January 1997).
[6] ibid para 25.
[7] Communication from the Commission, Guidelines on the application of Article 81(3) of the Treaty, OJ [2004] C 101/97.

Guidelines[8] and Technology Transfer Guidelines,[9] which included references to consumer welfare.

It is with the 2009 Guidance Paper on exclusionary abuses[10] that consumer welfare was given a prominent role, from a policy point of view, in Article 102 TFEU. Paragraph 19 of the Guidance Paper, which refers to the general framework of analysis, is quite explicit:

> The aim of the Commission's enforcement activity in relation to exclusionary conduct is to ensure that dominant undertakings do not impair effective competition by foreclosing their competitors in an anti-competitive way, thus having an adverse impact on consumer welfare, whether in the form of higher price levels than would have otherwise prevailed or in some other form such as limiting quality or reducing consumer choice. In this document the term 'anti-competitive foreclosure' is used to describe a situation where effective access of actual or potential competitors to supplies or markets is hampered or eliminated as a result of the conduct of the dominant undertaking whereby the dominant undertaking is likely to be in a position to profitably increase prices to the detriment of consumers.

The Guidance Paper's references to consumer welfare are closely linked with the fundamental distinction between procompetitive and anticompetitive foreclosure of competitors.[11] The criticism that Article 102 TFEU enforcement was too formalistic was based precisely on the point that it tended to protect competitors without regard to the interests of consumers.

Since these early policy pronouncements, consumer welfare has now established itself as a prominent objective mentioned in all basic Commission policy documents.[12] However, the Commission's embracement of consumer welfare should not be seen as an espousal of the technical characteristics of the US 'standard', with its main focus on price, but rather as a guiding principle that brings economic rationale and discipline into enforcement. The Commission also clarifies that its concept of 'consumer' is a broad one and encompasses intermediaries[13]

[8] Guidelines on the assessment of horizontal mergers under the Council Regulation on the control of concentrations between undertakings, OJ [2004] C 31/3, para 61.

[9] Commission Notice, Guidelines on the application of Article 81 of the EC Treaty to technology transfer agreements, OJ [2004] C 101/2, paras 5, 7.

[10] Communication from the Commission – Guidance on the Commission's enforcement priorities in applying Article 82 of the EC Treaty to abusive exclusionary conduct by dominant undertakings, OJ [2009] C 45/7.

[11] ibid, para 6.

[12] See eg Communication from the Commission – Guidelines on the applicability of Article 101 of the Treaty on the Functioning of the European Union to horizontal co-operation agreements, OJ [2011] C 11/1, para 52 and numerous references to benefits to 'consumers'; Guidelines on Vertical Restraints, OJ [2010] C 130/1, para 7; Communication from the Commission – Guidelines on the application of Article 101 of the Treaty on the Functioning of the European Union to technology transfer agreements, OJ [2014] C 89/3, para 5. These texts sometimes use language that does not include the word 'welfare' but there is no doubt that they mean to refer to the consumer welfare objective.

[13] See eg Communication from the Commission – Guidance on the Commission's enforcement priorities in applying Article 82 of the EC Treaty to abusive exclusionary conduct by dominant undertakings, OJ [2009] C 45/7, para 19 *in fine*, fn 15 ('The concept of 'consumers' encompasses all direct

and that, apart from price, other elements, such as quality, innovation and choice are constituent elements of competition.[14]

III. EU Case Law – No Love at First Sight

The reception of the consumer welfare objective in the case law of the EU Courts has had a different history, which is not difficult to understand, bearing in mind the courts' conservative nature and their different task vis-à-vis the Commission: the EU Courts will only interpret the law as such and will review the legality of Commission decisions; they cannot introduce policy changes. Only the Commission and the enforcement agencies can design policy changes.

Initially, from the 1960s to the 1990s, there were no references to consumer welfare in the case law. When the question of the objective of the competition rules arose, the EU Courts did not refer to consumer welfare or indeed to the protection of consumers as such, although, to be fair, the word 'consumers' appears both in primary law – Article 101(3) TFEU ('allowing consumers a fair share of the resulting benefit') – and in secondary law – the EU Merger Regulation.[15] Instead, the EU Courts saw the competition rules in a functionalist way and always in conjunction with the single market objectives. With particular reference to Article 102 TFEU, the mantra was that it 'is aimed not only at practices which may cause prejudice to consumers directly, but also at those which are detrimental to them through their impact on an effective competition structure'.[16] In the words of AG Kokott in *British Airways*,

> The starting-point here must be the protective purpose of Article 82 EC. The provision forms part of a system designed to protect competition within the internal market from distortions (Article 3(1)(g) EC). Accordingly, Article 82 EC, like the other competition

or indirect users of the products affected by the conduct, including intermediate producers that use the products as an input, as well as distributors and final consumers both of the immediate product and of products provided by intermediate producers. Where intermediate users are actual or potential competitors of the dominant undertaking, the assessment focuses on the effects of the conduct on users further downstream'); Guidelines on the assessment of horizontal mergers under the Council Regulation on the control of concentrations between undertakings, OJ [2004] C 31/3, fn 55 and para 84; Guidelines on the assessment of non-horizontal mergers under the Council Regulation on the control of concentrations between undertakings, OJ [2008] C 265/6, para 16.

[14] See eg Communication from the Commission, Guidelines on the application of Article 81(3) of the Treaty, OJ [2004] C 101/97, para 16; Communication from the Commission – Guidance on the Commission's enforcement priorities in applying Article 82 of the EC Treaty to abusive exclusionary conduct by dominant undertakings, OJ [2009] C 45/7, paras 5, 6, 11, 19; Guidelines on the assessment of horizontal mergers under the Council Regulation on the control of concentrations between undertakings, OJ [2004] C 31/3, para 8.

[15] Council Regulation 139/2004 of 20 January 2004 on the control of concentrations between undertakings, OJ [2004] L 24/1, Art 2(1)(b) and Recital 29. The reference to 'consumers' in Art 2(1)(b) was already included in the first Merger Regulation (Council Regulation 4064/89 of 21 December 1989 on the control of concentrations between undertakings, OJ [1989] L 395/1).

[16] See eg Case 6/72, *Europemballage Corporation and Continental Can Company Inc. v Commission*, ECLI:EU:C:1973:22 [26]; Case C-95/04 P, *British Airways plc v Commission* ECLI:EU:C:2007:166 [106];

> rules of the Treaty, is not designed only or primarily to protect the immediate interests of individual competitors or consumers, but to protect the *structure of the market* and thus *competition as such (as an institution)*, which has already been weakened by the presence of the dominant undertaking on the market. In this way, consumers are also indirectly protected. Because where competition as such is damaged, disadvantages for consumers are also to be feared.[17]

We would have to wait until 1999 for the first reference to consumer welfare in an Advocate General (AG) Opinion in a very unlikely case, that had little to do with substantive competition law questions. This was the *Eco Swiss* case, which concerned arbitration and EU competition law. The AG was referring to the importance of the competition rules in the Treaty and stressed that 'while they govern the conduct of individuals, also pursue objectives of a general nature such as the smooth functioning of the common market and the well-being of consumers'.[18] It may not be coincidence that the first judicial pronouncement on consumer welfare is almost cotemporaneous with the first ever use of the term in a Commission policy document, the 1996 Green Paper on vertical restraints.

From the 2000s onwards, the term started to be used quite often in AG Opinions, especially by those AGs that seemed more open to the new economic approach. The trend started with AG Jacobs in *Syfait*[19] and continued with AG Trstenjak in *Irish Beef*,[20] AG Wahl in *Treuhand*,[21] *AKKA/LAA*,[22] *Skanska*[23]

Case C-52/09, *Konkurrensverket v TeliaSonera Sverige AB* ECLI:EU:C:2011:83 [22], [108]; Case C-307/18, *Generics (UK) Ltd and Others v Competition and Markets Authority* ECLI:EU:C:2020:52 [147].

[17] Case C-95/04 P, *British Airways plc v Commission*, Opinion of AG Kokott, ECLI:EU:C:2006:133 [68] (emphasis in the original).

[18] Case C-126/97, *Eco Swiss China Time Ltd v Benetton International NV*, Opinion of AG Saggio, ECLI:EU:C:1999:97 [42]. The reference to 'well-being of consumers' as opposed to 'consumer welfare' is a translation glitch from the French 'bien-être des consommateurs', which obviously refers to consumer welfare. This is a common problem in judgments and opinions that refer to consumer welfare.

[19] Case C-53/03, *Synetairismos Farmakopoion Aitolias & Akarnanias (Syfait) and Others v GlaxoSmithKline plc and GlaxoSmithKline AEVE*, Opinion AG Jacobs, ECLI:EU:C:2004:673 [91]–[92]. AG Jacobs referred to consumer welfare in the course of his argumentation that too restrictive an approach vis-à-vis the imposition of some limitations to parallel trade would disincentivise pharmaceutical companies to offer their products in low-priced countries. In his words, 'The levels of output and consumer welfare generated by some pharmaceutical products would therefore fall within the Community. Similarly, the regulatory negotiation of prices in low-price Member States would almost certainly become more difficult. There would be considerable pressure for prices to rise in those States if they were to be generalised, by process of parallel trade, across the Community. Such price rises as were agreed would again reduce output and consumer welfare in the States where they occurred'.

[20] Case C-209/07, *Competition Authority v Beef Industry Development Society Ltd and Barry Brothers (Carrigmore) Meats Ltd*, Opinion of AG Trstenjak, ECLI:EU:C:2008:467. AG Trstenjak stressed that 'Article 81 EC protects competition in particular in regard to its function of forming a single market with conditions akin to an internal market and its function of supplying consumers as well as possible' and referred in fn. 16 of her Opinion to 'consumer welfare'. At [56]–[57] of her Opinion, she made a distinction between the first and second paragraphs of Article 101 TFEU: 'different aspects of consumer welfare are taken into account under Article 81(1) EC and under Article 81(3) EC. Under Article 81(1) EC, agreements which restrict competition between market participants and thus its function of supplying consumers optimally with a product at the lowest possible price or with innovative products are prohibited in principle. Such agreements directly affect consumer welfare and as such are prohibited in principle. Nevertheless, Article 81(3) EC recognises that agreements which restrict

and *MEO*,[24] and AG Bobek in *Budapest Bank*.[25] In particular AG Wahl's Opinions were quite rich in their references to consumer welfare and were also linking that concept to the more economic approach in the analysis of pro- and

competition between market participants result in particular in a reduction in production costs, and the reduction in production costs can contribute indirectly to consumer welfare'.

[21] Case C-194/14 P, *AC-Treuhand AG v Commission*, Opinion of AG Wahl, ECLI:EU:C:2015:350 [1]: 'The rules applicable to undertakings under Articles 81 EC and 82 EC (now Articles 101 TFEU and 102 TFEU) are intended to prohibit restrictions on free competition. The identification of a restriction of competition presupposes that it has been established, following an economic analysis, that, by its conduct, the undertaking in question has fully or partially ceased to constitute a constraint – the defining feature of effective competition – for the other operators on the market or markets concerned, to the detriment, ultimately, of economic efficiency and consumer welfare'. See also [45]: 'The overall objective of the competition rules is to ensure that the effects of freedom of competition, which are the counterpart of the opening up of markets, are not distorted by measures, in the broadest sense of that term, which have the consequence of favouring or putting at a disadvantage certain undertakings and, ultimately, operate to the detriment of consumers'.

[22] Case C-177/16, *Biedrība 'Autortiesību un komunicēšanās konsultāciju aģentūra – Latvijas Autoru apvienība' v Konkurences padome*, Opinion of AG Wahl, ECLI:EU:C:2017:286 [101]: 'At the outset, let us start by recalling the economic rationale of the unfair pricing abuse: when a dominant undertaking applies prices above competitive levels, there is an inefficient allocation of resources and consumer welfare is reduced (part of the welfare is transferred to the dominant company, whereas part is simply lost). Accordingly, from a theoretical point of view, any deviation from the competitive price in a regulated market might justify an intervention of the competition authorities. Indeed, any difference between the benchmark price and the actual price implies a certain loss in consumer welfare that would not have been there had the market been competitive'. See also [105].

[23] Case C-724/17, *Vantaan kaupunki v Skanska Industrial Solutions Oy and Others*, Opinion of AG Wahl, ECLI:EU:C:2019:100 [50]: 'Fundamentally, however, the real harm caused by illegal restrictions of competition is the dead weight loss resulting from such restrictions, that is to say a loss of economic efficiency caused by the anticompetitive conduct in question. This means that the harm identified in actions for damages based on an infringement of competition law is in reality a proxy for the economic inefficiencies resulting from the infringement and the corollary loss to society as a whole in terms of reduced consumer welfare'.

[24] Case C-525/16, *MEO – Serviços de Comunicações e Multimédia SA v Autoridade da Concorrência*, ECLI:EU:C:2017:1020 [61], [62], [64]: 'On a general note, it is important to bear in mind that discrimination, including discrimination in the charging of prices, is not in itself problematic from the point of view of competition law. The reason for that is that price discrimination is not always harmful to competition. On the contrary, as is evidenced in particular by the (vain) official attempts made in the United States to repeal the provision in the Robinson-Patman Act of 1936 which prohibits such discrimination, purely and simply prohibiting price discrimination may prove injurious to economic efficiency and the well-being of consumers. Indeed, it is well established that a practice of discrimination, and a differential pricing practice in particular, is ambivalent in terms of its effects on competition. Such a practice may have the consequence of increasing economic efficiency and thus the well-being of consumers. These are goals which, to my mind, should not be overlooked in the application of the rules of competition law, and they are, in any event, quite distinct from considerations of fairness. As the Court has repeatedly held, the rules of competition law are designed to safeguard competition, not to protect competitors … even where an undertaking is charged higher prices than those applied to other undertakings and, as a result, suffers (or considers that it suffers) discrimination, the conduct in question will be caught by Article 102 TFEU only if it is established that it is likely to restrict competition and diminish the well-being of consumers'. Again, the reference to 'well-being of consumers' as opposed to 'consumer welfare' is a translation glitch.

[25] Case C-228/18, *Gazdasági Versenyhivatal v Budapest Bank Nyrt. and Others*, Opinion of AG Bobek, ECLI:EU:C:2019:678 [40]: 'As the Court has emphasised in recent case-law, the concept of a restriction of competition 'by object' must be interpreted restrictively, and can be applied only to certain types of coordination between undertakings which reveal a sufficient degree of harm to competition and for which it is thus unnecessary examine their effects. That approach is justified by the fact that certain

anticompetitive conduct. AG Wahl never considered that consumer welfare should be an operational test to deal with competition law infringements, but clearly thought that it was a guiding principle that ought to influence also the legal tests.

The use of the term in an EU Court judgment took more time and was rather traumatic at the beginning. It was the then Court of First Instance (CFI) that first relied in the 2000s on consumer welfare as an objective of competition law. This first happened in *Österreichische Postsparkasse*, a procedural case, where the CFI put emphasis on the interests of 'final consumers':

> It should be pointed out in this respect that the ultimate purpose of the rules that seek to ensure that competition is not distorted in the internal market is to increase the well-being of consumers. That purpose can be seen in particular from the wording of Article 81 EC. Whilst the prohibition laid down in Article 81(1) EC may be declared inapplicable in the case of cartels which contribute to improving the production or distribution of the goods in question or to promoting technical or economic progress, that possibility, for which provision is made in Article 81(3) EC, is inter alia subject to the condition that a fair share of the resulting benefit is allowed for users of those products. Competition law and competition policy therefore have an undeniable impact on the specific economic interests of final customers who purchase goods or services. Recognition that such customers – who show that they have suffered economic damage as a result of an agreement or conduct liable to restrict or distort competition – have a legitimate interest in seeking from the Commission a declaration that Articles 81 EC and 82 EC have been infringed contributes to the attainment of the objectives of competition law.[26]

Cotemporaneously with *Österreichische Postsparkasse*, the CFI also rendered its judgment in the *Spanish Glaxo* case, where the above principles were cited and developed further. The CFI referred on numerous occasions to the 'welfare of final consumers'. In particular:

> 118. In effect, the objective assigned to Article 81(1) EC, which constitutes a fundamental provision indispensable for the achievement of the missions entrusted to the Community, in particular for the functioning of the internal market, is to prevent undertakings, by restricting competition between themselves or with third parties, from reducing the welfare of the final consumer of the products in question. At the hearing, in fact, the Commission emphasised on a number of occasions that it was from that perspective that it had carried out its examination in the present case, initially concluding that the General Sales Conditions clearly restricted the welfare of consumers, then considering whether that restriction would be offset by increased efficiency which would itself benefit consumers.

types of coordination between undertakings can be regarded, by their very nature, as being harmful to the proper functioning of normal competition since they normally produce inefficient economic outcomes and reduce consumer welfare'.

[26] Joined Cases T-213/01 and T-214/01, *Österreichische Postsparkasse AG and Bank für Arbeit und Wirtschaft AG v Commission* [115]. Again, the reference to 'well-being of consumers' instead of 'consumer welfare' is a translation glitch.

> 119. Consequently, the application of Article 81(1) EC to the present case cannot depend solely on the fact that the agreement in question is intended to limit parallel trade in medicines or to partition the common market, which leads to the conclusion that it affects trade between Member States, but also requires an analysis designed to determine whether it has as its object or effect the prevention, restriction or distortion of competition on the relevant market, to the detriment of the final consumer
>
> …
>
> 121. While it has been accepted since then that parallel trade must be given a certain protection, it is therefore not as such but, as the Court of Justice held, in so far as it favours the development of trade, on the one hand, and the strengthening of competition, on the other hand, that is to say, in this second respect, in so far as it gives final consumers the advantages of effective competition in terms of supply or price. Consequently, while it is accepted that an agreement intended to limit parallel trade must in principle be considered to have as its object the restriction of competition, that applies in so far as the agreement may be presumed to deprive final consumers of those advantages.
>
> 122. However, if account is taken of the legal and economic context in which GSK's General Sales Conditions are applied, it cannot be presumed that those conditions deprive the final consumers of medicines of such advantages. In effect, the wholesalers, whose function, as the Court of Justice has held, is to ensure that the retail trade receives supplies with the benefit of competition between producers, are economic agents operating at an intermediate stage of the value chain and may keep the advantage in terms of price which parallel trade may entail, in which case that advantage will not be passed on to the final consumers.
>
> …
>
> 171. … as the objective of the Community competition rules is to prevent undertakings, by restricting competition between themselves or with third parties, from reducing the welfare of the final consumer of the products in question (paragraph 118 above), it is still necessary to demonstrate that the limitation in question restricts competition, to the detriment of the final consumer. Incidentally, the Commission itself explained, at the hearing, that the limitation of the freedom of action of the Spanish wholesalers was difficult to envisage in isolation and constituted only the starting-point of its examination.
>
> 172. Consequently, GSK is correct to maintain that, after relying on the effect of Clause 4 of the General Sales Conditions on the freedom of action of the Spanish wholesalers, the Commission was still required to demonstrate how that provision had the effect of restricting competition to the detriment of the final consumer.[27]

However, the Court of Justice, on appeal, severely criticised the CFI's zeal, in particular because of the latter's emphasis on the welfare of '*final* consumers' and substituted the reasoning of the CFI judgment with text that echoed the traditional conservative approach. The Court of Justice, in particular, held that the CFI erred

[27] Case T-168/01, *GlaxoSmithKline Services Unlimited v Commission*, ECLI:EU:T:2006:265. See also references in [134], [135], [147], [185], [190] and [194]. This is probably the first and last judgment ever with so many references to 'final consumers'.

in its findings that the objective of the competition rules was to protect the 'final consumers'. In particular:

> 62. With respect to the Court of First Instance's statement that, while it is accepted that an agreement intended to limit parallel trade must in principle be considered to have as its object the restriction of competition, that applies in so far as it may be presumed to deprive final consumers of the advantages of effective competition in terms of supply or price, the Court notes that neither the wording of Article 81(1) EC nor the case-law lend support to such a position.
>
> 63. First of all, there is nothing in that provision to indicate that only those agreements which deprive consumers of certain advantages may have an anti-competitive object. Secondly, it must be borne in mind that the Court has held that, like other competition rules laid down in the Treaty, Article 81 EC aims to protect not only the interests of competitors or of consumers, but also the structure of the market and, in so doing, competition as such. Consequently, for a finding that an agreement has an anti-competitive object, it is not necessary that final consumers be deprived of the advantages of effective competition in terms of supply or price.
>
> 64. It follows that, by requiring proof that the agreement entails disadvantages for final consumers as a prerequisite for a finding of anti-competitive object and by not finding that that agreement had such an object, the Court of First Instance committed an error of law.[28]

The words of the Court of Justice were quite harsh. They need to be seen as more targeted against the CFI's excessive zeal to focus on '*final* consumers' rather than against the concept of consumer welfare. Still, this whole incident must have proved a rather traumatic experience for the CFI, which did not mention consumer welfare again until the Court of Justice itself started to refer to that concept.

IV. EU Case Law: Falling in Love

After a silence following the *Spanish Glaxo* incident, the Court of Justice gave the first indications that it was now more willing to follow its AG Opinions and refer approvingly to consumer welfare, while discussing the objectives of the competition rules. This happened in *Post Danmark I*, a Grand Chamber judgment that is credited as being the first judgment that showed an openness towards the new economic approach in Article 102 TFEU and a positive stance vis-à-vis the Commission's 2009 Guidance Paper. This first reference was relatively timid. The Court referred to 'negative effects on competition and consumer welfare'[29]

[28] Joined Cases C-501/06 P, C-513/06 P, C-515/06 P and C-519/06 P, *GlaxoSmithKline Services Unlimited v Commission, Commission v GlaxoSmithKline Services Unlimited, European Association of Euro Pharmaceutical Companies (EAEPC) v Commission* and *Asociación de exportadores españoles de productos farmacéuticos (Aseprofar) v Commission*, ECLI:EU:C:2009:610.

[29] Case C-209/10, *Post Danmark A/S v Konkurrencerådet* ECLI:EU:C:2012:172 [41].

and also stressed the importance of consumer harm resulting from competition law violations.[30] These quotes were again repeated in *Post Danmark II*,[31] which followed a few years later.

In the meantime, the Court of Justice's case law became less formalistic and more attuned to economics both in Article 101 TFEU and Article 102 TFEU. In Article 101 TFEU cases such as *Cartes Bancaires*, *Maxima Latvija* and *Budapest Bank*, the Court spoke of the anticompetitive consequences of conduct that 'leads to falls in production and price increases, resulting in poor allocation of resources to the detriment, in particular, of consumers'.[32] In Article 102 TFEU, the *Intel*[33] revolution meant that an effects-based approach was now the default position. As soon as the Union's highest judge started using the 'prohibited' term, the General Court felt at ease to restart citing consumer welfare albeit within the confines of the Court of Justice's terminology. Thus, in *Google Shopping*,[34] the General Court used the terms 'negative effects on competition and consumer welfare', exactly as the Court of Justice did.

However, it is at the Court of Justice level where the most recent pronouncements indicate a rather enthusiastic embracement of consumer welfare as a leading or indeed 'the ultimate' objective of the competition rules. Thus, AG Pitruzzella in his SABAM Opinion went as far as stating that '[u]ltimately, therefore, it is consumer welfare – the main (and some would say the only) objective of competition law – that suffers', while speaking of excessive pricing abuses. He went on to say:

> [T]he Commission, the national competition authorities and the national courts, when applying the concept of excessive prices, are faced with a Procrustean dilemma. On the one hand, there is the risk of antitrust over-enforcement based on false positives, which ultimately erode efficiency and consumer welfare. On the other, there is the risk of under-enforcement due to false negatives, which, in addition to eroding consumer welfare, may have, as mentioned in the previous point, wider negative repercussions.[35]

Perhaps the most detailed analysis on the role of consumer welfare is found in the recent AG Rantos Opinion in *Servizio Elettrico Nazionale*. The case at issue related to conduct by the former electricity state monopoly in Italy. After the liberalisation of the electricity market, generation and sale were opened to

[30] ibid, paras 20, 24.
[31] Case C-23/14, *Post Danmark A/S v Konkurrencerådet* ECLI:EU:C:2015:651, [49], [69].
[32] Case C-67/13 P, *Groupement des cartes bancaires (CB) v Commission* ECLI:EU:C:2014:2204 [51]; Case C-345/14, *SIA 'Maxima Latvija' v Konkurences padome* ECLI:EU:C:2015:784 [19]; Case C-227/14 P, *LG Display Co. Ltd and LG Display Taiwan Co. Ltd v Commission* ECLI:EU:C:2015:258 [62]; Case C-228/18, *Gazdasági Versenyhivatal v Budapest Bank Nyrt. and Others* ECLI:EU:C:2020:265 [36].
[33] Case C-413/14 P, *Intel Corporation Inc. v Commission* ECLI:EU:C:2017:632.
[34] Case T-612/17, *Google LLC and Alphabet, Inc. v Commission* ECLI:EU:T:2021:763 [553], [568], [572].
[35] Case C-372/19, *Belgische Vereniging van Auteurs, Componisten en Uitgevers CVBA (SABAM) v Weareone.World BVBA and Wecandance NV*, Opinion of AG Pitruzzella, ECLI:EU:C:2020:598 [22], [27].

competition, whereas transmission and distribution were still operated under a monopoly system. The former state monopoly – Enel – was structurally separated in three companies: Enel Energia (EE), electricity supplier for the deregulated market; Servizio Elettrico Nazionale (SEN), supplier of the 'enhanced protection service'; and e-distribuzione, concessionaire for electricity distribution activities. The Italian Competition Authority condemned the Enel Group for illegally using commercially sensitive information by operators to transfer customers from SEN to EE, in view of the announced market change. In particular, SEN obtained the consent of users to receive commercial proposals in a discriminatory manner, involving a request for initial authorisation for the processing of personal data by companies within the Enel Group and a second request in favour of third-party operators. The customers usually gave the initial consent, believing that this was necessary for managing the existing relationship with their supplier, while they usually refused the second consent, intended for other operators. Consent for third-party operators was only given in 30 per cent of cases. The Italian authority considered this a '*sui generis* abuse' and imposed fines on EE, SEN and the parent undertaking.

The case was an academic's paradise and a judge's nightmare. In this preliminary reference case, the referring court, the Italian Consiglio di Stato, sent some very abstract and theoretical questions to the Court of Justice that touched upon the basic objective of Article 102 TFEU. One of the specific questions asked was whether

> the purpose of the concept of abuse [is] to maximise the well-being of consumers, with the court being responsible for determining whether that well-being has been (or could be) reduced, or does the concept of an infringement of competition law have the function of preserving in itself the competitive structure of the market, in order to avoid the creation of economic power groupings that are, in any case, considered harmful for the community.

In proposing a response to that question, AG Rantos took a bold and principled position: protecting the structure of competition cannot be an objective alternative to consumer welfare.[36] In his view, protecting consumer welfare is a more central objective than the preservation of a competitive structure, although it would be unwise to view the two objectives as unconnected to each other. Indeed,

> Article 102 TFEU aims at the end of the day at maximising consumer welfare, in particular through the protection of the competitive structure of the market. Therefore, that protection may well constitute an objective pursued by Article 102 TFEU, not

[36] Case C-377/20, *Servizio Elettrico Nazionale SpA, ENEL SpA and Enel Energia SpA v Autorità Garante della Concorrenza e del Mercato*, Opinion of AG Rantos, ECLI:EU:C:2021:998 [94]–[95]. Unfortunately, the English text of the Opinion is not reflecting the nuances of the French text. Again, the reference to the 'well-being of consumers' instead of 'consumer welfare' is the result of a translation glitch.

> autonomously but only if in a specific case is integrated in the ultimate rationale of the (direct or indirect) protection of the consumers.[37]

AG Rantos added that effects on the structure of competition on a specific market can be considered a good 'proxy' of the effects that a certain exclusionary practice may have on consumer welfare. But an effect on the structure of competition does not necessarily mean a reduction of consumer welfare.[38]

The Court of Justice, in its judgment did not go as far as AG Rantos but included for the first time an express acknowledgement that consumer welfare is the ultimate objective of Article 102 TFEU:

> It follows that, as observed in essence by the Advocate General in point 100 of his Opinion, the well-being of both intermediary and final consumers must be regarded as the ultimate objective warranting the intervention of competition law in order to penalise abuse of a dominant position within the internal market or a substantial part of that market.[39]

This is a more far-reaching statement than the previous references of the Court of Justice to the objective of the competition rules being the 'protection of competition and consumer welfare'. The Court of Justice did retain its long-standing position that an authority only needs to show harm to the structure of competition, not harm to consumers as such,[40] but the protection of an 'effective competitive structure' is seen more as a proxy for that broader ultimate objective.[41] Thus, it can be seen as subservient to consumer welfare. At the same time, the Court's words make clear that consumer welfare is not seen in a technical sense that can have a direct bearing on which legal/operational tests need to be followed to find an abuse of dominance. The Court of Justice also clarifies that the concept of 'consumer' encompasses final consumers but also intermediaries. In other words, this amounts to a development though not a reversal of the *Spanish Glaxo* case law.[42]

[37] ibid [100].

[38] ibid [106].

[39] Case C-377/20, *Servizio Elettrico Nazionale SpA, ENEL SpA and Enel Energia SpA v Autorità Garante della Concorrenza e del Mercato* ECLI:EU:C:2022:379 [46].

[40] ibid [47]: 'Therefore, a competition authority discharges its burden of proof if it shows that a practice of an undertaking in a dominant position could impair, by using resources or means other than those governing normal competition, an effective competition structure, without it being necessary for that authority to prove that that practice may also cause direct harm to consumers. The dominant undertaking concerned may nevertheless escape the prohibition laid down in Article 102 TFEU by showing that the exclusionary effect that could result from the practice at issue is counterbalanced or even outweighed by positive effects for consumers.'

[41] [47] is linked with the broader pronouncement of [46] with the words 'des lors' ('therefore'), which mean that the standing of consumer welfare as 'ultimate objective' of competition law is not put in question by the references to 'effective competitive structure'.

[42] The inclusion of intermediaries into the concept of 'consumers' is also in line with the Commission guidelines and policy papers. See above.

V. Conclusions

This chapter has demonstrated that, irrespective of the discussions in the US, there has been no 'tyranny' of the consumer welfare standard in EU competition law. Protection of an 'effective competitive structure' has always been, and remains, a valid objective and is seen as a good proxy of the broader consumer welfare principle, which is the 'ultimate objective' of the competition rules but does not amount to an operational-technical test that can be applied to specific cases. At the same time, the EU case law makes it clear that consumer welfare is not just about prices but also pertains to quality, innovation and choice.[43]

Nonetheless, a more 'ideological' approach that advocates the repudiation of consumer welfare, echoing the current state of affairs in the US, would not conform with the more recent case law of the Court of Justice and its repeated and enthusiastic references to that objective behind the competition rules. Indeed, we can consider this an *acquis*. Bearing in mind that the EU case law relates to the interpretation of primary Union law (Articles 101 and 102 TFEU), only a change of the Treaty would make a departure from that *acquis* possible. In that sense, quite paradoxically, consumer welfare, currently under persecution in the US, has found a refuge in Europe. Time will tell whether such a refuge is temporary or here to stay.

[43] Case C-413/14 P, *Intel Corporation Inc. v Commission* ECLI:EU:C:2017:632 [134]: 'not every exclusionary effect is necessarily detrimental to competition. Competition on the merits may, by definition, lead to the departure from the market or the marginalisation of competitors that are less efficient and so less attractive to consumers from the point of view of, among other things, price, choice, quality or innovation'.

6

Antitrust and the Golden Thread

Balancing the Presumption of Innocence with the Public Interest in Competition Enforcement

NIAMH DUNNE[1]

I. Introduction

In the introduction to *Antitrust and the Bounds of Power: The Dilemma of Liberal Democracy in the History of the Market*, Amato sets out the fundamental tension at the core of his concise and masterful work: 'In a democratic society ... there are two bounds that should never be crossed: one beyond which the unlegitimated power of individuals arises, the other beyond which legitimate public power becomes illegitimate'.[2] The dilemma referenced in the book's subtitle is, of course, how to manage the intersection of these contrasting concerns: 'the boundary between the risk of market power and the risk of intrusive antitrust measures'.[3] The challenge is thus to implement an effective competition law system that protects the public interest without oppressing private interests unduly. In the quarter-century since the book's publication, the first of these concerns – the role of competition law in controlling undesirable private market power – has become ever more prominent in public discourse, prompted by fears about rising concentration levels generally[4] and the problems of Big Tech more specifically.[5] This has led, amongst other

[1] London School of Economics.

[2] G Amato, *Antitrust and the Bounds of Power: The Dilemma of Liberal Democracy in the History of the Market* (Hart Publishing, 1997) 3.

[3] Amato, *Antitrust and the Bounds of Power* (1997) 123.

[4] See, eg J de Loecker, J Eeckhout and G Unger, 'The Rise of Market Power and the Macroeconomic Implications' (2020) 135 *Quarterly Journal of Economics* 561, and focusing on the EU, G Koltay, S Lorincz and TM Valletti, 'Concentration and Competition: Evidence from Europe and Implications for Policy' (2022) CESifo Working Paper No 9640.

[5] European Commission, 'Competition Policy for the Digital Era. A report by Jacques Cremer, Yves-Alexandre de Montjoye & Heike Schweitzer' (April 2019).

things, to demands for more aggressive public enforcement. Concomitantly, there have been calls to drop some of the obstacles – others might call them safeguards – to be found within the existing case law, suggestions which bring the second aspect of Amato's dilemma into play. This focus of this chapter is, accordingly, the question of what 'legitimate' public enforcement entails today, focusing on the antitrust activity of the European Commission.

The past few decades have seen numerous efforts to develop a more 'effective'[6] competition regime in the EU: from steeper penalties,[7] to greater decentralisation of public enforcement to national authorities,[8] to efforts to facilitate private enforcement,[9] to the much-feted adoption of a 'more economic approach' to substantive assessment,[10] and even its apparent abandonment in recent practice.[11] Missing from this raft of innovations, however, is one of the most straightforward and sensible suggestions in Amato's book: namely, to entrust EU-level action to an independent authority rather than the politically controlled Commission.[12] Instead, the Commission itself has met demands for enhanced legitimacy in its decision-making by placing greater emphasis on issues of procedural fairness;[13] the Court of Justice has demonstrated more overt willingness to engage in full merits review of Commission infringement decisions;[14] and the advent of the Charter of Fundamental Rights has imbued these administrative processes with the language and logic of human rights protections.[15] Competition enforcement in the EU today is, accordingly, a complex and technically sophisticated enterprise. Yet it is also one which has become ever more consequential for defendants, who are subject to far-reaching public intervention against their private business activities.

[6] This concept has specific importance in developing the EU competition jurisprudence, see eg Cases C-453/99, *Courage and Crehan* ECLI:EU:C:2001:465 [26]; C-194/14, P *AC-Treuhand AG* ECLI:EU:C:2015:717 [36]; and C-547/16 *Gasorba SL* ECLI:EU:C:2017:891 [29].

[7] Particularly following adoption of the Commission's Guidelines on the method of setting fines imposed pursuant to Article 23(2)(a) of Regulation No 1/2003 (OJ C 210/2, 1 September 2006).

[8] As provided by Council Regulation (EC) No 1/2003 of 16 December 2002 on the implementation of the rules on competition laid down in Articles 81 and 82 of the Treaty (OJ L 1/1, 4 January 2003) ('Regulation 1/2003') and Directive (EU) 2019/1 of the European Parliament and of the Council of 11 December 2018 to empower the competition authorities of the Member States to be more effective enforcers and to ensure the proper functioning of the internal market (OJ L 11/3, 14 January 2019).

[9] In particular, through Directive 2014/104/EU of the European Parliament and of the Council of 26 November 2014 on certain rules governing actions for damages under national law for infringements of the competition law provisions of the Member States and of the European Union (OJ L 349/1, 5 December 2014) and accompanying Commission guidance.

[10] See, eg, AC Witt, 'The European Court of Justice and the More Economic Approach to EU Competition Law – Is the Tide Turning?' (2019) 64 *The Antitrust Bulletin* 172.

[11] As discussed by this author previously in 'Fairness and the Challenge of Making Markets Work Better' (2021) 84 *MLR* 230.

[12] Discussed in Amato (n 2), esp 119–24.

[13] European Commission, Notice on best practices for the conduct of proceedings concerning Articles 101 and 102 TFEU (OJ C 308/6, 20 October 2011).

[14] Relevant recent cases, discussed further below, include Cases C-67/13, P *Groupement de Cartes Bancaires v Commission* ECLI:EU:C:2014:2204, C-413/14, P *Intel v Commission* ECLI:EU:C:2017:632, and T-691/14, *Servier and Others v Commission* ECLI:EU:T:2018:922.

[15] See, eg Case C-386/10, *Chalkor v Commission* ECLI:EU:C:2011:815 [51]–[53].

This contribution examines the balance currently struck within the EU competition framework, which aims to ensure that the exercise of public power that is inherent within these rules and their application remains legitimate in all senses. Our focus is the enforcement by the Commission of what are now Articles 101 and 102 TFEU, prohibiting anticompetitive agreements and abuse of dominance respectively. The chapter begins with a brief overview of the structure of enforcement at EU level. Developments within the last few decades emphasise the nature of antitrust enforcement as an exercise in 'law enforcement',[16] marshalling the coercive power of the state (or, in the EU, the supranational authority) against individual economic interests. Such an incursion into private freedom is undoubtedly justifiable by reference to the need to curtail 'the unlegitimated power of individuals'.[17] Yet it nonetheless raises important questions about the fair and proper exercise of public power, and how this is scrutinised and controlled in the context of enforcing the relatively open-textured competition prohibitions. The remainder of the chapter explores the legal framework that conditions the Commission's exercise of its enforcement powers, considering its compatibility with the 'golden thread' of any justice system, the presumption of innocence. The chapter addresses, in particular, the burden of proof and standard of review in competition cases, the Commission's substantive obligations with respect to the application of Articles 101 and 102 respectively, the treatment of novel theories of harm, and the shifting landscape of negotiated settlements as a means to conclude investigations. Finally, the chapter concludes with some brief reflections.

II. The Structure of Contemporary EU-Level Competition Enforcement

Amato's book was prescient, among many reasons, for foreshadowing a switch from more 'regulatory' to 'decisional' enforcement practice in Europe.[18] The regulatory archetype positions antitrust decision-making as 'the outcome of political discretion';[19] the decisional one sees enforcement activity as 'primarily antitrust and no longer "multi-purpose"'[20] in nature. In the quarter-century since the book's publication, this shift has become ever more entrenched in both Commission enforcement practice, discussed in this section, and its review by the Union courts, discussed in section IV below.

[16] S Weber Waller, 'Prosecution by Regulation: The Changing Nature of Antitrust Enforcement' (1998) 77 *Oregon Law Review* 1383, 1384.

[17] See n 2 above.

[18] Amato (n 2)120.

[19] ibid 121.

[20] ibid 122.

Arguably the key development, from this perspective, has been the abandonment of the centralised notification system for potentially anticompetitive agreements, which provided the focus of much of Amato's frustration with the existing enforcement structure in Europe. This disappeared with the entry into force of the modernising Regulation 1/2003 in May 2004. Freed of the obligation to scrutinise any and all claims for application of the now Article 101(3) TFEU exception,[21] the Commission was free to developing increasingly aggressive and robust anti-cartel enforcement as the 'primary target of the antitrust rules'.[22] This included a beefed-up leniency programme,[23] and quite deliberately higher fines[24] for practices that were explicitly portrayed as 'cancers on the open market economy'.[25] The resulting redeployment of agency resources also enabled the Commission to expand its sector inquiry work,[26] which translated into rich streams of enforcement activity under both Articles 101 and 102 in sectors including telecommunications, energy, pharmaceuticals and e-commerce. The emergence of the digital economy, and with it the rise of powerful and chronically under-regulated Big Tech giants, has provided a further area for scrutiny and action, a focus matched by competition agencies elsewhere.

Importantly, Regulation 1/2003 also saw the bifurcation of the Commission's decision-making capacity into Article 7 infringement decisions and Article 9 commitment decisions. Article 7 decisions are formal findings of violation of Article 101 or 102, accompanied by fines absent exceptional circumstances. Article 9 decisions, by contrast, are voluntarily agreed with defendants, without any formal finding of breach, and require the undertaking concerned to modify its behaviour or structure to address the competition concerns. The nominal division between consensual and non-consensual case disposition under Regulation 1/2003 has been complicated, however, by the Commission's increasing enthusiasm for negotiating settlements which ultimately take place under Article 7.[27] In cartel cases, this occurs under the Leniency Notice[28] and the Cartel Settlement Notice,[29]

[21] Undertakings instead self-assess their compliance, using the Commission's Guidelines on the application of Article 81(3) of the Treaty (OJ C 101/97, 27 April 2004) ('Article 81(3) Guidelines').

[22] European Commission, Communication from the Commission – A pro-active Competition Policy for a Competitive Europe, COM(2004) 293 final (20 April 2004) 6.

[23] European Commission, Notice on Immunity from fines and reduction of fines in cartel cases (OJ C 298/17, 8 December 2006).

[24] See n 7.

[25] Competition Commissioner Mario Monti, 'Fighting Cartels – Why and How? Why should we be concerned with cartels and collusive behaviour?' (speech at the 3rd Nordic Competition Policy Conference, Stockholm, 11 September 2000).

[26] Conducted under Regulation 1/2003, Art 17.

[27] This shift has been explored by this author previously in 'From Coercion to Cooperation: Settlement within EU Competition Law' in D Gerard an A Komninos (eds), *Remedies in EU Competition Law: Substance, Process and Policy* (Wolters Kluwer, 2020).

[28] See n 23.

[29] Commission Notice on the conduct of settlement procedures in view of the adoption of Decisions pursuant to Article 7 and Article 23 of Council Regulation (EC) No 1/2003 in cartel cases (OJ C 167/1, 2 July.2008).

each of which make formal provision for discounts on fines for cooperation. In non-cartel cases, this takes the shape of an essentially informal practice, first used in 2016,[30] by which the Commission similarly gives significant discounts for assistance and admissions of guilt by defendants.[31] In practice, neither Article 9 decisions nor informal Article 7 settlements are appealed by defendants; and cartel settlements are typically challenged, if at all, only in respect of the amount of the fine. The overall impact of this 'transactionalisation'[32] of enforcement has been a parallel dejudicialisation, restricting Court of Justice oversight to a comparatively narrow slice of EU-level enforcement today.

III. EU Competition Enforcement and the Exercise of Public Power

Yet, notwithstanding the shift from regulatory to decisional – and now negotiated – enforcement practice, the EU competition rules and their application by the Commission remain an indisputable example of coercive (supranational) public power: used to restrain and direct and occasionally punish the profit-making activities of private market actors. For individual defendants, the consequences of a formal finding of breach can be draconian: high punitive fines of up to 10 per cent of an undertaking's annual turnover;[33] legally binding requirements to desist from the impugned business practices and to refrain from repeating these in future;[34] and obligations to take specific actions to remedy the resulting market problems.[35] Formal infringement decisions also undergird follow-on private damages claims, serving to satisfy the first element of the legal test for recovery under the *Courage* jurisprudence.[36] The latter is not the case for commitment decisions, which similarly do not attract fines.[37] Yet defendants who opt to settle by commitments are often required to offer significant concessions, which, legally, can go far beyond the obligations that could be imposed in equivalent Article 7 cases.[38] Moreover, regardless of whether a defendant chooses to fight or to settle

[30] Case AT.39759 – *ARA Foreclosure*, Decision of 20 September 2016.

[31] Non-cartel Art 7 settlements are not governed by secondary legislation, though the Commission provided an informal FAQ when it settled with Guess in 2020: see European Commission, 'Cooperation – FAQ' Factsheet (December 2020), available at ec.europa.eu/competition/publications/data/factsheet_guess.pdf.

[32] D Geradin and E Mattioli, 'The Transactionalization of EU Competition Law: A Positive Development?' (2017) 8 *Journal of European Competition Law & Practice* 634.

[33] Regulation 1/2003, Art 23(2).

[34] ibid Art 7(1).

[35] ibid.

[36] Case C-453/99, *Courage and Crehan* ECLI:EU:C:2001:465. The binding effect of infringement decisions is provided by Regulation 1/2003, Art 16.

[37] These distinctions proved pivotal in Case C-441/07 P, *Commission v Alrosa* ECLI:EU:C:2010:377 [48].

[38] ibid [40]–[48].

an investigation, competition cases today attract considerable public opprobrium, generating 'stigma' and negative reputational effects for prosecuted undertaking.[39]

The coercive impact of the EU competition rules extends beyond the implications for individual defendants. At their most basic, the competition provisions impose well-established limits on the default freedom of private enterprises to conduct a business, guaranteed by Article 16 of the Charter of Fundamental Rights. Article 101 limits a firm's ability to contract and collaborate in important ways.[40] A firm with significant market power, however lawfully acquired, has a weighty 'special responsibility' under Article 102, to ensure that its own profit-maximising behaviour does not unduly impede its competitors' ability to stay afloat.[41] There are also more systemic chilling effects associated with legally binding limitations on market activity, in particular the possibility that firms may refrain from aggressive competitive behaviour that would ultimately benefit consumers, for fear of falling foul of ill-defined or overly expansive prohibitions.[42] This dissuasive effect is further heightened by the prospect of private enforcement piggybacking on public efforts.[43]

Thus, the EU competition framework today, both as it is conceived and implemented, represents an unambiguous deployment of public power to circumscribe the private power of individual market actors. It does so directly, by proscribing and punishing the behaviour of specific defendants, and indirectly, by shaping and limiting the market freedom of traders more generally. This, in and of itself, is fairly unremarkable. As Amato noted, in a democratic society, the mere exercise of public power does not trouble us as such; it is only when power becomes *illegitimate* that we have cause for concern. On the one hand, the competition rules are firmly established in the Treaty framework, and indeed have the status of primary (and thus hierarchically superior) EU law. On the other, few would doubt that the practices that have been the focus of Commission enforcement activity in recent years – such as hardcore cartels, or exclusionary conduct by super-dominant firms – have at least the potential to cause significant harm to European economies and consumers. Indeed, many argue that current market dynamics make robust antitrust intervention even *more* essential today.[44]

[39] Opinion in Case C-272/09 P, *KME Germany and Others v Commission* ECLI:EU:C:2011:63 [64].

[40] Including the manner in which it organises its distribution network (see European Commission, Guidelines on Vertical Restraints, OJ C 130/1, 19 May 2010 ('Vertical Guidelines')) and horizontal cooperation with rivals (see European Commission, Guidelines on the applicability of Article 101 of the Treaty on the Functioning of the European Union to horizontal co-operation agreements (OJ C 11/1, 14 January 2011) ('Horizontal Cooperation Guidelines').

[41] Case C-322/81, *Michelin (I)* ECLI:EU:C:1983:313 [57].

[42] Described, with respect to the previous notification system for the exception rule, in BE Hawk, 'System Failure: Vertical Restraints and EC competition law' (1995) 32 *Common Market Law Review* 973.

[43] See n 9.

[44] See, eg, I Lianos, 'Competition Law for the Digital Era: A complex systems' perspective' (2019) UCL Centre for Law, Economics and Society Research Paper Series, 6/2019.

Yet even if the required legal tools exist in law, and even if public interest concerns can be identified to justify their deployment, it is necessary to ensure that the *exercise* of public power inherent in the application of Articles 101 and 102 by the Commission is legitimate in itself. Legitimacy, in this context, has several dimensions. Most basically, the requirements of the relevant legal provision must be infringed on the facts of a case. The EU competition rules, mirroring the approach of the US Sherman Act, do not gift to public enforcers a set of plenary powers by which to design and direct the operation of markets. Instead, Articles 101 and 102 each comprise discrete (if fairly wide-ranging) prohibitions, outlawing defined types of behaviour, and thus are only infringed only where it is demonstrated that a defendant undertaking has in fact engaged in the proscribed conduct. Competition law is somewhat remarkable insofar as it is subject to a multifaceted enforcement framework. Infringements of Articles 101 or 102 can be the subject of administrative decision-making by the Commission and national competition authorities, can form the basis of private civil – typically tortious – litigation before national courts, and in certain Member States, can lead to criminal prosecution of individual firm officers or employees.

Yet regardless of the precise procedural lens through which an enforcement case is pursued, the starting point is always the need to demonstrate the occurrence of the proscribed conduct. That is, while the competition prohibitions do not hinge on the existence of 'fault' in the sense of moral culpability[45] – there is no *mens rea* requirement as such – they are not no-fault rules in the sense that, for instance, the mere presence of market power or consumer harm can trigger their application. This point is underlined by the fate of the proposed 'new competition tool',[46] which would have introduced a generalised no-fault regulatory instrument in the EU along the lines of the UK's market investigation procedure.[47] The subsequent jettisoning of the new competition tool in favour of sector-specific no-fault legislation *only* for digital gatekeepers[48] reiterates the need to demonstrate prohibited conduct – broadly, an *actus reus* – to establish a violation of the ordinary competition rules.

The procedures and processes employed by the Commission to establish that such conduct has occurred raise more granular legitimacy concerns. It is uncontentious that fundamental rights protections apply to competition enforcement by the Commission,[49] including the right to good administration,[50] the right to

[45] In Case C-280/08 P, *Deutsche Telekom* ECLI:EU:C:2010:603 [89], the Court of Justice confirmed that the absence of any perceived 'fault' on the part of a defendant is no barrier to a finding of liability.

[46] European Commission, 'Antitrust: Commission consults stakeholders on a possible new competition tool' press release (2 June 2020).

[47] See, eg, A Fletcher, 'Market Investigations for Digital Platforms: Panacea or Complement?' (2021) 12 *Journal of European Competition Law & Practice* 44.

[48] Proposal for a Regulation of the European Parliament and of the Council on contestable and fair markets in the digital sector (Digital Markets Act) COM/2020/842 final (15 December 2020). Formal political agreement was reached to enact the DMA on 24 March 2022.

[49] See n 9.

[50] Charter of Fundamental Rights, Art 41.

a fair trial,[51] the presumption of innocence and right of defence,[52] and protection against double jeopardy.[53] Fair and open processes are especially important in light of the high profile of competition enforcement under the stewardship of the crusading Commissioner Vestager, raising attendant concerns that the EU rules may be deployed to further political objectives. There is also an increasing recognition within the jurisprudence of the Court of Justice of the counterproductive harms that can result where the rules are applied too broadly or bluntly against behaviour that is welfare-enhancing overall.[54] While error cost concerns must not prevent the progressive evolution of the jurisprudence,[55] any such development nonetheless cannot be wholly inconsistent with the existing case-law nor with the acknowledged objectives of competition policy.

This understanding of the limits of competition law and its legitimate application has been criticised.[56] A 'legalistic'[57] approach has the unavoidable effect of narrowing the range of market problems that come within the regulatory scope of the competition rules, thus increasing the likelihood that objectionable behaviours or harmful market structures will remain unchallenged. This returns us, of course, to the dilemma at the heart of *Antitrust and the Bounds of Power*: namely, whether it is possible to impose adequate controls on private market power, without requiring levels of public intervention that are incompatible with the 'social *market* economy' ideal.[58] The very existence of the competition rules represents a departure from the default freedom to conduct a business within the EU – albeit a departure foreseen within Article 16 of the Charter itself, which acknowledges that the right must be exercised 'in accordance with Union law'. Yet the integrity of the competition law enterprise, in addition to fidelity to the circumscribed coverage of the discrete Treaty provisions, means that application of the rules in practice may fall short of delivering 'genuine, undistorted competition'[59] in all instances.

The remainder of this chapter explores the balance that has been struck within contemporary EU-level enforcement practice: on the one hand, empowering the Commission to address competition problems in the public interest, effectively and efficiently; and on the other, protecting individual defendants and the market

[51] ibid Art 47.

[52] ibid Art 48.

[53] ibid Art 50.

[54] See, eg, Opinions of Advocate General Wahl in Case C-413/14 P, *Intel v Commission* ECLI:EU:C:2017:632 [119], and Advocate General Pitruzzella in Case C-132/19 P, *Groupe Canal+ v Commission* ECLI:EU:C:2020:355 [88], both making direct reference to error cost analysis and the perils of false positive findings in competition law.

[55] See n 5, 4.

[56] A remarkable example is found in an interview with former Chief Economist of DG Competition, Tommaso Valletti, who excoriated the current EU-level enforcement framework, from its 'useful fool' economists, to 'toxic' private lawyers, 'unambitious' agency officials and 'brainwashed' judges: see 'The European System of Monopoly … and how to fix it' *The Counterbalance Newsletter* (21 April 2021), available at ecounterbalance.substack.com/p/the-european-system-of-monopoly?s=r.

[57] ibid.

[58] Treaty on European Union, Art 3(3) (emphasis added).

[59] Case C-413/14 P, *Intel v Commission* ECLI:EU:C:2017:632 [135].

economy more generally against unfair and even counterproductive public intervention in private economic activity. The title of the chapter borrows the golden thread metaphor, developed within English criminal law, which posits that a justice system is (or at least should be) designed and implemented to protect the presumption of innocence, broadly construed.[60] Accordingly, the question considered here is the extent to which the current legal framework respects and reflects the propositions that the Commission holds the burden of establishing that a violation of Article 101 or 102 has occurred, and that undertakings are entitled to be treated as innocent unless and until anticompetitive conduct contrary to those rules has been established.

IV. The 'Golden Thread' in Practice: The Presumption of Innocence and Beyond in Contemporary EU Competition Enforcement

We thus start with the presumption of innocence itself, a general principle of EU law,[61] which requires that defendants 'shall be presumed innocent until proved guilty according to law'.[62] The presumption of innocence is a key component of the bundle of fair trial rights recognised and protected under the European Convention of Human Rights and the Charter of Fundamental Rights.[63] Together, these rights serve to ensure that the administration of justice within the EU system is compatible with the principle of the rule of law.[64] Under the European Convention, fair trial rights attach only to criminal proceedings; this is the case with certain protections in the Charter, although the presumption of innocence and general right to a fair trial are drafted more broadly. In any event, although the Commission's enforcement powers are expressly stated to *not* be criminal in nature,[65] the severity of the sanctions that can be imposed, alongside the stigma that attaches to prosecution, nevertheless means that the Commission's administrative decision-making is acknowledged to come within the scope of fair trial protections.[66]

[60] First articulated by Viscount Sankey in *Woolmington v DPP* [1935] AC 462, 481. A useful discussion of the 'golden thread' metaphor, and the importance of the presumption of innocence more generally, is A Hooper, 'Fair Trial: "One Golden Thread"' in L Blom-Cooper, B Dickson, and G Drewry (eds), *The Judicial House of Lords 1876–2009* (OUP, 2009).

[61] Opinion of Advocate General Hogan in Case C-440/19 P, *Pometon SpA v Commission* ECLI:EU:C:2020:816 [58]. See also Case C-199/92 P, *Hüls v Commission* EU:C:1999:358 [149].

[62] Charter of Fundamental Rights, Art 48(1); and European Convention on Human Rights, Art 6(2).

[63] The relevant provisions of the Charter are considered to 'implement', and thus cover the same ground as, equivalent rights contained with the European Convention on Human Rights: *Chalkor* (n 15) [51].

[64] See Preamble to the Charter of Fundamental Rights, 'the Union … is based on the principles of democracy and the rule of law'.

[65] Regulation 1/2003, Art 23(5).

[66] See, in particular, the discussion in the Opinion of Advocate General Sharpston in Case C-272/09 P, *KME Germany v Commission* ECLI:EU:C:2011:63 [60]–[67].

The presumption of innocence, as noted, is but one component of the suite of fair trial rights recognised in EU law. Yet as the golden thread metaphor suggests, its rationale and implications permeate the panoply of fair trial rights. The obligation to hold a fair and public hearing before an independent and impartial tribunal,[67] for instance, ensures that public enforcers face a sufficiently rigorous challenge to discharge their duty to establish the guilt of a defendant. Rights of defence,[68] similarly, ensure that the presumption is not too easily rebutted and thus that it imposes a meaningful constraint on the exercise of public coercive power. The principle of legality[69] – 'no punishment without law'[70] – prohibits the retrospective recharacterisation of otherwise 'innocent' behaviour as offending in nature. Accordingly, the discussion in this section extends beyond the strict confines of the case law addressing the presumption of innocence, to consider the wider framework that conditions the Commission's exercise of its competition powers, and in particular, those elements that ensure 'the fair examination of the charges brought against'[71] defendants in Article 101 or 102 investigations.

A. Burden of Proof and Standard of Review in Competition Cases

Our starting point is the burden of proof in competition cases, governed formally by Regulation 1/2003. 'In any national or [EU-level] proceedings … the burden of proving an infringement of [Article 101(1) or Article 102] shall rest on the party or the authority alleging the infringement'.[72] Conversely, 'The undertaking or association of undertakings claiming the benefit of [the Article 101(3) exception] shall bear the burden of proving that the conditions … are fulfilled'.[73] In EU-level enforcement activity, however, the Commission combines the roles of investigator, prosecutor and initial adjudicator: a contentious institutional set-up which nonetheless persists a quarter-century after Amato's cogent criticism in *Antitrust and the Bounds of Power*.[74] This means, of course, that it is the Commission itself which decides whether it has discharged its own burden of proof at first instance. Its freedom to do so is tempered by the review powers of the General Court, which conducts an 'in-depth review … in law and in fact' of any findings by the Commission,[75] with unlimited jurisdiction with respect to fines.[76] General Court

[67] Charter of Fundamental Rights, Art 47.
[68] ibid Art 48.
[69] ibid Art 9(1).
[70] ibid Art 7.
[71] Opinion in *Pometon* (n 61) [74].
[72] Regulation 1/2003, Art 2.
[73] ibid.
[74] See also Opinion in *KME* (n 66) [68].
[75] Case T-612/17, *Google and Alphabet v Commission (Google Shopping)* ECLI:EU:T:2021:763 [130].
[76] Regulation 1/2003, Art 31.

judgments can be further appealed to the higher Court of Justice on points of law.[77] The case law moreover makes it clear that the presumption of innocence requires that, in enforcement cases, the Commission must avoid any 'potential prejudgment'[78] or 'premature expression'[79] of guilt prior to any formal (and thus appealable[80]) finding of infringement. Yet legitimate concerns remain regarding the acceptability of requiring defendants to appeal an infringement decision to access their full fair trial rights, and about the extent to which subsequent full merits review provides an adequate safeguard against abuses of enforcement power at first instance.[81]

Under Article 263 TFEU, the Union courts are empowered to 'review the legality' of Commission decisions. Whether adopted under Article 7 or Article 9, direct addressees have automatic standing to seek review, whereas non-addressees must demonstrate sufficient 'direct and individual' concern to challenge a decision.[82] Article 263(2) provides an arcane-sounding list of grounds of review,[83] which permits, inter alia, challenges to be brought on the basis of errors in the substantive antitrust assessment, as well as procedural defects or violations of fair trial rights. Yet Article 263 does not specify a precise legal standard for the envisaged review of legality. Nor, for that matter, is the Commission's underlying legal burden addressed in either the Treaties or relevant secondary legislation. The Court's case law requires the Commission to 'produce sufficiently *precise and consistent evidence* to support the *firm conviction* that the alleged infringement took place'.[84] It is unnecessary, however, 'for every item of evidence produced by the Commission to satisfy those criteria in relation to every aspect of the infringement,' it being sufficient 'if the body of evidence relied on, … as a whole, meets that requirement'.[85]

When challenged before the Court of Justice, Commission decision-making is subject to what the Commission itself has described as 'a comprehensive review, in which the Court is expected to thoroughly scrutinise the decision for errors in the factual findings or the interpretation of the legal rules'.[86] The Court, somewhat notoriously, purports to grant a margin of discretion to the Commission with respect to 'complex evaluations on economic matters'.[87] It is increasingly accepted,

[77] Case C-440/19 P, *Pometon v Commission* EU:C:2021:214 [50]–[51].

[78] ibid [63].

[79] ibid [66].

[80] Purely 'provisional' measures cannot be challenged; the measure must have 'binding' legal effect on the defendant, thus 'bringing about a distinct change in his legal position': Case C-60/81, *IBM v Commission* ECLI:EU:C:1981:264 [9]–[10].

[81] See, eg, I Forrester, 'Due process in EC competition cases: A distinguished institution with flawed procedures' (2009) 34 *European Law Review* 817.

[82] TFEU, Art 263(4).

[83] Namely, 'lack of competence, infringement of an essential procedural requirement, infringement of the Treaties or of any rule of law relating to their application, or misuse of powers'.

[84] Case T-286/09 RENV, *Intel Corporation v Commission* ECLI:EU:T:2022:19 [163] (emphasises added).

[85] ibid.

[86] European Commission, Note by the EU on The standard of review by courts in competition cases, Submission to OECD Roundtable, DAF/COMP/WP3/WD(2019)9 [19].

[87] Case C-56/64, *Consten and Grundig v Commission* ECLI:EU:C:1966:41 [347].

however, that this leeway is more apparent than actual in current practice.[88] The courts are thus required to

> establish, among other things, whether the evidence relied on is factually accurate, reliable and consistent [and] also whether that evidence contains all the information which must be taken into account in order to assess a complex situation and whether it is capable of substantiating the conclusions drawn from.[89]

Ultimately, in exercising its review powers, 'The Court cannot … conclude that the Commission has established the infringement at issue to the requisite legal standard if it still entertains any doubts on that point'.[90]

A complicating factor, however, is the Commission's enthusiastic use of presumptions to structure and assist the task of determining whether a competition violation has occurred. This enables the Commission to short-circuit its burden of proof, at least initially, by essentially inferring an illegitimate distortion of competition (or constitutive element thereof) from sufficiently proximate facts. This then shifts the burden back to defendants, to introduce suitably compelling arguments and evidence to call into question the legal finding behind the presumption, which requires the Commission to provide *further* substantive support for its claims. Because of this, use of presumptions can raise concerns from a presumption of innocence perspective. The lower the threshold for the Commission to infer an infringement, and/or the more difficult for defendants to adduce arguments or evidence to rebut that prima facie finding, the higher the risk that an undertaking's guilt might be simply assumed from the circumstances rather than proven by the prosecutor. The use of presumptions can nonetheless be defended on grounds of common sense, to reflect past enforcement experience, to enhance the efficiency of adjudication by requiring the party most likely to have access to evidence to adduce it, and to enhance the 'effectiveness' of enforcement[91] – the latter being, essentially, a euphemism for making it easier to establish an infringement. Presumptions respect the presumption of innocence, as that principle is understood in EU law, provided that the presumption is rebuttable by the defendant at least in principle,[92] even if it is difficult to do so in practice.[93]

It is important however to distinguish two broad scenarios where a defendant may be called upon to introduce evidence to rebut a prima facie finding of infringement. On the one hand, where this conclusion is 'based on the supposition that the facts established cannot be explained other than by the existence of anticompetitive

[88] See n 86 [21]–[25].

[89] *Chalkor* (n 15) [54].

[90] RENV *Intel* (n 84) [161].

[91] C Ritter, 'Presumptions in EU Competition Law' (2018) 6 *Journal of Antitrust Enforcement* 189, 203–08.

[92] ibid 202, citing in particular the judgments in Cases T-144/07, *ThyssenKrupp Liften* ECLI:EU:T:2011:364 [114], and C-521/09 P, *Elf Aquitaine* ECLI:EU:C:2011:620 [62].

[93] Ritter (n 91) 203, argues that the fact that a presumption is difficult to rebut is proof of its underlying soundness: 'Since evidence contrary to the presumption rarely comes up, it was correct to presume'.

behaviour', it is sufficient for defendants merely to present arguments that provide 'another plausible explanation' of those facts, in order successfully to rebut the initial presumption of breach.[94] An example is the presumption of a cartel arising from evidence of parallel market behaviour, which can be rebutted, inter alia, by demonstrating that the relevant market may be susceptible to oligopoly dynamics.[95] On the other, where the Commission introduces substantive evidence that is, in itself, sufficient to support a finding of infringement, then it is not enough for defendants merely to raise the 'possibility' of an alternative explanation for the relevant facts. Instead, to the extent that a defendant claims that a particular circumstance serves to refute the Commission's interpretation, 'it is for the undertaking concerned to prove … the existence of the circumstance on which it relies and … that that circumstance calls into question the probative value of the evidence relied on by the Commission'.[96] Accordingly, though the Commission bears the burden of establishing that the defendant has in fact violated the prohibition set out in Article 101 or 102, it is not required to furthermore demonstrate the absence of alternative explanations for the resulting market harm.

B. Commission Practice under Article 101

The Court's jurisprudence further develops the more granular requirements of the Commission's substantive obligations when discharging its burden of proof under Regulation 1/2003. Article 101 is the wordier of the two antitrust provisions, identifying numerous categories of potentially problematic coordination under the prohibition rule in the first paragraph, and providing an explicit exception rule premised on four cumulative requirements in the third paragraph.[97] The case law makes it clear, however, that a formalistic reading of the prohibition rule is not required, paying little notice to the distinction between types of coordination – whether agreements, concerted practices or decisions of associations of undertakings[98] – and essentially none to the division between the enumerated categories of harm, namely the prevention, restriction or distortion of competition.

Closer attention is paid to the 'object or effect' criterion, which has been the focus of much recent case law. The Commission's earlier enforcement practice faced criticism for an over-reliance on and formalistic approach to the object limb – 'very rigid',[99] was Amato's assessment – which essentially absolved it of

[94] RENV *Intel* (n 84) [165].

[95] Case C-89/85 etc, *Ahlström Osakeyhtiö and Others v Commission ('Woodpulp')* ECLI:EU:C:1993:120 [126]–[27]. See the critique of this 'more sharply presumptive' approach in Amato (n 2) 56–58.

[96] RENV, *Intel* (n 84) [166].

[97] The language of 'prohibition rule' and 'exception rule' comes from the Article 81(3) Guidelines (n 21).

[98] See, eg, Case C-238/05, *ASNEF-EQUIFAX* ECLI:EU:C:2006:734 [32].

[99] Amato (n 2) 117.

the obligation to take account of the actual or even anticipated impact of conduct that took certain prohibited forms.[100] The *Cartes Bancaires* judgment in 2014 thus represented a high-profile loss for the Commission, in which the Court of Justice emphasised that it must do more than merely identify a potentiality for restrictiveness to discharge its burden under the object limb.[101] Instead, to establish that conduct is 'by its very nature, harmful to the proper functioning of competition',[102] the Commission must demonstrate that it 'pose[s] a sufficient degree of harm to competition on [a relevant] market'.[103] Posing harm is not quite the same as actually *causing* harm, however, and the Court has subsequently upheld findings by the Commission of object restrictions in more ambiguous circumstances, including pay-to-delay agreements[104] and the rules of the International Skating Union.[105] The more demanding effects limb remains available where the object test cannot be satisfied,[106] and this provided the vehicle by which the Commission ultimately succeeded in prohibiting the membership scheme in *Cartes Bancaires*.[107] The Commission has also adopted a belt-and-braces approach in some recent practice, of establishing that conduct is restrictive of competition *both* by object *and* by nature of its effects,[108] an approach permitted under Article 101 despite the ostensibly disjunctive nature of the object or effect criterion.[109]

The Article 101(3) exception is, under Regulation 1/2003, the qualification to the rule that the prosecutor bears the burden of establishing the existence of an antitrust violation.[110] Instead, the party seeking the benefit of the exception must demonstrate, by means of convincing arguments and evidence, that the conditions for obtaining an exemption are satisfied'.[111] This burden is not unqualified, however, as

> the facts relied on by that undertaking may be such as to oblige the other party to provide an explanation or justification [for refusing an exemption], failing which it is permissible to conclude that the burden of proof has been discharged.[112]

[100] See, eg, A Jones, 'Left Behind by Modernisation? Restrictions by Object Under Article 101(1)' (2010) 6 *European Competition Journal* 649.
[101] *Cartes Bancaires* (n 14) esp [65]–[71].
[102] Case C-228/18, *Budapest Bank* ECLI:EU:C:2020:265 [76].
[103] ibid [78].
[104] Case T-472/13, *Lundbeck v Commission* ECLI:EU:T:2016:449, upheld on appeal in Case C-591/16 P *Lundbeck v Commission* ECLI:EU:C:2021:243.
[105] Case T-93/18, *International Skating Union v Commission* ECLI:EU:T:2020:610; appeal pending at time of writing, in Case C-124/21 P, *International Skating Union v Commission*.
[106] See n 175.
[107] Confirmed in Case T-491/07 RENV, *CB v Commission* ECLI:EU:T:2016:379.
[108] Case AT.39612 – *Perindopril (Servier)*, Decision of 9 July 2014; confirmed with respect to most of the Article 101 aspects in Case T-691/14, *Servier and Others v Commission* ECLI:EU:T:2018:922.
[109] *Budapest Bank* (n 102) [33]–[44], confirms that an agreement can be held to violate Article 101 under the object and effects limbs simultaneously.
[110] Regulation 1/2003, Art 2.
[111] Case C-501/06 P, *GlaxoSmithKline v Commission* ECLI:EU:C:2009:610 [82].
[112] ibid [83].

Accordingly, while the Commission need not demonstrate an absence of countervailing benefits stemming from otherwise anticompetitive coordination, it cannot simply ignore plausible claims raised by defendants.

That being said, the exception rule plays a minor role in contemporary enforcement, at EU level at least.[113] The abolishment of the notification system has resulted in a dearth of recent decisional practice. Moreover, formal Commission guidance issued in 2004 adopted a notably restrictive approach to application of the exception rule, premised solely on notions of economic efficiency.[114] While this mitigates concerns that an overly 'permissive'[115] approach may take the exception into territory that is far from the purview of antitrust proper, it nonetheless creates conflict with existing case law,[116] and with proposals to open the exemption to a wider range of public interest objectives.[117] Though one can find reasons to be cautious about the latter prospect, the narrow – indeed sceptical[118] – approach of the Commission to Article 101(3) is hard to square with the exception rule's formal role as an integral element of the overall prohibition.

In cartel cases, the issues with respect to the Commission's burden of proof are rather different. The obviously anticompetitive nature of the classic cartel behaviours is well established,[119] and the Court of Justice has been receptive to placing more novel conduct within the object category where the requisite underhand or deceptive character is present.[120] It is also undisputed that, absent exceptional circumstances, the exception rule cannot apply to cartel behaviour, due at an absence of indispensability or of sufficient consumer benefit.[121] Instead, 'clandestine'[122] cartel cases revolve primarily around the Commission assembling a sufficiently compelling body of factual evidence to establish the existence of the cartel, its participants and its duration. This body of evidence must be convincing when viewed as a whole, though its individual elements need not be decisive in themselves: the jurisprudence acknowledges that the evidence assembled 'will normally be only fragmentary and sparse'.[123] The single continuous infringement

[113] See, eg, D Bailey, 'Reinvigorating the Role of Article 101(3) under Regulation 1/2003' (2016) 81 *Antitrust Law Journal* 111. The exception rule plays a greater role in Member State practice: see O Brook, 'Struggling with Article 101(3) TFEU: Diverging approaches of the Commission, EU Courts, and five Competition Authorities' (2019) 56 *Common Market Law Review* 121.

[114] Article 81(3) Guidelines (n 21) [48]–[72].

[115] Amato (n 2) 117.

[116] See, eg Case T-528/93, *Métropole v Commission* ECLI:EU:T:1996:99 [118].

[117] Including collective efforts to further sustainability and labour rights.

[118] For instance, the Vertical Guidelines (n 40) [96], imply that object restrictions are presumed to fall outside the scope of the Art 101(3) exception, an approach unsupported by the case-law (see Cases T-17/93, *Matra Hachette* ECLI:EU:T:1994:89 [85], and more recently, Opinion of Advocate General Bobek in Case C-228/18, *Budapest Bank* EU:C:2019:678 [34]–[35]).

[119] Confirming that the *Cartes Bancaires* decision has not impacted the prohibition of secret market-sharing and price-fixing, see Cases C-373/14, P *Toshiba Corporation* ECLI:EU:C:2016:26 and C-469/15, P *FSL Holdings NV* ECLI:EU:C:2017:308, respectively.

[120] See, eg, Case C-179/16, *Hoffmann-La Roche v AGCM* ECLI:EU:C:2018:25.

[121] See, eg, the Commission's discussion of this point in the Article 81(3) Guidelines (n 21) [46], and the Horizontal Cooperation Guidelines (n 40) [74], [190] and [248].

[122] Case T-53/03, *BPB v Commission* ECLI:EU:T:2008:254 [63].

[123] ibid.

rule, moreover, makes defendants responsible not only for their own behaviour but also conduct of fellow cartelists that occurs intentionally within the agreed parameters of the cartel.[124] The upshot is that, despite the acknowledged gravity of cartel offences and the severity of the penalties they can attract, the Commission is not subject to a beyond reasonable doubt standard.[125] The General Court has nonetheless proven itself willing to engage in fairly rigorous reassessment of factual findings made by the Commission in cartel cases and of the inferences derived from such evidence.

C. Commission Practice under Article 102

While enforcement practice under Article 102 has been less plentiful, the Commission's most high-profile (and contentious) activity now occurs in this area. This has generated a concomitant increase in the jurisprudence delimiting its obligations under the provision. The text of Article 102 is notoriously open-ended, and while the enumerated examples offer broad guidance on potentially problematic behaviour – exploitation, discrimination, exclusion – its application is not restricted to practices fitting neatly within these categories.[126] Despite influential calls for a more holistic assessment,[127] the Commission's defeat in *Servier* reiterates the necessity of establishing dominance as the threshold requirement.[128] Yet in relation to what behaviours may constitute *abuse* – a concept that hinges on the abstruse notion of methods of competition *other than competition on the merits*[129] – the Commission has greater scope to engage in regulatory policymaking.

Exclusionary conduct comprises the focus of enforcement. Here, the key point of contention is the existence and propriety of object-type approaches to the abuse criterion: namely, whether Article 102 does and should prohibit certain forms of dominant conduct, solely because it is assumed to be harmful given an absence of structural competition.[130] This concern is coupled with the opacity of the 'special responsibility,' which, although it does not outlaw dominance as such, imposes on dominant firms a wide-ranging obligation 'not to allow [their] conduct to impair genuine undistorted competition'.[131] The Commission's practice under Article 102 has long faced criticism as being unduly formalistic and expansive in nature – and

[124] Case C-99/17 P, *Infineon Technologies v Commission* ECLI:EU:C:2018:773 [172]–[73].
[125] *BPB* (n 122) [64].
[126] Case C-6/72, *Continental Can Company v Commission* ECLI:EU:C:1973:22 [26].
[127] Most notably, n 5, ch 3.
[128] Case T-691/14, *Servier v Commission* ECLI:EU:T:2018:922.
[129] See, eg, Case C-457/10 P, *AstraZeneca v Commission* ECLI:EU:C:2012:770 [75].
[130] Contrast, eg, W Wils, 'The Judgment of the EU General Court in Intel and the So-Called "More Economic Approach" to Abuse of Dominance' (2014) 37 *World Competition* 405 and L Peeperkorn, 'Coherence in the Application of Articles 101 and 102: A Realistic Prospect or an Elusive Goal?' (2016) 39 *World Competition* 389.
[131] See n 41.

thus protecting competitors potentially at the expense of the competitive process itself.[132] Yet there are trade-offs involved in whichever approach one favours: object-type abuses may, conversely, enhance the effectiveness of competition intervention, insofar as they are more straightforward both to establish at first instance and to defend on appeal.

In 2008, the Commission published its Enforcement Priorities informing its application of Article 102 to exclusionary abuses.[133] In it, the Commission ostensibly embraced an effects-based 'anticompetitive foreclosure' standard for intervention.[134] The rationale was a desire to improve the quality of decision-making, and in particular, to address concerns that the formalistic approaches seen in earlier jurisprudence could generate negative impacts in efficiency terms. The guidance was deliberately at odds with the case law in certain areas, though the Commission acknowledged that it is the Court, ultimately, which determines the parameters of the competition rules.[135] This generated a tension within the Commission's enforcement practice, however, insofar as the methodological innovations anticipated by the Enforcement Priorities potentially raised the evidentiary requirements that the Commission itself faced when applying Article 102 in practice.

These tensions boiled over in the *Intel* saga. The Commission's infringement decision, coming just months after the Enforcement Priorities, contained an in-depth assessment of the potential of the suspect conduct – loyalty rebates – to exclude as-efficient competitors (AEC).[136] Yet ultimately, the case was based on the venerable, formalistic *Hoffmann-La Roche* precedent which, it was assumed, prohibited loyalty rebates as such.[137] While this uncompromising approach was upheld by the General Court,[138] its trenchant defence of formalism did not survive further appeal. A Grand Chamber sitting of the Court of Justice 'clarified' that, where a defendant 'submits, during the administrative procedure, on the basis of supporting evidence, that its conduct was not capable of restricting competition and, in particular, of producing the alleged foreclosure effects',[139] the Commission must consider the circumstances and likely impact of the impugned practice to determine its 'capacity to foreclose', rather than relying upon an abstract presumption of harm.[140] The Court did not prescribe a particular methodology to assess

[132] Discussed, eg, in EM Fox, 'We Protect Competition, You Protect Competitors' (2003) 26 *World Competition* 149.

[133] European Commission, Guidance on the Commission's enforcement priorities in applying Article 82 of the EC Treaty to abusive exclusionary conduct by dominant undertakings (OJ C45/7, 24 February 2009) ('Enforcement Priorities').

[134] ibid [19].

[135] ibid [3].

[136] Case AT.37990 – *Intel*, Decision of 13 May 2009.

[137] Case C-85/76, *Hoffmann-La Roche v Commission* ECLI:EU:C:1979:36 [89]–[90].

[138] Case T-286/09, *Intel v Commission* EU:T:2014:547.

[139] Case C-413/14 P, *Intel v Commission* EU:C:2017:632 [138].

[140] *Intel* (ibid) [139]–[40].

capacity to foreclose;[141] but because the Commission had conducted a detailed AEC analysis, this ought to have been reviewed on appeal.[142] The case was thus reconsidered by the lower court,[143] which, reflecting the scepticism of the Grand Chamber judgment, identified numerous deficiencies in the AEC assessment, and annulled the finding of abusive rebates and the *entire* fine imposed as a result.

Yet, though *Intel* represents a high watermark for judicial scrutiny of decision-making under Article 102, we should be wary of overly confident predictions regarding its impact on the Commission's burden of proof going forward. The second General Court judgment can be contrasted, in particular, with the outcome in the *Google Shopping* appeal,[144] decided several months previously. Here, a differently constituted General Court upheld the Commission's infringement decision for abusive self-preferencing,[145] essentially a new type of leveraging abuse that requires dominant firms to provide equal treatment to competitors.[146] The General Court disputed aspects of the Commission's assessment, in particular its approach to the earlier *Bronner* case law.[147] Yet it upheld the thrust of the treatment of self-preferencing as a freestanding abuse, premised upon the deliberate favouring of a dominant undertaking's products compared with rival products, coupled with a potential for anticompetitive effects.[148]

In doing so, the General Court confirmed that, in exclusionary cases, the Commission must pay due attention to the anticipated effects of conduct: 'a practice cannot be categorised as abuse of a dominant position unless it is demonstrated that there is an anticompetitive effect, or at the very least a potential anticompetitive effect'.[149] This would, accordingly, appear to preclude the Commission from adopting a purely formalistic or object-type approach to the abuse criterion in future.[150] Yet the Court was relaxed in its understanding of what sorts of effects might satisfy this requirement. It emphasised that *potential* anticompetitive effects are sufficient: 'which, although it must be realistic, effectively describes a probable situation'.[151] Moreover, since actual anticompetitive effects are not required, it is similarly unnecessary to demonstrate tangible consumer harm stemming from the practice.[152] Instead, it could merely be assumed that 'the weakening of competition

[141] As confirmed by the General Court in RENV *Intel* (n 84) [126].
[142] *Intel* (n 139) [141]–[47].
[143] RENV, *Intel* (n 84).
[144] Case T-612/17, *Google and Alphabet v Commission (Google Shopping)* EU:T:2021:763.
[145] Case – AT.39740 *Google Search (Shopping)*, Decision of 27 June 2017.
[146] Though the term 'self-preferencing' is not used in the infringement decision or General Court judgment, it has become accepted terminology extrajudicially: see, eg, n 5, 65–68.
[147] *Shopping* (n 145) [244]–[246].
[148] ibid, esp [166]–[185].
[149] ibid [438] (emphasis added).
[150] Reaching similar conclusions, see JL da Cruz Vilaça, 'The intensity of judicial review in complex economic matters – recent competition law judgments of the Court of Justice of the EU' (2018) 6 *Journal of Antitrust Enforcement* [173].
[151] *Shopping* (n 145) [377].
[152] ibid [443].

is highly likely to have such consequences'.[153] And in notable contradistinction to the probing reassessment of the Commission's analysis in *Intel*, the Court in *Shopping* was happy to grant the Commission significant latitude with respect to market dynamics and the presumed impact of the conduct.

Deciphering the Commission's obligations in Article 102 cases, following the difficult-to-reconcile judgments in *Intel* and *Shopping*, is not straightforward. It is possible to rationalise the dissonance in several ways. First, *Intel* involved a well-established theory of harm, and a storied strand of the Court's own jurisprudence. Though the clarification ultimately departed from the previously understood parameters of the *Hoffmann-La Roche* rule,[154] in doing so the Grand Chamber continued an ongoing process of curating the law in this area.[155] *Shopping*, by contrast, involved a novel theory of harm, and the General Court was content merely to confirm that the Commission had approached the task of devising a new legal standard in a satisfactory manner. To the extent that the Commission considered existing precedents in *Shopping*, the General Court offered a more critical assessment, even if the points of disagreement did not invalidate the finding of infringement.[156] Thus the Commission appears to have correspondingly greater wiggle room to determine the requirements of Article 102 in areas not yet delineated by prior case law.

Second, the Commission considered the treatment of loyalty rebates in its *Enforcement Priorities*,[157] and the *Intel* decision contained a detailed effects assessment along the lines of what it had previously advised. The novel abuse in *Shopping*, by contrast, was not covered in the guidance, and the General Court rejected efforts to shoehorn the treatment of self-preferencing into the assessment framework for other types of anticompetitive conduct.[158] The Court does not consider itself to be bound by the Enforcement Priorities,[159] and has supported the Commission in departing from the guidance previously.[160] The juxtaposition of the *Intel* and *Shopping* cases nonetheless suggests that the guidance remain relevant for the future assessment of the enumerated theories of harm – or, insofar as the Commission no longer wishes to be constrained by its prescriptions, ought to be modified or withdrawn.

Third, the contrasting fates of these defendants can be seen from a more politically focused perspective. The Grand Chamber judgment in *Intel*, while nominally

[153] ibid.

[154] As discussed by Advocate General Wahl in his Opinion in Case C-413/14 P, *Intel v Commission* ECLI:EU:C:2016:788 [60]–[71].

[155] ibid [74]–[105].

[156] See n 147 above.

[157] n 133 [37]–[45].

[158] *Shopping* (n 145) [538]–[539].

[159] For instance, adopting a different approach to the treatment of margin squeeze: see Case C-52/09, *TeliaSonera Sverige* ECLI:EU:C:2011:83.

[160] Most notably, in treating constructive and outright refusals to supply as distinct abuses (C-165/19, P *Slovak Telekom* ECLI:EU:C:2021:239) despite their combined treatment in n 133 [79].

preserving the *Hoffmann-La Roche* rule, can be seen as a deliberate, near-seismic shift within Article 102 jurisprudence, towards a more economic approach.[161] It was thus unsurprising that the General Court subsequently followed the overtly sceptical and demanding steer of the higher court. The *Shopping* decision, by contrast, is the opening gambit in a spate of high-profile, explicitly aggressive enforcement activity in the digital economy by the Commission. The General Court judgment can thus be seen as an exercise in regulatory restraint, whereby the first instance court declined to interrupt the progressive development of the competition rules, even if it did not necessarily agree with every aspect of the more granular assessment. The General Court notably endorsed the notion of 'fair competition'[162] – and not merely 'undistorted competition'[163] – as the undergirding principle, a linguistic shift that has been a key pillar of Commission efforts to articulate a more expansive ambitious vision for competition enforcement.[164] This does not mean, however, that the higher court will necessarily agree in either instance: both the *Intel* and *Shopping* judgments have been appealed, by the Commission and the defendant respectively.[165]

Finally, it is firmly established that, although the text of Article 102 does not provide an exception rule, defendants can offer objective justifications to take their conduct outside the scope of the prohibition.[166] This defence can take the form of claims about the objective necessity of the impugned conduct, whether arising from legitimate commercial considerations or technical requirements of the product.[167] Or it can involve efficiency gains, which benefit consumers and serve to outweigh the harm caused by the exclusionary effects of the abusive conduct.[168] Like the Article 101(3) exception rule, the burden of raising and establishing a claim of objective justification lies with defendants;[169] though, as with Article 101(3), the Commission must engage with claims that are supported with 'arguments and evidence' and, where necessary, explain its decision to reject a proffered defence.[170] Perhaps unavoidably, because successful claims are unlikely to culminate in infringement decisions that are then appealed, there is a dearth of court jurisprudence demarcating the parameters of the objective justification limb. This creates at least a perception that defendants face insurmountably high hurdles if seeking to defend their conduct on commercial, technical or efficiency-based

[161] See, eg, N Petit, 'The Judgment of the EU Court of Justice in Intel and the Rule of Reason in Abuse of Dominance Cases' (2018) 43 *European Law Review* 728.

[162] *Shopping* (n 145) [433]–[434].

[163] ibid [432], citing Protocol 27 to the Lisbon Treaty.

[164] See n 11.

[165] Pending Cases C-240/22 P, *Commission v Intel Corporation* and C-48/22 P, *Google and Alphabet v Commission (Google Shopping)*.

[166] Case C-209/10, *Post Danmark (I)* ECLI:EU:C:2012:172 [40]–[42].

[167] Shopping (n 145) [551]–[552].

[168] ibid [551] and [553].

[169] ibid [554].

[170] ibid.

grounds – a perception, it must be said, that is unlikely to have been altered by the treatment of these issues in *Shopping*.

D. New Theories of Harm in Commission Enforcement Practice

Freedom to compete has been described as the ability 'to assert with vigour, imagination, devotion, and ingenuity whatever economic muscle [an undertaking] can muster'.[171] Imagination and ingenuity can be double-edged swords, however, where undertakings ultimately devise new methods by which to restrict competition in their own private interests. Given this prospect, and the unpredictable nature of market competition, antitrust law requires sufficient flexibility to meet future competition challenges. Put simply, because it is impossible to foresee *ex ante* the range of ways in which firms may seek to harm competition through coordination or the abuse of market power, it is vital that the Commission is not inhibited from developing new theories of harm to encapsulate these emerging anticompetitive behaviours.

Helpfully in this regard, Articles 101 and 102 are open-textured provisions, described by Amato as akin to 'magic boxes, capable of expanding their contents'.[172] The enumerated examples are starting points for assessment, but these neither dictate nor confine the parameters of liability. Our discussion of *Shopping* demonstrated that novelty is no barrier to substantive liability under Article 102, provided that the Commission can advance a plausible argument about how the behaviour is incompatible with the general thrust of the prohibition. The same position arises under Article 101. While the case law indicates that the object category should be interpreted restrictively,[173] it does not preclude the recognition of newer types of object restraints.[174] The residual effects category also remains available where it can be demonstrated 'that competition has in fact been prevented, restricted or distorted to an appreciable extent' by the suspect coordination.[175]

It was noted above, however, that the suite of fair trial rights that condition competition enforcement includes the principle of legality. A question arises about the extent to which the recognition of new theories of competition harm raises the prospect of retrospective criminalisation, to the extent that undertakings are punished for behaviour that was, to all intents and purposes, 'legal' when it occurred. Of course, a simple answer is that the mere fact that conduct has not yet been condemned by a competition authority does not guarantee its continued

[171] *US v Topco*, 405 US 596 (1972), 610.
[172] Amato (n 2) 43.
[173] *Cartes Bancaires* (n 14) [58].
[174] See, eg, Case C-32/11, *Allianz Hungária Biztosító* ECLI:EU:C:2013:160.
[175] *Cartes Bancaires* (n 14) [52].

immunity.[176] The residual nature of the antitrust provisions means that, in theory, almost all forms of coordination between undertakings, and of exclusionary conduct by dominant firms, must be considered fair game for future condemnation. Yet there is a difference between adding new categories of conduct to a list of prohibited (or at least problematic) behaviours going forward, and punishing a firm *ex post* for behaviour that it could quite legitimately have been considered innocent *ex ante*. Even if the progressive development of the competition rules can and should be supported, punitive penalties in novel cases may not sit so comfortably. Thus German law, for instance, forbids the use of fines in novel cases, which explains why Facebook was subject to prospective behavioural requirements but no financial penalties following the well-known Bundeskartellamt investigation.[177]

The position in EU law is more equivocal. Fines can be imposed where the Commission concludes that anticompetitive conduct is performed 'intentionally or negligently',[178] with most decisional practice hinging on the former.[179] The mere fact that a type of behaviour has not previously been held to violate the competition rules does not preclude a finding of intentional breach. Instead, the criterion is whether 'the undertaking concerned could not have been unaware of the *anticompetitive nature* of its conduct',[180] a standard that obliges defendants to do more than simply ask whether the same conduct has been proscribed previously.[181] This uncompromising approach is tempered by the Commission's practice of refraining from fining, or of imposing notably lower penalties, in cases involving novel theories of harm.[182] Yet discounts for novelty are discretionary, lying outside the formal rules on fines under Regulation 1/2003.[183] Moreover, the General Court in *Shopping* rejected the claim that the principle of equal treatment has any implications for fines in novel cases, on the basis that that principle applies only in 'comparable' situations.[184] Yet novel cases, by definition, involve new theories of harm that have not arisen in decisional practice previously, so that this formalistic approach had the effect of emptying the principle of equal treatment of any meaning in this context. (An incongruous outcome, given its importance to the substantive holding in *Shopping*.) One may have limited sympathy for the defendant in *Shopping*,

[176] While Regulation 1/2003 Art 10 empowers the Commission to make findings of 'inapplicability', to the effect that particular behaviour does *not* violate Arts 101 or 102, it has only very rarely exercised its power to do so. National competition authorities cannot take non-infringement decisions: Case C-375/09, *Tele2 Polska* ECLI:EU:C:2011:270.

[177] Bundeskartellamt Decision of 6 February 2019, B6-22/16 – *Facebook*.

[178] Regulation 1/2003, Art 23(2).

[179] The fact that anticompetitive behaviour was committed negligently constitutes a mitigating circumstance: n 7 [29].

[180] *Shopping* (n 145) [608].

[181] In *Shopping*, for instance, the General Court upheld the finding of intentional breach, on the basis that Google's (super)-dominance should have been apparent, the case-law recognised numerous categories of abusive leveraging even if self-preferencing is novel, and 'Google must have known that its conduct undermined equality of opportunity': *Shopping* (n 145) [614]–[616].

[182] ibid [624].

[183] ibid [628].

[184] ibid [623]. Comparability means past cases involving equivalent 'sectors and issues': [624].

and the case certainly aligns with the present antitrust zeitgeist of hostility to Big Tech. Yet coupled with the absence of any fault requirement within the substantive liability rules, the normalisation of very high fines in novel cases is one of the more troubling aspects of contemporary EU competition practice.

E. The Presumption of Innocence and Negotiated Settlements

Fair trial concerns apply with fullest force to cases within the law enforcement paradigm: that is, where the facts or their legal characterisation are disputed; where the Commission proceeds to a formal determination on the merits that is likely to be challenged before the Union courts; and where punitive penalties are imposed. Yet, as noted, enforcement practice has moved steadily towards a more consensual paradigm, whereby investigations are concluded by negotiated settlements. Whether decided under Article 7 or Article 9, settlement is voluntary for defendants, so that fair trial concerns have lower prominence. Put simply, we tend to have fewer worries about the legitimacy of proceedings where these are willingly – though probably not eagerly – accepted by defendants. Moreover, the choice to settle itself represents compromise in many senses; meaning that we cannot be too squeamish about formal procedural niceties to the extent that this makes it impossible for parties to achieve the mutually sought benefits of settlement.[185] Yet settled cases at least contemplate an involuntary finding of infringement at their outset, and thus remain connected to the Commission's legitimate exercise of its coercive enforcement powers. In this final subsection we consider several settlement-specific concerns that may arise.

As explained, Regulation 1/2003 makes express provision for settlement in the guise of Article 9. The commitment procedure is premised on the prima facie existence of an infringement of Article 101 or 102: commitments can be accepted only 'in the course of proceedings which might lead to an agreement or practice being prohibited',[186] and 'Where the Commission [otherwise] intends to adopt a decision requiring that an infringement be brought to an end'.[187] Yet Regulation 1/2003 expressly rules out the possibility of including a formal finding of infringement within the final binding decision.[188] The absence of a definitive statement regarding breach, and the consensual nature of Article 9 settlements, also make it less likely that such cases will come before the Union courts subsequently.

Accordingly, Article 9 cases pose a conundrum in fair trial and legitimacy terms. By definition, the commitment procedure cannot result in a finding of guilt

[185] On the benefits of settlement, see Director-General for Competition Alexander Italianer, 'To commit or not to commit, that is the question' (speech at CRA Competition Conference, Brussels, 11 December 2013).

[186] Regulation 1/2003 Recital 13.

[187] ibid Art 9(1).

[188] 'Commitment decisions should find that there are no longer grounds for action by the Commission *without* concluding whether or not there has been or still is an infringement': ibid Recital 13.

as such, though the Commission has comparatively broad discretion should it ultimately choose to ditch Article 9 and proceed to an infringement decision.[189] But the procedure is only available, in principle, where a prima facie breach is identified. Indeed, as the Grand Chamber recognised in *Alrosa*, it is knowledge of the potential consequences that can follow should the Commission proceed under Article 7 that typically motivates a defendant to offer commitments to deflect a formal finding of infringement.[190] Article 9 settlements thus occur in the shadow of the Commission's coercive competition law powers; yet it is difficult to characterise a voluntarily accepted bargain as an instance of *coercion* as such.

The law and practice regarding Article 9 decisions reflects this uneasy compromise. Commitment decisions are the product of formal Commission investigations,[191] during which the full range of the Commission's evidence-gathering powers is available.[192] Consensual Article 9 settlements can also follow the adoption of mandatory interim measures.[193] Yet because commitment decisions are not (necessarily) preceded by a statement of objections,[194] the protections concerning the right to be heard and access to file that are provided by the Implementing Regulation are not formally applicable.[195] While it can be argued that the fair trial rights as general principles of EU law impose broadly equivalent obligations, the extent to which commitment decisions can be equated to quasi-criminal proceedings is more questionable. In any event, once defendants choose the Article 9 route, they have thus far invariably waived their right to challenge the concluded decision subsequently. This means that not only is the Court unable to supervise compliance with fair trial rights during the administrative procedure; it is also prevented from scrutinising the soundness of the underlying theory of antitrust harm reflected in the final decision. This generates a potential 'paucity of precedent',[196] but also the more troubling risks, from a legitimacy perspective, that Article 9 decisions might disguise investigations that are supported by weak evidence, that involve shaky theories of harm, or that are settled for political rather than principled reasons. And even if, exceptionally, an Article 9 decision comes before the Court, the Commission benefits from a deferential standard of review

[189] *Shopping* (n 145) [633]–[638].

[190] *Alrosa* (n 37) [48].

[191] Which require the formal initiation of proceedings by the Commission under Regulation 1/2003, Art 11(6).

[192] In particular, its powers to request information, take statements and conduct dawn raids, provided by Regulation 1/2003, Arts 18–21.

[193] Adopted under Regulation 1/2003 Art 8. For an example of interim measures preceding an Art 9 decision, see Case AT.40608 – *Broadcom*, Decision of 16 October 2019.

[194] Regulation 1/2003, Art 9(1) requires only a concise 'preliminary assessment' setting out the Commission's competition 'concerns'. Where a fuller statement of objections has been issued in a case subsequently concluded under Art 9, unsurprisingly it can serve as a substitute assessment.

[195] See Commission Regulation (EC) No 773/2004 of 7 April 2004 relating to the conduct of proceedings by the Commission pursuant to Articles 81 and 82 of the EC Treaty (OJ L 123/18, 27 April 2004), Arts 10–15.

[196] M Wathelet, 'Commitment Decisions and the Paucity of Precedent' (2015) 6 *Journal of European Competition Law & Practice* 553, 554.

which permits intervention only if the commitments do not meet the competition concerns identified by the Commission, if the defendant has offered less onerous commitments that also address those concerns adequately,[197] and/or if the agreed commitments empty the pre-existing rights of third parties of all content.[198]

The counterargument, of course, is that defendants in Commission investigations are typically large and powerful companies; if they choose to settle on palatable terms, then it is not the proper role of the fundamental rights protections to second-guess that self-interested choice. And if they decide against settlement, then the full protections of the infringement procedure come into play.

Yet considerable settlement also takes place today under Article 7. Most analogous to the commitment procedure is the Commission's informal practice of settling certain non-cartel cases, where the defendant is prepared to admit its participation in the infringement and to assist in the investigation, in return for often quite significant discounts on fines. The practice has no basis in formal Commission legislation, though it borrows quite obviously from the cartel settlement and leniency programmes.[199] As infringement decisions, the fair trial protections more clearly apply to the procedure leading to these settlements; but again, the point is somewhat moot, as no such decisions have been appealed by defendants thus far. As Article 7 decisions, and thus formal statements of the requirements of the competition rules, this more recent practice nominally addresses the problem of the paucity of precedent. Yet, at times, the cure may be worse than the disease, as a number of cases have relied unquestioningly upon older, overtly formalistic case law that is difficult to square with the turn towards a more economic approach.[200]

The final category of settlements are infringement decisions concluded under the cartel settlement procedure.[201] This provides a 10 per cent discount on fines for defendants that admit their participation in secret cartels. The procedure reflects the fact that the prohibition on cartels is clear and unequivocal, making a successful defence unlikely where the Commission's evidence paints a convincing picture of participation. It raises distinct presumption of innocence concerns, nonetheless, in so-called hybrid situations. These arise where one or more defendants decline to join their fellow cartelists in settling, and instead proceed to an ordinary Article 7 decision under the standard procedure. In doing so, non-settling defendants gain access to the full panoply of rights of defence, including the rights of access to file, to receive and reply to a statement of objections, and to have an oral hearing.[202]

[197] *Alrosa* (n 37) [41].
[198] Case C-132/19 P, *Groupe Canal+ v Commission* EU:C:2020:1007.
[199] See n 31.
[200] For example, the 'object' condemnation of resale price maintenance, following the approach in Case C-243/83, *Binon* ECLI:EU:C:1985:284, in Cases AT.40181 – *Philips*, AT.40182 – *Pioneer*, AT.40465 – *ASUS*, AT.40469 – *Denon & Marantz*, Decisions of 24 July 2018, and Case AT.40428 – *Guess*, Decision of 17 December 2018.
[201] See n 29.
[202] Case C-411/15, P *Timab Industries and CFPR v Commission* EU:C:2017:11 [121].

In this manner, hybrid settlements, in principle, are not incompatible with fair trial protections.

The particular difficulty is that the parallel settlement decision, often concluded prior to the ordinary infringement decision,[203] may foreshadow the participation and thus the guilt of non-settling defendants. In *Icap*, which involved a standard infringement decision concluded several years after a cartel settlement, the General Court held that the Commission infringed the presumption of innocence by making repeated references to the non-settling defendant as a cartel facilitator.[204] In *Pometon*, however, the Court of Justice clarified that 'the question whether the Commission disregarded the presumption of innocence depends on the settlement decisions specific to each case, including their reasoning, and the particular circumstances in which those decisions have been adopted'.[205] The Court acknowledged that 'it may be objectively necessary … to address, in the [settlement] decision … certain facts and behaviour concerning participants in the alleged cartel which are the subject of the standard procedure'.[206] The crucial question, however, is whether these references amount to a 'premature expression of [the] guilt' of the non-settling defendant(s).[207] Careful drafting of the *Pometon* settlement convinced the Court (though not its Advocate General[208]) that the characterisation of the facts, and the non-settling defendant's role within them, was sufficiently circumscribed to avoid any potential prejudgment in the circumstances.

Settlement by its nature implies compromise, but hybrid settlements may trouble us particularly, because it is the choice of one party to settle that negatively impacts the prospects of another getting a fair trial. The difficulty, however, is that if we instead prioritise the protection of uncooperative defendants, this serves to deny both willing defendants *and* the public interest more generally the benefits of at least partial settlement. The Court of Justice has attempted to split the difference, in a sense, by making the propriety of any particular hybrid settlement depend upon a context-specific assessment of the facts of the case and the wording of the settlement decision. This, however, merely kicks the can down the road: hybrid settlements are permissible in principle, but in practice it is difficult to predict with certainty just what information pertaining to non-settling defendants can be deemed objectively necessary to establish the guilt of others.

[203] Settled cartel investigations are typically concluded more speedily: see K Hüschelrath and U Laitenberger, 'The Settlement Procedure in EC Cartel Cases: An Empirical Assessment' (2015) *ZEW – Centre for European Economic Research Discussion Paper* No 15-064.

[204] Case T-180/15, *Icap v Commission* ECLI:EU:T:2017:795 [256]–[268].

[205] Case C-440/19, P *Pometon v Commission* ECLI:EU:C:2021:214 [86].

[206] ibid [65].

[207] ibid [66].

[208] Opinion in ibid [70]–[81].

V. Concluding Remarks

Let us draw these disparate elements together. It is indisputable that, in the hands of the Commission, Articles 101 and 102 provide powerful tools by which to regulate markets generally, and to discipline and punish transgressing economic actors more specifically. These effects, both collective and individual, drive the characterisation of EU-level competition enforcement as the exercise of coercive supranational public power. The 'magic box' quality of the competition rules, coupled with the Commission's combined prosecutorial and adjudicatory functions, raise the spectre of amorphous and expanding liability. Yet the case law on Articles 101 and 102 imposes clear and fairly demanding substantive requirements on the Commission, whose burden of proof is policed by the increasingly exacting Union courts. The presumption of innocence, evidently applicable in competition proceedings, makes it incumbent upon the Commission to provide sufficient, and sufficiently compelling, evidence to establish that the necessary elements of each offence are made out on the facts. Moreover, while the Commission has no obligation to establish the absence of a legitimate justification for suspect conduct, it must engage with and where necessary explain its reasons for discarding any plausible defences raised by defendants.

Questions of legitimacy nonetheless continue to creep into the Commission's enforcement activities, despite the enhanced emphasis on procedural fairness and the more demanding economic approach of recent decades. The Commission itself has not been consistent in its integration of effects-based approaches; a problem that has been enabled and probably exacerbated by the Court's propensity for brief, sparsely argued judgments on review, sometimes with an almost Delphic quality. The continued absence of an independent adjudicator at first instance places defendants on the back foot, typically 'having their day in court' only after they have already been held to have infringed the competition rules by a decision that is presumed to be valid and enforceable, unless and until the defendant persuades the General Court otherwise. Moreover, swathes of current enforcement practice are, to all intents and purposes, immune from even this degree of judicial supervision, being encompassed in settlements that rarely reach the docket of the Union courts.

Undeniably, this account of Commission practice could be criticised as unduly legalistic in nature – or, perhaps more damningly in a post-Brexit landscape, as framed from the perspective and thus reflecting the prejudices of a common lawyer. Greater fondness for, or at least unavoidable reliance upon, adversarial legalism is famously one of the hallmarks of the American system.[209] This may go some way towards explaining many of the transatlantic differences that continue

[209] R Kagan, *Adversarial Legalism. The American Way of Law* (Harvard University Press, 2003).

to persist in the antitrust arena. In cases like *Trinko*,[210] *Leegin*[211] and *linkLine*,[212] the US Supreme Court explicitly invoked institutional concerns, stemming from the overwhelming predominance of private enforcement in the US, to justify a minimalist reading of the scope of the substantive rules. The recent appointment of top US antitrust enforcers steeped in the progressive New Brandeisian tradition raises the question of whether these jurisprudential constraints should bind public enforcement agencies, an issue that will ultimately be determined by an increasingly conservative Supreme Court.

It is important, however, to resist characterising fundamental questions about the legitimacy of competition enforcement by reference to an overly simple left/right political division. Competition law, it has been acknowledged, provides an indispensable weapon in the struggle to control private market power in the broader public interest. Yet Amato's dilemma remains as compelling and challenging today as it was 25 years ago, or indeed back in 1957 when the Treaty of Rome was first enacted. The concept and implications of the rule of law similarly reflect pivotal public interest concerns, which cannot be sacrificed at the altar of some nominal quest for greater effectiveness in competition enforcement. Fair trial protections, and the presumption of innocence in particular, do not exist solely to frustrate and delay the work of virtuous public enforcers. Instead, they reflect more systemic efforts to uphold the integrity of the EU legal system, ensuring to the greatest extent possible that decision-making is *proper* in all senses. An appropriate balance must be struck: a measured right to fair treatment must not segue inadvertently into an absolute right to immunity. Yet to ignore or minimise the coercive aspects of competition enforcement simply because the defendant can afford to pay the (often eye-watering) fine incurred risks bringing the competition law enterprise into disrepute.

We thus return to the central issue of whether EU-level competition enforcement today manages to stay on the right side of the line 'beyond which legitimate public power becomes illegitimate', while still imposing effective controls on 'the unlegitimated power of individuals'.[213] Among its considerable virtues, *Antitrust and the Bounds of Power* provided the reader what is undoubtedly the clearest and most compelling articulation of this regulatory balancing act in academic writing to date: explaining not merely why it matters both in principle and in practice, but also how it has informed, in crucial ways, the development of what remain the two most influential systems of competition law globally. Amato's vision of antitrust and its role in law and society is, all things considered, optimistic. But it is also realistic, highlighting the complexity of the underlying considerations, and also the extent to which perceptions of 'legitimacy' may themselves betray an ideological bent. This chapter framed the question of the adequacy of the Commission's

[210] *Verizon v Trinko*, 540 US 398 (2004).
[211] *Leegin Creative Leather Products, Inc v PSKS, Inc*, 551 US 877 (2007).
[212] *Pacific Bell Telephone Co v linkLine Communications, Inc*, 555 US 438 (2009).
[213] See n 2.

current enforcement practice essentially in rule of law terms: asking whether the processes and safeguards that are in place to ensure that the Commission discharges its burden of proof are effective and sufficient. Yet this choice in itself arguably reveals a legalistic approach to competition law and its place within the social market economy; a perspective that perhaps sits uneasily with the concerns of contemporary advocates of more aggressive – usually meaning less legally constrained – intervention.

Nonetheless, the discussion in the chapter confirms that EU-level competition enforcement is indeed a law-heavy business today. The Commission may still investigate, try and decide its own cases at first instance; but its nominal freedom to do so is sharply curtailed by a complex tapestry of both substantive legal precedents, which delineate the requirements of the competition rules, and fair trial rights, which dictate the manner in which the Commission can exercise its enforcement powers. Reasonable observers may disagree over the extent to which the Commission (or perhaps its individual enforcement officials) feel, or at least act in a way which indicates that they feel, constrained by these formal legal requirements. Yet recent years have seen robust counter-action by the Union courts in circumstances where the Commission has paid inadequate attention to rule of law concerns. Accordingly, although the EU has by no means embraced unadulterated US-style adversarial legalism in the antitrust arena, its enforcement practices today are a good deal less 'impressionistic',[214] and thus from a rule of law perspective rather more legitimate, than they were a quarter-century ago.

Of course, as acknowledged, this understanding of competition law as an essentially legal, and thus legally constrained, market regulatory tool comes into conflict with the efforts of those who would afford it a more ambitious, inventive role in tackling urgent economic and social problems today. There is some irony that, 25 years ago, Amato felt obliged to emphasise the extent to which economic analysis makes competition law better and stronger – while nonetheless cautioning against its disguised, more ideological use as a means to preserve illegitimate and abusive private power.[215] Today, conversely, a vocal subset of the antitrust community advocates for essentially abandoning the effects-based approach, in a manner which suggests an almost pathological hostility to economics as a perceived obstacle to the untrammelled regulatory power of the competition rules. It is hard to argue that those who seek to deploy competition law to reduce inequality, to protect vulnerable workers or to address the climate crisis, for instance, are not well-intentioned. Yet there is a naïveté arguably bordering on egoism in the assumption that the suite of legal obligations and protections, honed by the Union courts in competition cases over many decades, should be discarded wholesale because they make it more difficult to reach a policy outcome preferred by that advocate in a particular instance.

[214] Amato (n 2) 122.
[215] ibid 125–26.

Instead, this chapter has sought to explore and evaluate the constraints faced by the Commission when exercising its enforcement powers from a more positive perspective: that is, as effective elements of an institutional structure that serves to ensure the 'legitimate' deployment of the competition rules only against behaviour that falls within the scope of the discrete prohibitions. Ultimately, the dilemma identified so cogently and influentially by Amato remains a source of tension in contemporary EU practice, and may be unsolvable in an objective sense within any antitrust jurisdiction. We might nonetheless conclude, somewhat optimistically, that in current EU practice such concerns are at least minimised, within a system that is undeniably complicated and slow-moving, but where substantive law, economics and wider rule of law concerns all have an integral part to play.

7

Procompetitive Effects in EU Competition Law[1]

STAVROS MAKRIS

I. Introduction

It would not be controversial to say that the purpose of crafting legal tests[2] in competition law is to distinguish anticompetitive effects from procompetitive or neutral effects.[3] Which practices, conduct or benefits count and should count as procompetitive under EU competition law? Is there a consistent meaning of 'procompetitive effects' across all key competition law provisions? What is their role in the legal analysis of restrictive agreements, abuses of dominance and anti-competitive mergers? How could the parties prove the actual or potential existence of procompetitive effects, and under what circumstances are they obliged to do so? Even though the so-called procompetitive gains or effects are ubiquitous in EU competition law, a systematic treatment of the concept and its legal role is missing.

This chapter teases out the key features and legal functions of procompetitive effects by examining their role under all three key competition law regimes: Articles 101 and 102 TFEU and Regulation 139/2004 (EUMR).[4] It argues that,

[1] Pursuant to the ASCOLA Transparency and Disclosure Declaration the author declares not to have any conflicts of interests to disclose. I am grateful to Oles Andriychuk, Or Brook, Elias Deutscher, Niamh Dunne, Magali Eben, Pablo Ibañez Colomo, Andriani Kalintiri, Giorgio Monti and Ryan Stones for their thoughtful suggestions. The usual disclaimer applies.

[2] The problem of legal tests relates to the rules v standards problem. See HLA Hart, *The Concept of Law*, 2nd edn (Clarendon Press, 1994) 124–54, L Kaplow, 'Rules v Standards: An Economic Analysis' (1992) 42 *Duke Law Journal* 557; A Christiansen and W Kerber, 'Competition Policy with Optimally Differentiated Rules Instead of "Per se Rules vs. Rule of Reason"' *Marburg Papers on Economics* No 06-2006; D Crane, 'Rules Versus Standards in Antitrust Adjudication' (2007) 64 *Washington & Lee Law Review* 49.

[3] In this study I use the term 'procompetitive effects' to refer to both beneficial and neutral effects on competition. If a practice or an agreement is only capable of or has only a neutral effect on competition then declaring it unlawful is not warranted in light of a general harm principle or a presumption of liberty (*in dubio pro libertate*). JS Mill, *On Liberty* [1859] (Dover Publications, 2002) ('The only purpose for which power can be rightfully exercised over any member of a civilized community, against his will, is to prevent harm to others'); P Schneider, 'In dubio pro libertate' in E von Caemmerer, E Friesenhahn and R Lange, *Hundert Jahre deutsches Rechtsleben* (Karlsruhe, 1960) 263.

[4] Council Regulation (EC) 139/2004 of 20 January 2004 on the control of concentrations between undertakings (EC Merger Regulation) OJ L 24 (29 January 2004) 1–22.

in accordance with the case law and the European Commission's practice, such effects, in principle, derive from practices that intensify (or at least do not harm) competition to the benefit of consumers. An analysis of the case law reveals that four key criteria are used to identify such effects (identification criteria). A practice or an agreement would be considered procompetitive if it: (i) addresses a market failure without employing anticompetitive means; (ii) intensifies a dimension or parameter of competition while softening another; (iii) makes possible a welfare-enhancing arrangement or increases the value of a product or a service without eliminating or overly restricting rivalry; or (iv) increases net consumer welfare without fully eliminating competition. Cases where procompetitive effects have been identified might fall into more than one of these categories. Yet, arguably, these criteria maintain their analytical autonomy and suggest that the concepts of market failure; productive, allocative and dynamic efficiency; consumer welfare; and rivalry serve as the key sources of procompetitive effects.

Furthermore, the present study identifies the legal role that procompetitive effects play in the competitive assessment of each relevant provision claiming that they feature either as a *counterindicators* of the existence of a restriction of competition or as *justifications* for it. In the context of Article 101(1) TFEU, if a practice or agreement is a plausible source of procompetitive effects, the characterisation of 'restriction by object' is not warranted, while the existence of actual or potential procompetitive effects suggests that a restriction by effect is absent.[5] When an effects analysis is conducted under Article 101(1) TFEU, the ancillarity doctrine is used to identify likely procompetitive effects and functions as an analytical shortcut[6] to avoid balancing and overenforcement.[7] A balancing exercise enters the scene under Article 101(3) TFEU once a restriction of competition is established. At this stage the crucial question is whether a restriction of competition can be justified on the basis of offsetting procompetitive effects (eg efficiency gains that are passed on to consumers and achieved

[5] This author takes the view that the notions of by object and by effect restriction do not refer to types of practices (the so-called 'black box' approach) but to modes of analysis organised around decision theory concerns and the key question: how much we need to know to condemn a practice as anti-competitive. See PE Areeda and H Hovenkamp, *Antitrust Law: An Analysis of Antitrust Principles and their Application*, 4th edn (Wolters Kluwer Law & Business, 2017) 1500, 1507 ('the modes of antitrust analysis represent a continuum, or "sliding scale," with different fact finding requirements for different situations'); R Whish and D Bailey, *Competition Law*, 10th edn (OUP, 2021) 125–31 and esp 130 (even though these authors seem to favour a black box approach, they recognise that 'irrespective of how large or small the object box might be, there remains a riddle: how much analysis should be undertaken when determining whether a particular agreement belongs to one box or the other?').

[6] A Kalintiri, 'Analytical Shortcuts in EU Competition Enforcement: Proxies, Premises and Presumptions' (2020) 16 *Journal of Competition Law & Economics* 392.

[7] European Commission, Guidelines on the application of Article [101(3) TFEU] OJ [2004] C 101/97, para 11: 'The balancing of anti-competitive and pro-competitive effects is conducted exclusively within the framework laid down by Article [101(3)]'. F Easterbrook, 'Limits of Antitrust' (1984) 63 *Texas Law Review* 1, 14–17, esp 13 (noting that 'in restricted distribution cases the "reduction in intrabrand competition" is the source of the competitive benefit that helps one product compete against another … The reduction in dealers' rivalry in the price dimension is just the tool the manufacturer uses to induce greater competition in the service dimension. There is no "loss" in one column to "balance" against a gain in the other').

without overly restricting competition). The Vertical Block Exemption Regulation (VBER) is another legal tool that reflects the role of procompetitive effects as counterindicators.[8] Relying on existing economic knowledge and experience, VBER uses various proxies, benchmarks and filters to single out a wide array of vertical restrains from a case-by-case analysis. According to VBER, under certain conditions most types of vertical restrains are considered presumptively lawful in light of the fact that they are more likely to generate procompetitive than anticompetitive effects. Hence, VBER incorporates and crystallises existing knowledge and experience with regards to the role of procompetitive effects as counterindicators in the treatment of vertical restraints. In doing so, it allows enforcers to avoid a case-by-case analysis and balancing procompetitive and anticompetitive effects in the assessment of most vertical restraints.

In the area of Article 102 TFEU, there are two pathways through which the dominant undertaking can use procompetitive effects to challenge a finding of abuse: one consists of disproving the negative effects (ie procompetitive effects as counterindicators) and another of showing offsetting positive effects once an abuse is established (ie procompetitive effects as justifications). Especially after *Intel* and *ENEL*, it has become clear that the dominant undertaking can escape a finding of abuse by showing that the practice at issue is incapable of restricting competition by producing foreclosure effects.[9] Arguably, showing foreclosure effects has become fairly demanding for the plaintiff as they have to use more economic evidence and engage in a deeper analysis.[10] As a result, the defendant has a greater leeway to argue the absence of anticompetitive effects or the existence of procompetitive aspects at the initial stage of the analysis, and to avoid a finding of harm by using procompetitive effects as counterindicators. If an abuse is established the dominant undertaking can still escape a finding of abuse by showing that the exclusionary effect is counterbalanced or outweighed by positive effects for the consumers that do not eliminate competition in a substantial part of the market.[11] In such a case, procompetitive effects would be used as justification of a prima facie abuse. Similarly in merger control, procompetitive effects could be used to show that the proposed transaction is unlikely to have non-coordinated or coordinated effects or that such effects are outweighed or counteracted by merger-specific and verifiable efficiencies that benefit consumers.[12]

[8] Commission Regulation (EU) No 330/2010 of 20 April 2010 on the application of Article 101(3) of the Treaty on the Functioning of the European Union to categories of vertical agreements and concerted practices [2010] (VBER) OJ L 102 (23 April 2010) 1–7.

[9] Case C-413/14 P, *Intel Corp v European Commission (Intel)* ECLI:EU:C:2017:632, [138]; C-377/20, *Servizio Elettrico Nazionale and Others (ENEL)* ECLI:EU:C:2022:379 [51]–[52], [77] (noting that if a practice has no plausible purpose other than the restriction of competition it can be inferred that it departs from competition on the merits).

[10] *Intel* (ibid) [139] (establishing a capacity to foreclosure requires examining five factors: extent of dominance, market coverage, granting conditions of the rebate scheme, duration and capacity to foreclose as-efficient competitors).

[11] ibid [140]; Case C-95/04 P, *British Airways v Commission* EU:C:2007:166 [86].

[12] European Commission, Guidelines on the assessment of horizontal mergers under the Council Regulation on the control of concentrations between undertakings (HMG) OJ C 31 (5 February 2004) 5–18; European Commission, Guidelines on the assessment of non-horizontal

Undoubtedly, the concept of procompetitive effects has always played an important role in competition assessments. Its meaning, though, has been incrementally developed by the European Court of Justice (ECJ) in tandem with the concepts of restriction of competition and anticompetitive effects. The four identification criteria presented here suggest that procompetitive effects are understood in a concrete and consistent manner across all competition norms and derive from the same epistemic cradle as they are tied to the notions of market failure; productive, allocative and dynamic efficiency; consumer welfare; and rivalry. Nonetheless, the concept of 'procompetitive effect' remains open-textured since its underlying conceptual elements remain in epistemic flux. Given the overall concrete and consistent way procompetitive effects are understood, though, this conceptual openness should not be deemed problematic. It allows the notion of procompetitive effects to be applied in a context-specific manner and incorporate new knowledge, thereby enhancing competition law's adaptability and capacity to set boundaries to power.[13]

In addition, the present analysis suggests that procompetitive effects play an increasingly prominent legal role in competition assessments. *Cartes Bancaires, Budapest Bank, Generics, Intel, Enel* and *CK Telekoms* suggest that the EU courts are frontloading procompetitive effects in their analysis of Articles 101 and 102 TFEU, and Article 2 EUMR, rather than leaving their analysis to the assessment of Article 101(3) TFEU, or Article 102 TFEU's and merger control's efficiency defence. In other words, procompetitive effects have come to play a more prominent role as counterindicators than as justifications of a restriction of competition. This change in the sequencing of procompetitive effects is indicative of the moving boundaries of EU competition law.[14] Such development may make competition analysis less formulaic and more accurate,[15] increase the evidentiary burden for

mergers under the Council Regulation on the control of concentrations between undertakings (NHMG) OJ C 265 (18 October 2008) 6–25.

[13] S Makris, 'EU Competition Law as Responsive Law' (2021) *Cambridge Yearbook of European Legal Studies* 1 (arguing that EU competition law is a field in constant epistemic change that needs to remain relatively open conceptually to secure its integrity. The latter is understood as value-laden consistency and coherence aligned to rule of law principles. Openness does not mean nor does it entail that EU competition is indeterminate. Interpretive struggles, institutional practices and input from extra-legal knowledge (eg economics) is what allows EU competition law to secure its integrity and be relatively determinate: to pursue its core mission in a relatively coherent and consistent way. Inevitably, though, frictions (manifestations of law's openness) remain. Arguably, instead of being a necessary evil, such frictions and uncertainties allow the law to adapt to new knowledge, different values, and market contexts.

[14] CF Beckner III and SC Salop, 'Decision Theory and Antitrust Rules' (1999) 67 *Antitrust Law Journal* 41 (sequencing is inevitable since courts are essentially decision-makers operating under limited and imperfect information. Two key questions affect or should affect sequencing: (i) what is an optimal decision and (ii) which information should be gathered, how much and in what order).

[15] A usual criticism of certain decisions of the Commission and EU courts has been that they adopt a formulaic approach especially to TFEU, Art 102, when they condemn practices of dominant undertakings that may have been procompetitive Whish and Bailey, *Competition Law* (2021) 198, 205; A Jones, B Sufrin and N Dunne, *EU Competition Law: Text, Cases, and Materials*, 7th edn (OUP, 2019) 295–99; N Petit, 'From Formalism to Effects – The Commission's Communication on Enforcement Priorities in Applying Article 82 EC' (2009) 32 *World Competition* 485.

the plaintiffs and reduce the risk of overenforcement. Yet, it can increase administrative and enforcement costs and the risk of underenforcement.

The chapter unfolds as follows. Section II discusses the notion of procompetitive effects in its association with other fundamental concepts such as 'restriction of competition', 'abuse of dominance', 'merger that leads to a significant impediment of effective competition' and 'anticompetitive effects', suggesting that in principle a practice that enhances or does not affect rivals' ability and incentives to compete and benefits consumers would be considered as procompetitive. Section III analyses the existing case law to flesh out the four substantive criteria used to identify procompetitive effects. In doing so, this section highlights the types and range of procompetitive effects recognised under the existing case law, shows that there is coherence across the board, and suggests that procompetitive effects derive from four fundamental concepts: market failure; efficiency; consumer welfare; and rivalry. Section IV discusses the legal techniques through which procompetitive effects are considered, arguing that procompetitive effects can function as either counterindicators of the existence of an anticompetitive practice or agreement, or as justification for it. Section V concludes with some observations about the evolving meaning and role of procompetitive effects and a discussion of the potential causes of this development. The ultimate purpose of the study is to contribute to the broader discussion about what are and what should be the boundaries of EU competition law. To this discussion, Amato's *Antitrust and the Bounds of Power: The Dilemma of Liberal Democracy in the History of the Market*, written a quarter of a century ago, continues to offer an essential reading.[16]

II. The Notion of Procompetitive Effects

It is hard to provide an uncontroversial definition of 'competition', or to obtain consensus about the reasons for having competition law.[17] Since the core objective of EU competition law, namely the protection of market competition, is multifaceted and elusive, this law is bound to remain relatively open to new understandings of what is competition, under which conditions it operates effectively, and under which circumstances can it be restricted.[18] Competition could be understood as 'dynamic' or 'static', 'price-driven' or 'non-price-driven', and a restriction of competition might have an impact not only on output and prices, but also on innovation, product quality, sustainability, income/wage inequalities and employment.[19]

[16] G Amato, *Antitrust and the Bounds of Power: The Dilemma of Liberal Democracy in the History of the Market* (Hart Publishing, 1997).

[17] G Monti, *EC Competition Law* (CUP, 2007) 2.

[18] For the reasons why EU competition law must be open see S Makris, 'Openness and Integrity in Antitrust' (2021) 17 *Journal of Competition Law & Economics* 1, 14–31; Makris, 'EU Competition Law' (2021) 19–25.

[19] I Lianos, 'Competition Law for the Digital Era: A complex systems; perspective' (2019) CLES Research Paper Series, 3 and 15–31.

Market players may compete not only on the basis of price or output, but also in terms of brand positioning, choice, quality, innovation or another scarce resource that consumers appreciate.[20] Market players might, for instance, compete to provide products or services that fare better in terms of privacy, sustainability, environmental protection and labour standards. To these it should be added that competition could be understood in consequentialist terms, namely as a device that maximises efficiency (defined for instance as total or consumer welfare)[21] or in deontological terms, namely as a process of meritorious rivalry,[22] or as decentralised information processing.[23] It can also be understood in a hybrid way[24] as a 'plebiscitary' coordination process for the allocation of resources resting upon freedom, equality of opportunity, and efficiency.[25]

The way competition is understood inevitably affects the interpretation of the key competition rules and predicates how competition law sets bounds to public and private power.[26] For instance, Article 101 TFEU prohibits agreements that restrict competition by object or by effect, Article 102 TFEU prohibits abuses of dominance, whereas Article 2 EUMR prohibits concentrations[27] with an EU dimension[28] that could significantly impede effective competition (SIEC). Fleshing out a conception of the concept[29] of competition and understanding how a particular practice or agreement might or actually affects this conception is necessary for finding a restriction of competition, an abuse of dominance, or a merger leading to a SIEC.[30] In a similar vein, different understandings of the idea of competition can affect what types of effects are recognised as procompetitive and how much weight is attributed to them. Furthermore, untangling the core concepts of competition norms can shed light on the meaning of anti- and procompetitive effects, and, vice versa, investigating the meaning of such effects can elucidate when and under what conditions a commercial activity restricts or promotes competition.

Despite the relative indeterminacy of the concept of competition and the open-textured nature of virtually all key competition law terms, an analysis of the case law reveals some clear-cut definitions.[31] A restriction of competition could

[20] OECD, 'Considering non-price effects in merger control – Background note by the Secretariat', DAF/COMP(2018)2; N Averitt and R Lande, 'Consumer Choice: The Practical Reason for Both Antitrust and Consumer Protection Law' (1998) 10 *Loyola Consumer Law Review* 44.

[21] R Posner, *Antitrust Law*, 2nd edn (University of Chicago Press, 2001) 11–17, 73; R Bork, *The Antitrust Paradox* (Free Press, 1993) 91.

[22] O Black, *The Conceptual Foundations of Antitrust* (CUP, 2005) 8–16.

[23] FA Hayek, 'Competition as a Discovery Procedure' (2002) 5 *The Quarterly Journal of Austrian Economics* 9.

[24] As an ideal that combines consequentialist and deontological elements.

[25] F Böhm, 'Freiheit und Ordnung in der Marktwirtschaft' [1971] in N Goldschmidt (ed), *Grundtexte zur Freiburger Tradition der Ordnungsökonomik* (Mohr Siebeck, 2008) 305.

[26] Amato, *Antitrust and the Bounds of Power* (1997) 108–29.

[27] EUMR, Art 3.

[28] EUMR, Art 1.

[29] For the distinction between concept and conception see Hart, *The Concept of Law* (1994) 1149–159.

[30] An abuse of dominance and a SIEC-inducing merger equally amount to a restriction of competition.

[31] Makris (n 13) 22; Makris, 'Openness and Integrity' (2021) 27–31.

be understood as a practice that is capable of having or actually has a net negative impact on firms' ability and incentives to compete.[32] Such reduction of rivals' ability and incentives to compete to the detriment of consumers can be achieved through either exclusion or collusion.[33] An abuse of dominance could be understood as covering any practice[34] pursued by a dominant[35] undertaking that has as actual or potential effect either the elimination of a competitor with means that deviate from competition on the merits,[36] or the exploitation of consumers by charging them excessively high and unfair prices.[37] Put differently, a practice that is at least capable of restricting competition and either has no plausible procompetitive rationale or its actual or potential anticompetitive effects outweigh any procompetitive gains, will count as an abuse of dominance.[38] A merger can lead to an SIEC either by generating non-coordinated (ie increasing market power or leading to a non-collusive oligopoly) or coordinated effects (ie tacit collusion), if horizontal,[39] or by leading to market foreclosure (ie input or customer foreclosure) or tacit collusion, if non-horizontal.[40]

[32] P Ibañez Colomo and A Lamadrid, 'On the Notion of Restriction of Competition: What We Know and What We Don't Know We Know' in D Gerard, M Merola and Bern Meyring (eds), *The Notion of Restriction of Competition: Revisiting the Foundations of Antitrust Enforcement in Europe* (Bruylant, 2017) 21, 35, 44.

[33] For instance, a horizontal agreement that allows various players to coordinate their behaviour and fix prices or reduce output leads to collusion, whereas a vertical agreement that guarantees exclusivity to a supplier's product might deny their rivals access to the market and lead to market foreclosure. See R Posner, *Antirust Law*, 2nd edn (University of Chicago Press, 2019) 132–64 and 449–56.

[34] Abuse could be understood as any behaviour that deviates from competition on the merits and is possible due to substantial market power. Case 85/76, *Hoffmann-La Roche & Co AG v Commission* (*Hoffmann-La Roche*) [1979] ECR 461, [91] (defining abuse as 'an objective concept relating to the behaviour of an undertaking in a dominant position which is such as to influence the structure of a market where, as a result of the very presence of the undertaking in question the degree of competition is weakened and which, through recourse to methods different from those which condition normal competition in products or services on the basis of the transaction of commercial operators, has the effect of hindering the maintenance of the degree of competition still existing in the market or the growth of that competition').

[35] ibid [39] (noting that 'such a position enables the undertaking which profits by it if not to determine at least to have an appreciable influence on the conditions under which competition will develop and in any case to act largely in disregard of it so long as such conduct does not operate to its detriment').

[36] C-209/10, *Post Danmark A/S v Konkurrencerådet (Post Danmark I)* ECLI:EU:C:2012:172 [21] (noting that Art 102 prohibits a dominant undertaking from, among other things, adopting practices that have an exclusionary effect by using methods other than those that are part of competition on the merits).

[37] Case 27/76, *United Brands v Commission (United Brands)* ECLI:EU:C:1978:22 [65]. Typically, abuses are classified as either exploitative or exclusionary. The first including abuses have as their object or effect to harm the customer of the dominant undertaking (eg excessive pricing) while the latter have as their object or effect the exclusion of rivals on the market in which the dominant firm operates or on a neighbouring one. Excessive pricing as an abuse does not fit into Posner's taxonomy mentioned in ft 31 and is not cognizable as antitrust offence under US law. See *Berkey Photo, Inc v Eastman Kodak Co*, 603 F.2d 263, 297 (2d Cir 1979); *US v. Aluminum Co of America*, 148 F.2d 416, 430 (2d Cir 1945).

[38] P Ibañez Colomo, 'What is an Abuse of a Dominant Position? Deconstructing the Prohibition and Categorizing Practices' forthcoming in P Akman, O Brook and K Stylianou (eds), *Research Handbook on Abuse of Dominance and Monopolization* (Elgar, 2022) 32–33.

[39] HMG (n 12) 24–57.

[40] NHMG (n 12) 29–81.

All these practices are considered unlawful under EU competition law either because they are capable of generating anticompetitive effects, as they are not a plausible source of procompetitive gains, or because (and when) their actual or potential anticompetitive effects outweigh the procompetitive ones. Against this backdrop, it could be argued that procompetitive effects refer to practices or other factual elements that cancel out a restriction of competition, an abuse of dominance or an SIEC-inducing merger. In principle, an agreement or a practice that enhances or does not affect rivals' ability and incentives to compete and that benefits consumers would be considered procompetitive. In line with this abstract definition, the analysis of the case law in the following section suggests that there are four substantive criteria used by the EU courts to infer procompetitive effects.

III. Four Identification Criteria

A. Avoiding Market Failures Through Non-Anticompetitive Means

One question used by the EU courts to identify procompetitive effects is whether the practice or agreement at stake deals with a market failure in a non-anticompetitive manner, ie without unnecessarily diminishing rivals' ability and willingness to compete. Article 101 TFEU case law is illuminating in this regard. To establish a restriction of competition within the meaning of this provision the plaintiff must show that the agreement restricts competition either by object or by effect.[41] To show the existence of a restriction by object the plaintiff would have to analyse the content of the provisions of the agreement and its objective purpose within the economic and legal context of which it forms a part[42] and the intentions of the parties.[43] The plaintiff must also show that the relevant agreement is by its very nature 'injurious to the proper functioning of normal competition'[44] or – in less ontological and more analytical vocabulary – that it 'reveals in itself a sufficient degree of harm to competition'[45] in light of the existing experience and economic knowledge.[46] On such an occasion the agreement would be considered

[41] The two categories are alternative. Case C-209/07, *Beef Industry Development and Barry Brothers (BIDS)* ECLI:EU:C:2008:643 [15], [16].

[42] ibid [15]–[21] (when determining the context, it is also relevant to look at the nature of the goods or services affected, the real conditions of the functioning of the market, and the structure of the market. The subjective intention of the parties is not determinative, but just one factor that may indicate a by object restriction); Case C-32/11, *Allianz Hungária Biztosító and Others* ECLI:EU:C:2013:160 [48]; Case C-67/13P, *Groupement des Cartes Bancaires v European Commission (Cartes Bancaires)* ECLI:EU:C:2014:2204 [53].

[43] *BIDS* (n 41) [21].

[44] ibid [17].

[45] *Cartes Bancaires* (n 42) [57].

[46] ibid [51]; Case C-228/18, *Gazdasági Versenyhivatal v Budapest Bank Nyrt. and Others (Budapest Bank)* ECLI:EU:C:2020:265 [36], [76], [79].

presumptively unlawful on the basis that it is *more* than capable of having anticompetitive effects.[47] Hence, if the multifactored and context-sensitive analysis of an agreement reveals that it can in itself harm competition on the market to a sufficient degree, then the agreement will qualify as a restriction by object and its anticompetitive effects will be presumed.[48] The plaintiff would not have to establish actual or potential anticompetitive effects. If it is established that the agreement constitutes a plausible source of procompetitive effects then it will not be considered as revealing in itself a sufficient degree of harm to competition, and it will escape a 'restriction by object' characterisation.

In *Bids*, the ECJ assessed whether an industry-wide agreement to reduce the processing capacity of Irish beef sector constituted a restriction by object.[49] Beef producers suffering from an overcapacity crisis[50] sought to set up an industry-wide rationalisation plan which would fix the number of meat producers (stayers) by encouraging the exit of goers through a compensation fund.[51] To find out whether such an agreement constituted a restriction by object, the Court followed the method described above.[52] Even though the agreement had a commercial rationale and was pursuing other legitimate objectives,[53] the Court found it to restrict competition by object since its object was 'to change, appreciably, the structure of the market through a mechanism intended to encourage the withdrawal of competitors'.[54] Specifically, 'the BIDS arrangements [were] intended to improve the overall profitability of undertakings supplying more than 90% of the beef and veal processing services on the Irish market by enabling them to approach, or even attain, their minimum efficient scale'.[55] Therefore, these arrangements were aimed

[47] How capable is a matter of degree and remains a controversial issue indicative of the moving boundaries of EU competition law. Compare *T-Mobile* or *Allianz Hungaria* and subsequent case law such as *Cartes Bancaires*, *Budapest Bank* and *Generics*. Case 8/08, *T-Mobile Netherlands BV, KPN Mobile NV, Orange Nederland NV and Vodafone Libertel NV v Raad van bestuur van de Nederlandse Mededingingsautoriteit (T-Mobile)* ECLI:EU:C:2009:343 [31] ('in order for a concerted practice to be regarded as having an anti-competitive object, it is sufficient that it has the potential to have a negative impact on competition'); Case C-307/18, *Generics (UK) Ltd v Competition and Markets Authority (Generics)* ECLI:EU:C:2020:52 [18], [82]; *Cartes Bancaires* (n 42) [69] ('although the General Court thereby set out the reasons why the measures … are capable of restricting competition and, consequently, of falling within the scope of the prohibition laid down in Article [101(1)], it in no way explained … in what respect that restriction of competition reveals a sufficient degree of harm in order to be characterised as a restriction 'by object' within the meaning of that provision').

[48] *T-Mobile* (ibid) [29] ('in deciding whether a concerted practice is prohibited by Article 81(1) EC, there is no need to take account of its actual effects once it is apparent that its object is to prevent, restrict or distort competition').

[49] *BIDS* (n 41) [6]–[14].

[50] ibid [4].

[51] ibid [8].

[52] ibid [15]–[17].

[53] ibid [21] (noting that 'an agreement may be regarded as having a restrictive object even if it does not have the restriction of competition as its sole aim but also pursues other legitimate objectives').

[54] ibid [31].

[55] ibid [32], [33] (these arrangements were intended 'to enable several undertakings to implement a common policy which has as its object the encouragement of some of them to withdraw from the market and the reduction, as a consequence, of the overcapacity which affects their profitability by preventing them from achieving economies of scale').

at solving a market failure (ie overcapacity) and could generate some productive efficiencies (eg enable the transition to a more efficient equilibrium at lower transaction costs). Yet, they would do so by substituting 'practical cooperation for the risks of competition'[56] and by inhibiting independent action by each economic operator.

In the absence of these agreements, rivalry would be intensified in the market and lead – in a less organised manner – to the higher concentration levels necessary for the efficient operation of producers.[57] Instead, the Irish producers were seeking to set up a cartel-like arrangement and plan the exit and presence of market players in the market. They had an efficiency rationale, ie to address a market failure by allowing the stayers to reach minimum efficient scale. But, they were seeking to achieve this efficient outcome in an anticompetitive manner, by fully eliminating rivalry or by cooperating instead of competing. On this basis the Court considered their agreement a restriction by object. Hence, simply generating economies of scale or scope or solving a market failure does not suffice to establish a procompetitive effect under Article 101(1) TFEU, if such outcome is to be achieved by excessively restricting the competitive process.[58] On the contrary, an agreement that seeks to tackle a market failure without employing anticompetitive means would be considered as having procompetitive aspects or effects.

Other cases where a horizontal agreement is used to solve another type of market failure – ie collective action problems – are equally suggestive of this point.[59] In *Gøttrup-Klim* the Court had to assess a horizontal purchasing agreement in a market in which the price paid for supplies depended on the volume of the order and in which purchasers were in a relatively weak bargaining position. This agreement was not found to restrict competition by object in spite of the fact that it involved price-fixing, as it could 'make way for more effective competition'.[60] In *Luttikhuis* a withdrawal fee scheme of a cooperative association did not qualify as a restriction by object as it was considered necessary to ensure that the cooperative functions properly, has a sufficiently wide commercial base and stable membership.[61] In *Tournier* the refusal by the members of a copyright collecting society to license parts of their repertoire, ostensibly a restriction of output, was found to fall outside the scope of Article101(1) TFEU in that it pursued

[56] ibid [34].

[57] ibid [35].

[58] Opinion of Advocate General Trstenjak in *BIDS* (n 41) [101]: 'the aim of BIDS is to create production benefits through economies of scale. However, it is clear from the connection between Article 81(1) EC and Article 81(3) EC that such an aim can only be considered under Article 81(3)'. See also Case T-14/89, *Montedipe* v *Commission* ECLI:EU:T:1992:36 [265]; Case T-148/89, *Tréfilunion* v *Commission* [1995] ECR II-1063 [109]; and Case T-112/99, *M6 and Others* v *Commission* ECLI:EU:T:1995:68 [72]–[74].

[59] R Cooter and T Ulen, *Law & Economics*, 6th edn (Pearson, 2016) 41, 102–05.

[60] Case C-250/92, *Gøttrup-Klim and Others Grovvareforeninger v Dansk Landbrugs Grovvareselskab* ECLI:EU:C:1994:413 [31]–[34].

[61] Case C-399/93, *Oude Luttikhuis and Others v Verenigde Coöperatieve Melkindustrie Coberco* ECLI:EU:C:1995:434 [12]–[14] (since 'organizing an undertaking in the specific legal form of a cooperative association does not in itself constitute anti-competitive conduct').

a 'legitimate aim', namely it solved a collective action problem.[62] In the absence of the agreement, the search and enforcement cost would be prohibitively excessive.[63]

For similar reasons, standard-setting agreements enjoy a 'soft safe harbour', according to the Commission, and do not run counter to Article 101(1) TFEU, as long as participation in standard-setting is unrestricted; the procedure for adopting the standard in question is transparent; the agreements do not contain an obligation to comply with the standard; and access to the standard is provided on fair, reasonable and non-discriminatory terms.[64] These conditions are in place to ensure that the standard setting agreement will solve a collective action problem without eradicating or overly delimiting the competitive process.[65] Similarly agreements providing for the joint licensing of a technology through a pool of 'essential' patents[66] are prima facie lawful as long as they solve a collective action problem without employing anticompetitive means.[67]

Information asymmetries can be another type of market failure.[68] As long as an agreement can address the negative consequences of asymmetric information, it would be considered as a plausible source of procompetitive effects and

[62] Case 395/87, *Ministère public v Jean-Louis Tournier (Tournier)* ECLI:EU:C:1989:319 [29]–[31].

[63] ibid [31] ('Copyright-management societies pursue a legitimate aim when they endeavour to safeguard the rights and interests of their members vis-à-vis the users of recorded music. The contracts concluded with users for that purpose cannot be regarded as restrictive of competition for the purposes of Article 85 unless the contested practice exceeds the limits of what is necessary for the attainment of that aim. Those limits may be exceeded if direct access to a sub-division of a repertoire, as advocated by the discothèque operators, could fully safeguard the interests of authors, composers and publishers of music without thereby increasing the costs of managing contracts and monitoring the use of protected musical works').

[64] Communication from the Commission, Guidelines on the applicability of Article 101 of the Treaty on the Functioning of the European Union to horizontal co-operation agreements ('Guidelines on horizontal co-operation agreements') OJ C 11 (14 January 2011) [277]–[286].

[65] Collective action problems occur when there are disincentives that tend to discourage joint action by individuals in the pursuit of a common goal. Illustrative in this regard is the simple, one-shot 'prisoner's dilemma' game which shows that even when it would be in the interests of both players to cooperate, they could end up not cooperating when they can see the advantages of free-riding and fear the dangers of being taken for a ride. If a collective good is non-excludable a free-riding problem may block its provision. A supply-side response is to attempt to convince would-be free riders that if they do not contribute, the good will not be provided at all. See M Olson, *The Logic of Collective Action* (Harvard University Press, 1971) 5–52, 153–58.

[66] Communication from the Commission, Guidelines on the application of Article 101 of the Treaty on the Functioning of the European Union to technology transfer agreements OJ C 89 (28 March 2014) [220] ('When a pool is composed only of technologies that are essential and therefore by necessity also complements, the creation of the pool as such generally falls outside Article [101(1)] irrespective of the market position of the parties. However, the conditions on which licences are granted may be caught by Article [101(1)]').

[67] ibid [226] (the Commission requires that the pool licenses its technology on a fair, reasonable and non-discriminatory basis). As highlighted by Olson the relative costs of taking part into collective action can be determinative of whether the action will be undertaken or not. Olson, *Collective Action* (1971) 2, 3, 9, 21–36.

[68] This concept is defined as a situation in which the information about the features of the product subject to exchange is not evenly distributed among buyers and sellers. The archetypal example is of the seller of a good that has more information about its quality than does its buyer. Cooter and Ulen, *Law & Economics* (2016) 38–41, 87–88; G Akerlof, 'The Market for Lemons: Quality Uncertainty and the Market Mechanism' (1970) 84 *Quarterly Journal of Economics* 488.

escape the restriction by object characterisation.[69] In *T-Mobile*, the ECJ held that information-sharing can be a restriction by object when it affords the parties the possibility of 'removing uncertainties concerning the intended conduct of the participating undertakings' and engages in a concerted practice.[70] Yet, in *John Deere*, the ECJ and the General Court (GC) did not deny that, in light of a variety of factors, information exchanges may improve the conditions of competition on a particular market.[71]

In *Asnef-Equifax*, the ECJ stressed that information sharing agreements may fall outside the scope of Article 101(1) TFEU altogether when they are a proportionate reaction to a market failure.[72] In this case the Court had to assess whether an information exchange between competing credit organisations restricted competition by object.[73] The Court, after noting that Article 101 TFEU 'requires companies to determine their commercial policies autonomously and prohibits them from any direct or indirect contact which could influence the conduct of competitors', highlighted that this 'does not deprive companies of the right to adapt themselves intelligently to the existing or anticipated conduct of their competitors'. The Court then considered that the purpose of the registers in question was 'to increase the amount of information available to credit institutions on potential borrowers, reducing the disparity between creditor and debtor as regards the holding of information, thus making it easier for the lender to foresee the likelihood of repayment'.[74] By increasing the available information, the registers were in principle capable of reducing the rate of borrower default and of improving the functioning of the supply of credit. Hence, the purpose of the agreement was to tackle information asymmetries, reduce the risk of lending and the number of borrowers who default on repayments, and improve the functioning of the credit supply system as a whole. On this basis a finding of a restriction by object was not warranted.

Cases such as *BIDS Gøttrup-Klim, Luttikhuis, Tournier, John Deere, Asnef-Equifax* suggest that an agreement which addresses a market failure

[69] Guidelines on horizontal co-operation agreements (n 64) [95]–[100] (The Commission acknowledges that information exchange agreements may be a source of efficiency gains in this sense. The exchange of information in the insurance sector may allow competing firms to identify the risk profile of end-users and thus avoid adverse selection).

[70] *T-Mobile* (n 48) [35].

[71] Case C-7/95 P, *John Deere Ltd v Commission of the European Communities* ECLI:EU:C:1998:256 [89]–[90] (noting that crucial factors for this assessment are the nature of information, the frequency of dissemination, the persons to whom it is disclosed, whether the data is aggregated or individualised). See also Guidelines on horizontal co-operation agreements (n 4) [86]–[94].

[72] Case C-238/05, *Asnef-Equifax, Servicios de Información sobre Solvencia y Crédito, SL and Administración del Estado v Asociación de Usuarios de Servicios Bancarios (Asnef-Equifax)* ECLI:EU:C:2006:734, [55]–[56]. Guidelines on horizontal co-operation agreements (n 64) [75]–[94]. See also M Bennett and P Collins, 'The Law and Economics of Information Sharing: The Good, the Bad and the Ugly' (2010) 6 *European Competition Journal* 311.

[73] *Asnef-Equifax* (ibid) [7] (Asnef-Equifax, a group of financial organisations, set up a register to exchange solvency and credit information about their customers to evaluate the risks undertaken when engaging in credit or lending activities).

[74] ibid [47].

(eg excessive capacity, collective action and information asymmetry problems) without eliminating or restricting more than necessary market players' ability to act autonomously and independently should be deemed procompetitive and prima facie lawful.

B. Intensifying Rivalry

In a similar vein, when undertakings seek to achieve an efficient outcome by intensifying one dimension of rivalry while softening another, their behaviour might be deemed prima facie procompetitive. Rivalry is to be understood as referring to the competitive process as a means to preserve firms' incentives to create, invest and innovate. If overall rivalry is intensified, the practice would be safely assumed to be procompetitive regardless of any efficiencies. Such efficiencies would be assumed and not required to be demonstrated.[75] Hence, procompetitive effects can be identified by considering whether a practice or an arrangement affects positively net rivals' ability and incentives to compete.[76]

The treatment of vertical restraints provides a good illustration of how this second identification criterion works.[77] There is a stark difference in the treatment of horizontal and vertical agreements under the current system. Vertical restraints (eg exclusive dealing, exclusive distribution, selective distribution, non-compete clauses, territorial protection clauses) involve intra-value chains restrictions and complementary products or services. As a result, they are generally considered less harmful than horizontal ones since they are usually a plausible source of efficiency-enhancing effects, especially when the parties of the agreement do not

[75] Case T-111/08, *MasterCard, Inc and MasterCard Europe v European Commission* ECLI:EU:T:2012:260 [80] (noting that the analysis of the 'objective necessity' of a restraint under TFEU, Art 101(1) 'cannot be but relatively abstract'). In *Société Technique Minière*, *Metro I* and *Pronuptia* the restraints in question were found, in general, to be a plausible source of efficiency gains, and that fact alone allowed the Court to conclude that they were not restrictive by object. Case 56–65, *Société Technique Minière (LTM) v Maschinenbau Ulm GmbH (MBU) (Société Technique Minière)* ECLI:EU:C:1966:38 at 250; Case 26/76, *Metro SB-Großmärkte v Commission (Metro I)* EU:C:1977:167 [26]–[27], [32]–[45]; Case 161/84, *Pronuptia de Paris GmbH v Pronuptia de Paris Irmgard Schillgallis (Pronuptia)* EU:C:1986:41 [15]–[17], [21], [23], [27]. These cases suggest that if the defendant shows that the restraint is necessary, it would be deemed a plausible source of procompetitive effects. The *Metro I* criteria could be read as a more structured way to demonstrate procompetitive effects.

[76] Ibañez Colomo and Lamadrid, 'On the Notion of Restriction of Competition' (2017) 24–29; G Monti, 'EU Competition Law and the Rule of Reason Revisited' (2020) TILEC Discussion Paper, available at ssrn.com/abstract=3686619.

[77] European Commission, Guidelines on Vertical Restraints OJ C 130 (19 May 2010) [24] ('an agreement or concerted practice entered into between two or more undertakings each of which operates, for the purposes of the agreement or the concerted practice, at a different level of the production or distribution chain, and relating to the conditions under which the parties may purchase, sell or resell certain goods or services'). The most common types of such restraints are those for the supply, distribution, production, purchase and sale of goods, and research and development agreements. They tend to include restrictions relating to, inter alia, the number of buyers a seller will trade with within a specified territory, the number of providers a buyer is allowed to purchase from, and the conditions (price, location, customers) under which the goods can be resold. Whish and Bailey (n 5) 649–52.

enjoy market power.[78] Therefore, in principle vertical restraints are considered capable of boosting inter-brand competition even when they soften intra-brand competition.[79]

A cursory look at the relevant case law, the VBER and the Guidelines on Vertical Agreements suggests that, in principle, such restraints do not raise any competition concerns as long as the intensity of inter-brand competition compensates for the ensuing softening of intra-brand competition.[80] For instance, exclusive distribution or an exclusive territorial licensing agreement restricts intra-brand competition, and may lead to some price rigidity or increases. Yet, these agreements are likely to be found lawful where the parties to the agreement have low market shares (ie indication of lack of market power) and face competitive pressure by their rivals.[81] In addition, as discussed below, such restraints are lawful when they are necessary to intensify competition at some other segment of the value chain.[82] Consequently, as long as a contractual restriction delimits one dimension of competition only to intensify competition in another, it would be deemed as capable of generating procompetitive effects.[83]

Apart from the obvious example of vertical restraints, there are cases involving horizontal agreements suggesting that an agreement that softens one dimension (eg inter-brand vs intra-brand) or parameter (eg price vs quality) of competition

[78] VBER, Recital 7. Such requirement suggests that generating efficiencies alone does not suffice to establish procompetitive effects. This requirement is aimed at balancing efficiencies with rivalry. In this sense there is an interplay between criteria (ii) and (iii).

[79] Oxera Consulting LLP and Accent, 'Vertical restraints: new evidence from a business survey' (2016) survey prepared for the Competition and Markets Authority, available at www.gov.uk/government/publications/vertical-restraints-roundtable-discussion-and-business-survey (further suggests that vertical restraints may be used to limit the expansion of e-commerce).

[80] Guidelines on Vertical Restraints (n 77) [153] ('The market position of the supplier and its competitors is of major importance, as the loss of intra-brand competition can only be problematic if inter-brand competition is limited. The stronger the position of the supplier, the more serious is the loss of intra-brand competition').

[81] ibid [152] (exclusive distribution is exempted by the Block Exemption Regulation where both the supplier's and buyer's market share each do not exceed 30% and does not contain hardcore restrictions) and 154 ('The position of the competitors can have a dual significance. Strong competitors will generally mean that the reduction in intra-brand competition is outweighed by sufficient inter-brand competition. However, if the number of competitors becomes rather small and their market position is rather similar in terms of market share, capacity and distribution network, there is a risk of collusion and/or softening of competition').

[82] For instance, a reseller may not have distributed the products in the absence of mechanisms allowing it to capture the positive externalities generated by its activity; or a holder of an intellectual property right would not have accepted to license the rights without it being able to preserve the value of the public good in question. P Ibañez Colomo, 'Market Failures, Transaction Costs and Article 101 TFEU' (2012) 37 *European Law Review* 541, 555.

[83] Case 107/82, *Allgemeine Elektrizitäts-Gesellschaft AEG-Telefunken AG v Commission of the European Communities. Selective distribution system (AEG Telefunken)* ECLI:EU:C:1983:293 [33]; Case C-439/09, *Pierre Fabre Dermo-Cosmétique SAS v Président de l'Autorité de la concurrence and Ministre de l'Économie, de l'Industrie et de l'Emploi (Pierre Fabre)* EU:C:2011:649 [40] ('it has always been recognised in the case law of the Court that there are legitimate requirements, such as the maintenance of a specialist trade capable of providing specific services as regards high-quality and high-technology products, which may justify a reduction of *price competition* in favour of competition relating to *factors other* than price', italics added).

while it intensifies another, will be considered to have procompetitive effects. Illustrative in this regard is *Cartes Bancaires*.[84] In this case the main banks of France set up the CB Group which sought to ensure the interoperability of the systems for payment and withdrawal by bank cards issued by its members and to solve a free-riding problem.[85] That interoperability enabled, in practice, a CB card issued by a member of the CB Group to be used for payments to all traders affiliated to the CB system through any other member of the Group and/or to make withdrawals from automatic teller machines (ATMs) operated by all other members. The fees paid by CB Group members depended on the issuing/acquisition ratio of the members of the group.[86] The Commission considered that these measures artificially increased prices to the advantage of the major banks of the group and to the detriment of new entrants, and on this basis it argued that they constituted a by object restriction of competition.[87] The GC concurred.[88]

Nonetheless, the ECJ set aside the GC judgment, finding that the GC could not properly have concluded that the pricing measures adopted by CB had as their object the restriction of competition. The pricing measures were adopted in the context of a payment system and were to be applied in a two-sided market.[89] These measures sought to establish a certain balance between the issuing and acquiring activities of the members of the CB Group and to tackle a free-riding problem. Although capable of restricting competition, the ECJ noted, the measures did not reveal in themselves a sufficient degree of harm to competition to be characterised as restrictive by object.[90] The measures were aimed at intensifying overall rivalry, and thereby had a plausible procompetitive explanation. Hence, these measures could not qualify as a restriction by object, even though they restricted rivalry in a particular segment of the market. It should be noted that even though the said measures did not qualify as by object restrictions, on further review they were found to have restrictive effects.[91] Beyond the specificities of the case however

[84] *Cartes Bancaires* (n 42) [37].

[85] In this sense, *Cartes Bancaires* could be read as a case satisfying also criterion (i) as the said agreement was purported to solve a collective action problem.

[86] ibid [4] (banks had to pay a higher membership fee if their issuing activities were considerably larger than their acquiring activities, or if the stock of payment cards they had issued tripled over a defined period).

[87] Commission Decision C (2007) 5060 final of 17 October 2007 relating to a proceeding under Article [81 EC] (COMP/D1/38606 – Groupement des cartes bancaires 'CB').

[88] Case T-491/07, *Groupement des cartes bancaires (CB) v European Commission* ECLI:EU:T:2016:379.

[89] Two-sided markets provide a good example of the multi-dimensional character of competition and how restricting one dimension of rivalry might be justified on the basis of the ensuing intensification of rivalry on another dimension. J-C Rochet and J Tirole, 'Platform Competition in Two-Sided Markets' (2003) 1 *Journal of the European Economic Association* 990.

[90] *Cartes Bancaires* (n 42) [69], [73] (according to the ECJ, the GC was entitled 'at the most to infer … that those measures had as their object the imposition of a financial contribution on the members which benefit from the efforts of other members for the purposes of developing the acquisition activities of the system').

[91] The GC concluded that the Commission was correct in finding that the measures in question had restrictive effects on competition. Case T-491/07 RENV, *Groupement des cartes bancaires (CB) v European Commission* ECLI:EU:T:2016:379 [80]–[90], [105]–[214].

there is a key takeaway of the *Cartes Bancaires* saga that is relevant for the purposes of this study. This case suggests that if an agreement or a practice softens one dimension or parameter of competition to enhance rivals' ability and incentives to compete in another, it would be considered a plausible source of procompetitive effects, and escape the restriction by object characterisation.[92]

C. Making Possible a Welfare-Enhancing Arrangement or Increasing the Value of a Product or a Service without Eliminating or Overly Restricting Rivalry

Another criterion for identifying procompetitive effects is asking whether the practice or the agreement in question makes possible a welfare-enhancing arrangement which would not have existed otherwise or whether it increases the value of a product or a service, without eliminating or overly restricting rivalry.[93] This point could be exemplified by examining the treatment of vertical restraints. Such restraints are likely to enable better coordination within a chain of production or distribution; reduce transaction and distribution costs, promote non-price competition; improve quality of services; solve free-rider problems; open up or allow undertakings to enter new markets; solve hold-up problems or vertical externality problems; achieve economies of scale in distribution; correct capital market imperfections, and ensure product uniformity and quality standardisation.[94] Such efficiency-enhancing effects are likely to outweigh any potential anticompetitive effects especially when the undertakings involved enjoy a low degree of market power and face competition from other suppliers of goods or services.[95]

These requirements set by VBER suggest that generating efficiencies alone does not suffice to establish procompetitive effects and sustain a presumption of lawfulness: if certain efficiencies are expected, while competition as a process of rivalry is not likely to be diminished or is likely to be intensified, then, and only

[92] A similar conclusion can be inferred by General Courts reasoning in *O2 Germany*. The agreement in question was restricting rivalry in national roaming between the two network operators but allowed O2 to enter the 3G market. Hence, the Court said that the assessment of such an agreement requires an effects analysis and that both dimensions of competition had to be analysed to establish the restrictive effect. Case T-328/03, *O2 (Germany) GmbH & Co, OHG v Commission of the European Communities (O2 Germany)* ECLI:EU:T:2006:116 [71]–[79], [85]–[98].

[93] Communication from the Commission, Guidelines on the application of Article 81(3) of the Treaty OJ C 101 (27 April 2004) [33] (referring the achievement of 'procompetitive effects by way of efficiency gains, explaining that efficiencies may create additional value by lowering the cost of producing an output, improving the quality of the product or creating a new product. Criteria (ii) and (iii) might be two sides of the same coin and most cases that fall under the former can fall under the latter and vice versa. Arguably, though the two criteria retain their analytical autonomy as we could imagine a practice that simply intensifies a dimension of rivalry with demonstrated efficiencies).

[94] Guidelines on Vertical Restraints (n 77) [106]–[107].

[95] VBER, Recital 7 ('for most vertical restraints competition concerns can only arise if there is insufficient competition at one or more levels of trade').

then, can procompetitive effects be safely inferred.[96] This is the reason why market power, barriers to entry, the market position of the parties and of existing and potential competitors, the countervailing power of buyers, the maturity of the market, and the level of trade are factors that are regularly taken into consideration in the assessment of vertical restraints.[97] Such factors ensure that the expected efficiencies will not overly restrict rivalry, and that vertical restraints will remain procompetitive.

It is not surprising, thus, that in virtue of their procompetitive effects most types of vertical agreements (ie the ones that do not include hard-core restrictions) have been granted the VBER benefit and are considered to automatically satisfy the conditions of Article 101(3) TFEU.[98] Even among the restraints that do not qualify for the VBER benefit, only a handful would be considered as restrictive by object (eg absolute territorial protection,[99] minimum resale price maintenance,[100] restrictions of cross-supplies in selective distribution systems; and restrictions on the sale of components[101]), while the vast majority of them would be analysed under an effects analysis.[102] Notably, if a vertical agreement does not meet the VBER conditions,[103] and falls within the scope of Article 101(1) TFEU, it will be prohibited only if actual or potential anticompetitive effects are shown and as long as it cannot be justified under Article 101(3) TFEU. The reason behind this choice lies in the fact that vertical restraints, by being able to increase the value of a product or a service, are generally considered procompetitive, as long as they do not

[96] Guidelines on Vertical Restraints (n 77) [47], [161].

[97] ibid [97]–[99], [106], [110]–[121], [134], [156], [194], [215], [220], [223].

[98] VBER, Recital 5. In this sense there is an interplay between criteria (iii) and (iv).

[99] Joined cases 56 and 58–64 *Établissements Consten SàRL and Grundig-Verkaufs-GmbH v Commission of the European Economic Community (Consten Grundig)* ECLI:EU:C:1966:41. Note, though, that in *Coditel II*, the ECJ concluded that an exclusive territorial licensing agreement providing for absolute territorial protection was not restrictive by object, because that absolute territorial protection was necessary to ensure that the intellectual property rights exploited can be appropriated by the licensee. The value of a broadcast to a licensee may depend on its ability to prevent other operators from exploiting it at the same time. Case C-262/81, *Coditel SA, Compagnie générale pour la diffusion de la télévision v Ciné-Vog Films SA (Coditel II)* ECLI:EU:C:1982:334 [15]–[16], [19]–[20]. In *Nungesser* the ECJ held that exclusive territorial protection may be a necessary means to induce a licensee to engage in the necessary investments to manufacture the product. Case 258/78, *LC Nungesser KG and Kurt Eisele v Commission of the European Communities (Nungesser)* ECLI:EU:C:1982:211 [57]. Along similar lines, in *Erauw-Jacquery* the Court considered that an exclusive territorial licensing agreement was not restrictive by object, because when a licensor has undertaken financial effort to develop a new technology, the licensor should be allowed to protect itself against any improper handling of such technology. Case C-27/87, *SPRL Louis Erauw-Jacquery v La Hesbignonne SC* ECLI:EU:C:1988:183 [10].

[100] When the ECJ examined the status of vertical price fixing under TFEU, Art 101(1) in *Binon*, it did not deny that such a restraint is a potential source of substantial efficiency gains, yet it concluded that is restrictive of competition by their very nature, seemingly on account of the fact that it limits the freedom of the distributor to set prices in their dealings with third parties. Case 243/83, *SA Binon & Cie v SA Agence et messageries de la presse* ECLI:EU:C:1985:284 [44], [46]. This same position would be confirmed in *Pronuptia* (n 75) [25], [74]; *Erauw-Jacquery* (n 99) [15].

[101] VBER, Art 4.

[102] Guidelines on Vertical Restraints (n 77) [96]–[121].

[103] These conditions are: (i) the market share of each of the parties to the agreement does not exceed 30%; and (ii) the agreement does not contain hardcore restrictions. See VBER, Arts 3, 4.

overly restrict rivalry (eg they do not involve hardcore restrictions and the market share of each of the involved parties is below 30 per cent).

When the ECJ engaged in an effects analysis of specific types of vertical restraints (where the by object characterisation was found to be inappropriate), it clarified the conditions under which particular types of agreements will be lawful. A selective distribution system for luxury goods will be compatible with Article 101(1) TFEU provided that: (a) resellers are chosen on the basis of objective criteria of a qualitative nature, laid down uniformly for all potential resellers and not applied in a discriminatory fashion; (b) the characteristics of the product in question necessitate such a network in order to preserve its quality and ensure its proper use; and (c) the criteria laid down do not go beyond what is necessary (the *Metro I* criteria).[104] In *Pierre Fabre*, the Court held that a total ban on Internet sales in a selective distribution system is a by object restriction,[105] while in *Coty* it ruled that it is legal to limit online sales in order to preserve the luxury image of the goods, as long as the requirements are not applied in a discriminatory manner, and are proportionate to the objectives pursued.[106] According to *Pronuptia* the contractual restrictions of a franchise agreement that are 'indispensable' to protect the franchisor's know-how and maintain the identity and reputation of the franchise network are procompetitive and lawful, but the restrictions that carve up markets between the franchisor and its franchisees or fix retail prices are not.[107] These specific conditions under which particular types of vertical agreements are prima facie lawful can be viewed as a way to ensure that they will bring about the expected efficiencies without restricting rivalry more than necessary.[108]

In this regard, it could be said that an agreement that is likely to generate efficiencies (eg make possible a welfare-enhancing arrangement or increase the value of a product or a service), would be permissible as long as it does not overly restrict competition, or, to put it differently, as long as it does not dangerously increase the likelihood of collusion or exclusion.[109] Hence, if an agreement generates efficiencies without restricting rivalry more than necessary it will be considered as having procompetitive effects. This identification criterion seems to overlap with criterion (ii) discussed above, and indeed most of the actual cases where procompetitive effects were identified under criterion (iii) satisfy also criterion (ii). For instance, most vertical agreements are prima facie lawful as they are associated with both types of procompetitive effects.[110] Yet, the two criteria are distinct from

[104] *Metro I* (n 75) [20], [27].
[105] *Pierre Fabre* (n 83) [41], [47].
[106] Case C-230/16, *Coty Germany GmbH vs Parfümerie Akzente GmbH (Coty)* EU:C:2017:941 [36].
[107] *Pronuptia* (n 75) [12], [16], [17].
[108] As already indicated these cases could be read as also satisfying criterion (ii).
[109] Case C-234/89, *Stergios Delimitis v Henninger Bräu AG (Delimitis)* ECLI:EU:C:1991:91 [13]–[27]; Case C-345/14 SIA, *'Maxima Latvija' v Konkurences padome (Maxima Latvija)* ECLI:EU:C:2015:784 [25]–[31].
[110] *Maxima Latvija* (n 109) [21].

an analytical point of view, since under criterion (ii) efficiencies are assumed *in abstracto* and deduced from an intensification of overall rivalry.

D. Net Consumer Welfare Gains without Fully Eliminating Competition

A fourth analytical criterion for identifying procompetitive effects asks whether an agreement or a practice leads to net consumer welfare gains without fully eliminating competition. Even though this criterion includes the procompetitive effects recognised under criteria (i)-(iii), it is not necessarily included in them: an agreement might solve a market failure, intensify rivalry, or generate efficiencies without directly benefiting consumers, even though it can be safely assumed that such procompetitive effects will ultimately benefit consumers. This fourth criterion can be traced to the fact that under all three key competition law pillars, if the defendant manages to show that their conduct generates efficiencies that are passed on to consumers, counterbalance or outweigh the relevant anticompetitive effects, and do not eliminate competition in a substantial part of the market, their conduct will be deemed procompetitive and lawful.

In particular, according Article 101(3), an agreement that restricts competition could be justified if it contributes to improving the production or distribution of goods or to promoting technical or economic progress; ensues a fair share of the benefits to the consumers; includes restrictions that are essential to achieving these objectives; and does not give the parties any possibility of eliminating competition in respect of substantial elements of the products in question.[111] Along similar lines, a dominant undertaking can avoid a finding of abuse under Article 102 TFEU by demonstrating that its practice is objectively necessary or that its conduct produces substantial efficiencies which outweigh any anticompetitive effects on consumers.[112] To make out the latter defence the undertaking would have to show that the efficiencies have been or are likely to be realised as a result of the conduct; that the conduct is indispensable to the realisation of those efficiencies (ie there is no less restrictive alternative); that the likely efficiencies outweigh any likely negative effects on competition and consumer welfare; and that the conduct in question does not eliminate effective competition by removing all or most existing sources of actual or potential competition.[113]

[111] Guidelines on the application of Article 81(3) (n 93) [105]–[116].

[112] *United Brands* (n 37) [184]; Case 311/84, *Centre Belge d'études de marché – Télémarketing (CBEM) v Compagnie luxembourgeoise de télédiffusion (CLT) and Information publicité Benelux (IPB)* ECLI:EU:C:1985:394 [27]; Case T-30/89, *Hilti v Commission (Hilti)* ECLI:EU:T:1991:70 [102]–[119]; Case T-83/91, *Tetra Pak International v Commission (Tetra Pak II)* ECLI:EU:T:1994:246 [136], [207]; *British Airways v Commission* (n 11) [69], [86].

[113] *Hilti* (n 112) [118]–[119]; *Tetra Pak II* (n 2) [83], [84], [138]; *Intel* (n 9) [140]; *British Airways v Commission* (n 11) [86].

The latter condition needs to be satisfied irrespective of the magnitude and value of consumer benefits, since 'rivalry between undertakings is an essential driver of economic efficiency, including dynamic efficiencies in the form of innovation' and 'in its absence the dominant undertaking will lack adequate incentives to continue to create and pass on efficiency gains'.[114] Hence, 'where there is no residual competition and no foreseeable threat of entry, the protection of rivalry and the competitive process outweighs possible efficiency gains'.[115] Similarly, any merger likely to lead to anticompetitive effects can be cleared as long as the merging parties can demonstrate that there are likely and timely, merger-specific and verifiable efficiencies that benefit the consumers and outweigh or counteract the anticompetitive effects.[116] Yet, a merger to monopoly is unlikely to be found as generating efficiencies sufficient to counteract its potential anticompetitive effects.[117]

Consequently, the most clear-cut case of procompetitive effects is when a practice or an agreement necessarily and directly benefits consumers without eliminating competition. Under the current framework it is not possible to claim that a practice that does not eliminate competition and directly and unequivocally benefits consumers is anticompetitive. Therefore, the EU Courts will consider that procompetitive effects have been established if the defendant shows that their practice generates net consumer gains without overly restricting rivalry.

E. Coherence Across the Board

The analysis undertaken so far reveals that when the EU Courts seek to identify procompetitive effects they do not simply ask whether a practice or an agreement is associated with efficiency gains. Instead they use certain economically informed identification criteria as heuristic devices.[118] If the defendant shows that their agreement or practice is aimed at addressing a market failure without employing any anticompetitive means; intensifies a dimension or parameter of competition while softening another; generates efficiencies without overly restricting rivalry; or produces or is likely to produce net consumer welfare gains without eliminating

[114] Communication from the Commission, Guidance on the Commission's enforcement priorities in applying Article 82 of the EC Treaty to abusive exclusionary conduct by dominant undertakings (Guidance Paper) OJ C 45 (24 February 2009) [30] (in the Commission's view, exclusionary conduct which maintains, creates or strengthens a market position approaching that of a monopoly normally cannot be justified on the grounds that it also creates efficiency gains).

[115] ibid [30].

[116] HMG (n 12) [76]–[88]; NHMG (n 12) [53].

[117] HMG (n 12) [84].

[118] By doing so they also allocate the burden of showing procompetitive effects between the plaintiff and the defendant. For instance, the counterfactual test or the ancillarity doctrine could qualify as heuristic devices. For a broader and in-depth discussion of the role of presumptions, proxies and premises see Kalintiri, 'Analytical Shortcuts in EU Competition Enforcement' (2020) 395–401 (providing a taxonomy of analytical shortcuts and distinguishing between proxies, premise and presumptions); Easterbrook, 'Limits of Antitrust' (1984) 10–11.

residual competition, they would be able to credibly claim that the agreement or practice is a source of procompetitive effects.[119] The benchmark for finding procompetitive effects is the competition that would have otherwise existed in the market.[120]

These four identification criteria can also be traced in the abuse of dominance case law, even though the Court refers explicitly to procompetitive effects only in a handful of cases. Yet, the high-level interpretation of Article's 102 TFEU key terms, the treatment of individual categories of abuses and the general 'as-efficient competitor' principle reveal that Court's understanding of what is a procompetitive effect is similar under both provisions. These three issues will now be examined in turn.

First, the existence of the dominance threshold reveals a fundamental assumption that unilateral conduct by firms without substantial market power is generally considered procompetitive.[121] In other words, the way the Court interprets 'dominance' suggests that, in the absence of substantial market power, competition is considered to be sufficiently robust. By relying on such assumption the Court recognises the value of vigorous rivalry. In the absence of dominance, rivalry is vigorous enough to ensure that no market player would be able to alone restrict output and raise prices. Nonetheless, having a dominant position is not prohibited as such,[122] and finding an Article 102 TFEU violation requires an abuse, namely a conduct that deviates from competition on the merits. Hence the abuse component of Article 102 TFEU and the way it is interpreted reveals another fundamental assumption according to which dominance can be the by-product of 'performance competition'[123] and superior efficiency, and reflect consumer preferences. Consequently, the main architecture of Article 102 and the high-level interpretation of its key terms (ie dominance and abuse) suggest that behaviour that is constrained by a vigorous competitive process or intensifies rivalry, generates efficiencies and benefits consumers should be considered procompetitive, and thereby lawful.

[119] Cooter and Ulen (n 59) 87–91. Transaction costs are the costs of exchange and involve (i) search costs (ie the costs of finding a commercial partner selling the good in question); (ii) bargaining costs (ie those incurred to strike a deal); and (iii) enforcement costs (ie those that relate to ensuring that the terms of the deal are respected) and may create allocative inefficiencies.

[120] *Société Technique Minière* (n 75) at 250.

[121] Guidance Paper (n 114) [9–18] (where dominance is not understood in a static but in a dynamic way as an ability to prevent effective competition or raise prices profitably above the competitive level for a significant period of time. Such ability is conditioned upon the features of the market and the role of existing and potential rivals, as well as buyers).

[122] *Intel* (n 9) [135]; Case C-322/81, *NV Nederlandsche Banden Industrie Michelin v Commission of the European Communities* (*Michelin I*), ECLI:EU:C:1983:313 [10] (noting that 'a finding that an undertaking has a dominant position is not in itself a recrimination but simply means that, irrespective of the reasons for which it has such a position, the undertaking concerned has a special responsibility not to allow its conduct to impair genuine undistorted competition on the [internal] market').

[123] For the distinction between performance and impediment competition see also V Vanberg, The Freiburg School: Walter Eucken and Ordoliberalism, Freiburg Discussion Papers on Constitutional Economics 04/11 (2011) 13–14; E Deutscher and S Makris, 'Exploring the Ordoliberal Paradigm: The Competition-Democracy Nexus' (2016) 11 *Competition Law Review* 181, 192.

Second, a cursory look at individual categories of abuses reveals that the same analytical criteria are used to identify procompetitive effects under both Articles 101 and 102 TFEU. For example, providing misleading information to patent authorities to extend the length of a patent is considered a 'naked restriction' as it does not deal with any market failure, nor does it intensify rivalry; make possible a welfare-enhancing outcome; or directly and unequivocally benefit the consumers. In other words, this practice is considered a 'naked restriction' because of a lack of procompetitive benefits as these were defined above. Pricing below average variable cost (AVC) is considered abusive irrespective of its effects.[124] Such a presumption relies on the premise that this kind of behaviour does not solve any market failure, nor does it intensify rivalry among as-efficient rivals, generate efficiencies or benefit consumers. Hence, prohibiting such a practice on the basis that it is not a plausible source of procompetitive effects suggests that the Court understands the latter as discussed in section III.A-D above.

Another example is refusal to supply, a practice which is unlawful only under strict conditions.[125] The underlying premise of the so-called *Bronner* conditions is that a refusal of a dominant undertaking that: (a) does not eliminate all competition; (b) can be objectively justified; and (c) does not preclude access to an indispensable input or facility, is capable of intensifying competition, generating long-run efficiencies, stimulating innovation incentives, and benefiting consumers.[126] The refusal to deal case law suggests also that if a dominant undertaking makes impossible a welfare-enhancing outcome without any reasonable justification, its conduct is likely to be considered abusive.[127]

Moreover, according to *Intel*, if an undertaking offers rebates that are incapable of excluding an as-efficient competitor there is no abuse.[128] The underlying premise of such a holding is that exclusivity rebates are generally likely to intensify rivalry, generate efficiencies (eg address externalities, allow the manufacturer to cover some fixed costs) and increase consumer welfare.[129] Thus, by considering

[124] Case C-62/86, *AKZO Chemie BV v Commission (AKZO)* EU:C:1991:286 [64], [71]; Case C-202/07 P, *France Télécom SA v Commission of the European Communities* ECLI:EU:C:2009:214 [32], [36], [52], [109], [110]. Contrast with *Brooke Group v Brown & Williamson Tobacco Corp*, 509 US 209, 226 (1993) (which focused almost entirely on the recoupment requirement and consider it necessary element for finding predation). Note that the Commission uses average avoidance cost (AAC) as a better cost benchmark and does not narrow down predation only to pricing below AAC. Conduct that predictably leads to short term net revenue lower than the one that could have been expected from an alternative conduct could be also found to predatory. See Guidance Paper (n 114) [63–74].

[125] Case C-7/97, *Oscar Bronner GmbH & Co KG v Mediaprint Zeitungs- und Zeitschriftenverlag GmbH & Co KG, Mediaprint Zeitungsvertriebsgesellschaft mbH & Co KG and Mediaprint Anzeigengesellschaft mbH & Co KG (Oscar Bronner)* ECLI:EU:C:1998:569 [41]–[46].

[126] Opinion of Advocate General Jacobs in *Oscar Bronner* (ibid) [57]–[62].

[127] Joined cases C-241/91 P and C-242/91 P, *Radio Telefis Eireann (RTE) and Independent Television Publications Ltd (ITP) v Commission of the European Communities (Magil)* ECLI:EU:C:1995:98 [54]–[55].

[128] *Intel* (n 9) [138].

[129] D Ridyard, 'Interpreting the As-Efficient Competitor Test in the Abuse of Dominance Cases' (2014) 10 *Competition Law Review* 125, 134–36.

that exclusivity rebates are a plausible source of procompetitive effects as long as they lead to the exclusion of less efficient rivals, the Court shows that it understands procompetitive effects in the way defined here.[130]

Third, beyond individual categories of abuse, a consistent line of case law suggests that as a matter of principle[131] Article 102 does not seek 'to prevent an undertaking from acquiring, on its own merits, [a] dominant position' but to ensure that only firms willing and able to compete on the merits remain on the market.[132] In other words, the aim of this provision is not to protect market players that are less efficient than the dominant undertaking.[133] Only the exclusion of equally efficient rivals would count as inappropriate softening of competition.[134] This general principle applies to pricing and non-pricing abuses,[135] is distinct from the 'as efficient test' that is applicable to particular categories of abuse, and suggests that if a dominant undertaking marginalises a rival by providing more attractive products or services to consumers in terms of, among other things, price, choice, quality or innovation, this conduct will be deemed procompetitive.[136] Consequently, this general 'as-efficient competitor' principle suggests that the same criteria for identifying procompetitive effects are used under both Articles 101 and 102 TFEU. If a dominant undertaking achieves certain efficiencies that benefit consumers without diminishing the ability and incentives of equally efficient rivals to compete, it can credibly claim that its conduct is a plausible source of procompetitive effects. Similarly, if dominant undertaking's conduct intensifies rivalry between equally efficient rivals, makes possible products that would not have existed otherwise, or generates net consumer gains without eliminating residual competition, that conduct will be deemed as a source of procompetitive effects.[137]

The same identification criteria can be traced in merger control. Most mergers are deemed lawful because they can intensify rivalry, generate efficiencies and benefit consumers. On this basis they are presumed procompetitive.[138] The EUMR thresholds are a clear indication that under the current regime only mergers between sufficiently large undertakings can trigger structural changes in the

[130] ibid [133]–[134].

[131] For an exception to this principle see Case C-23/14, *Post Danmark A/S v Konkurrencerådet (Post Danmark II)* ECLI:EU:C:2015:651 [58]–[60].

[132] *Intel* (n 9) [133].

[133] *Post Danmark I* (n 36) [21].

[134] *ENEL* (n 9) [51]. Not all exclusionary effects are considered problematic; only the ones that hamper rivals' ability and incentives to compete to the detriment of consumers. *ENEL* makes it clear that the '*Intel* rule' (according to which where the dominant undertaking submits, on the basis of evidence, that its conduct is not capable of restricting competition, the Commission must examine this issue) applies to all exclusionary practices.

[135] *ENEL* (n 9) [45]–[46] (the case is about non-pricing conduct and the associated principle lies at its heart).

[136] *Post Danmark II* (n 131) [22]; *ENEL* (n 9) [46].

[137] Criterion (i) is less likely to be used under Art 102 TFEU as it requires cooperation between firms and Art 102 TFEU covers unilateral conduct.

[138] EUMR, Recitals 4, 29; HMG (n 12) [11], [12]; NHMG (n 12) [13], [16], [21], [22], [28].

market and raise competition concerns.[139] In addition, the market share and the Herfindahl-Hirschman Index (HHI) function as filters that screen out the mergers that although falling within the scope of EUMR are unlikely to harm competition.[140] The use of such filters suggests that most concentrations are unlikely to raise competition concerns due to their innate procompetitive virtues (as these are defined above). For instance, mergers between entities with insignificant market shares are unlikely to curtail rivalry or harm consumers; mergers reasonably raising the concentration levels within a market can resolve coordination problems or enable the undertakings to reach minimum efficient scale.[141] In general, mergers between market players with low market shares operating in modestly concentrated markets, can intensify rivalry, reduce merging parties' costs and increase consumer welfare. On this basis, such mergers are considered procompetitive and prima facie lawful.

Nevertheless, horizontal mergers can significantly impede effective competition by generating non-coordinated or coordinated effects.[142] For instance, a merger between two actual and close competitors with large market shares operating in a market where barriers to entry are high is likely to have anticompetitive effects, especially when the customers of the merging parties face high switching costs and the rivals of the merging parties are incapable of increasing output in case of a price increase.[143] Such a merged entity will have a strong incentive to reduce output below the combined pre-merger levels, thereby raising market prices. Thus, a merger that removes an important competitive constraint on one or more sellers, who consequently will acquire increased market power can have as direct effect the loss of competition between the merging firms and reduce competitive pressure between the non-merging parties.[144] This merger will be prohibited on the basis that it creates or solidifies a dominant position as long as it is unlikely to generate procompetitive effects.[145]

Another type of non-coordinated effects leading to a prohibition of a merger could be found in the following scenario. Imagine a merger in an oligopolistic market that eliminates important competitive constraints exerted by the merging parties upon each other, and reduces the competitive pressure on the remaining competitors. Such a merger would create a non-collusive oligopoly, and even where there is little likelihood of coordination between the members of the oligopoly, it will be considered unlawful as long as it is not accompanied by offsetting

[139] EUMR, Art 1.
[140] HMG (n 12) [14]–[21]; NHMG (n 12) [23]–[27].
[141] HMG (n 12) [18]; NHMG (n 12) [13]–[14].
[142] HMG (n 12) [24]–[57].
[143] ibid [24]–[36].
[144] ibid [24].
[145] Commission Decision of 27/06/2007 declaring a concentration to be incompatible with the common market and the EEA Agreement (Case No COMP/M.4439 – Ryanair / Aer Lingus).

consumer beneficial efficiencies.[146] In addition, a horizontal merger may make coordination within the market easier, more stable and more effective (ie tacit collusion), if it is relatively simple for the remaining players to reach, post-merger, a common understanding on the terms of coordination; monitor to a sufficient degree each other and easily spot deviators; retaliate or credibly threat to retaliate deviators; and outsiders remain unable to jeopardise the results of the said coordination.[147]

The three theories of harm (ie single dominance, non-collusive oligopoly, tacit collusion) discussed in the two previous paragraphs suggest that horizontal mergers that are likely to have non-coordinated or coordinate effects will be banned, in the absence of offsetting efficiencies benefiting consumers. The rationale behind such a ban is that these mergers diminish merging and non-merging parties' ability and incentives to compete without solving a market failure, generating efficiencies or benefiting consumers. In other words, the three theories of harm briefly discussed above seek to ensure that only mergers that are unlikely to have procompetitive effects (as these were defined in section III.A-D above) will be blocked under EUMR. Mergers likely to generate procompetitive effects, are unlikely to give rise to anticompetitive effects, and on this basis should not and will not be banned.

The same conclusion can be reached by examining the three main theories of harm pertaining to vertical or conglomerate mergers. Unlike horizontal mergers that bring together manufacturers of substitute products and could remove a direct competitive constraint, non-horizontal mergers bring together suppliers of complementary or unrelated products. Hence, they do not directly eliminate a competitive constraint. In addition, they are likely to generate efficiencies that increase consumer welfare (eg reduce prices, improve product quality, generate economies of scale/scope, reduce transaction costs).[148] Due to these procompetitive virtues, non-horizontal mergers are considered, in general, less harmful for competition than horizontal mergers.[149]

Nonetheless, non-horizontal mergers may alter existing market structures making coordination between the merged entity and its competitors more likely

[146] HMG (n 12) [25]; EUMR, Recital 25; Commission Decision of 26 April 2006 declaring a concentration compatible with the common market and the functioning of the EEA Agreement (Case COMP/M.3916 – T-Mobile Austria/tele.ring) (in this case the key concern of the Commission was that the proposed acquisition would remove from the Austrian mobile telephony market the operator that had offered the best prices for consumers in recent years. Hence, the Commission sought to remedy the loss of a maverick).

[147] HMG (n 12) [39]–[57]; Case T-342/99, *Airtours v Commission* ECLI:EU:T:2002:146 [62].

[148] NHMG (n 12) [12]–[14]; S Bishop, A Lofaro, F Rosati and J Young, 'The Efficiency-Enhancing Effects of Non-Horizontal Mergers' (2012) Report produced by RBB Economics on behalf of the Enterprise and Industry Directorate-General of the European Commission, available at www.researchgate.net/figure/3-Vertical-integration-between-upstream-and-downstream-sectors_fig2_265271786. For a more critical approach see SC Salop, 'Invigorating Vertical Merger Enforcement' (2018) 127 *The Yale Law Journal* 1962, 1974–82.

[149] NHMG (n 12) [11].

and they may lead to price increases or other competition harms.[150] Alternatively, such mergers can result in input or customer foreclosure when the merged entity has an ability and an incentive to foreclose access to its input or customer base. Such mergers can raise the costs of downstream rivals by restricting their access to an important input or to sufficient customer base.[151] These outcomes are likely to be manifested if the new entity post-merger has: (i) the ability to substantially foreclose access to inputs or customers; (ii) the incentive to do so; and (iii) the foreclosure strategy can have a significant detrimental effect on competition downstream (eg upward pricing pressure in the downstream market).[152] Such detrimental effect is likely when barriers to entry are high; downstream competitors do not pose any credible and sufficient threats; countervailing factors (eg buyer power or entry) are unable to discipline the merged entity; and there are no merger-specific and consumer-relevant verifiable efficiencies.[153]

Accordingly, like in the case of horizontal mergers, the theories of harm articulated for non-horizontal mergers seek to ensure that such concentrations will be unequivocally cleared (or cleared upon certain conditions), if and only if they are a plausible source of procompetitive effects as these were understood under criteria (i)-(iv) above. In other words, the said theories of harm use various criteria, filters and benchmarks to sort out when non-horizontal mergers are likely to have procompetitive virtues. The less likely the latter are, the more likely a finding of a SIEC would be. Consequently, not only horizontal but also vertical or conglomerate mergers that intensify a dimension or parameter of competition while softening another, solve a market failure without overly restricting rivalry, or generate efficiencies that benefit consumers without eliminating residual competition will be considered a credible source of procompetitive gains. Simultaneously, they will also be considered unlikely to have anticompetitive effects and on these grounds will be deemed lawful.

F. The Sources of Procompetitive Effects

The analysis of the case law undertaken above fleshed out four analytical criteria that have been used by the EU courts to identify procompetitive effects. In doing so it identified the range and types of procompetitive effects. In most of the cases discussed above, it could reasonably be argued that the EU courts used more than one of these analytical criteria to infer procompetitive effects. In this sense, the examples of the case law used might satisfy more than one of the identified criteria. Arguably, though, it suffices to satisfy only one to demonstrate procompetitive effects. All four identification criteria clearly suggest that fundamental economic

[150] ibid [79]–[90].
[151] ibid [30].
[152] ibid [31]–[57] (input foreclosure), [58]–[77] (customer foreclosure).
[153] ibid [47]–[57], [72]–[77].

concepts such as market failure,[154] efficiency,[155] and consumer welfare[156] are the key sources from which procompetitive effects flow.

Furthermore, the notion of rivalry, even though less concrete from an economic standpoint, makes its way into the notion of procompetitive effects, and features in all identification criteria. For instance, under criterion (i) the Court does not simply ask whether the agreement addresses a market failure, but whether it does so without unnecessarily[157] restricting the competitive process. If, for instance, a collecting society as in *Tournier* or a patent pool as per Commission's Guidelines on technology transfer agreements is necessary to solve a collective action problem, then competition is not restricted. The same applies to information exchange schemes as suggested by *Asnef-Equifax*. On the contrary, a coordination scheme capable of addressing a market failure but aiming to do so by substituting cooperation for rivalry will not pass the procompetitive effects test as hinted at by *BIDS*. Criterion (ii) compares different dimensions of the competitive process and does so by using certain economic indicators, benchmarks and filters.[158] In criterion (iii), rivalry features through concerns about market power, barriers to entry, the position of existing and potential competitors, and buyers' countervailing power that play a role in the analysis of well-recognised welfare-enhancing arrangements such as vertical restraints. Rivalry is also relevant under criterion (iv) because a practice that eliminates effective competition by removing all or most existing

[154] On the notion of market failure in general, see eg Cooter and Ulen (n 59) 38–41, and Gregory Mankiw, *Principles of Economics* (6th edn, Stamford, CT:Southwestern 2012) 135–51, 195–229.

[155] On the notion of efficiency see S Bishop and M Walker, *The Economics of EC Competition Law: Concepts, Application and Measurement*, 3rd edn (Sweet & Maxwell, 2010). As already noted, efficiency includes productive, allocative and dynamic efficiency, and reductions of transaction costs counts as an efficiency enhancement. Cooter and Ulen (n 59) 87. Efficiency can be understood as Pareto efficiency (ie an allocation of resources is Pareto optimal if no individual can be made better off without making someone worse off) or as Kaldor-Hicks efficiency (ie an allocation that results in some persons being better off and some worse off, and the winners could compensate the losers in such a way that, on balance, everybody is better off. AM Feldman, 'Welfare Economics' in SN Durlauf and LE Blume (eds), *The New Palgrave Dictionary of Economics*, 2nd edn (Palgrave Macmillan, 2008) 721, 722–23; D Winch, *Analytical Welfare Economics* (Penguin, 1971) 143. Efficiency or total welfare 'refers to the aggregate value that an economy produces, without regard for ways that gains or losses are distributed'. See Areeda and Hovenkamp, *Antitrust Law* (2017) 114a.

[156] Consumer welfare refers to the aggregate welfare of consumers as consumers, disregarding the welfare of producers. Under such a standard, if consumers lose from a practice it is counted as inefficient, or anticompetitive, even if producers gain more than consumers lose. SA Salop, 'Question: What is the Real and Proper Antitrust Welfare Standard? Answer: The True Consumer Welfare Standard' (2010) 22 *Loyola Consumer Law Review* 336, 348–53. Consumer welfare can capture short-term and long-term effects on price and output, as well as the non-price dimensions or parameters of competition such as privacy, innovation, and quality OECD, Considering Non-Price Effects in Merger Control – Background Note By the Secretariat, DAF/COMP (2018) 25–32.

[157] A proportionality test is used in this respect. Cases such as *Gøttrup-Klim, Luttikhuis, Tournier, John Deere, Asnef-Equifax* suggest that the agreement should not go beyond what is necessary in restricting competition to solve the relevant market failure. *Société Technique Miniere, Metro I, Pronuptia, Perre Fabre* are also indicative of a proportionality or necessity assessment for identifying procompetitive effects under criterion (ii).

[158] Easterbrook (n 7) 14–17.

sources of actual or potential competition cannot be justified as procompetitive even if it generates efficiencies that are passed on to the consumers.

Against this backdrop, the following section discusses the legal function that procompetitive effects play, suggesting that they function either as counterindicators of prima facie unlawful conduct or as justifications of evidently anticompetitive conduct. In other words, procompetitive effects are used (i) to deny an object finding under either Article 101(1) or 102 TFEU; (ii) to show no harm to competition under an effects analysis under both provisions; or (iii) to provide a justification of a restrictive agreement under Article 101(3) TFEU or of an abuse under Article 102 TFEU.[159] Similarly, when it comes to merger control, procompetitive effects can be used to cast doubt to the existence of non-coordinated or coordinated effects, or to excuse a merger likely to produce such anticompetitive effects in virtue of offsetting procompetitive benefits.

IV. The Role of Procompetitive Effects in Competition Analysis

A. Procompetitive Effects as Counterindicators under Article 101(1) TFEU

When it comes to Article 101 TFEU, procompetitive effects can either cast doubt to the characterisation of an agreement or a practice as a restriction by object or effect under paragraph (1), or once if an agreement or a practice is found to have a restrictive object or effect, they can provide a justification for it under paragraph (3). In the former case procompetitive effects play the role of counterindicators of what would otherwise be a restriction of competition, while in the latter they provide a justification for an evidently anticompetitive agreement or practice.

A long line of case law highlights how procompetitive effects operate as counterindicators under paragraph (1) of Article 101 TFEU. In *Société Technique Minière*, the Court ruled that an agreement that is 'really necessary' for a supplier to enter a new market is not restrictive of competition, whether by object or effect.[160] In *Asnef-Equifax* the information exchange system among credit providers did not qualify as a restriction by object, since it was 'in principle capable of improving the functioning of the supply of credit' and 'of increasing the mobility of consumers of credit'.[161] In *Gottrup-Klim* a joint purchasing agreement was not

[159] Even though Art 102 TFEU does not contain an Art 101(3) equivalent, it is well recognised in the case law that a prima facie abusive practice can be justified. See *United Brands* (n 37) [184]; *Tetra Pak II* (n 112) [136], [207]; *Hilti* (n 112) [102]–[109].

[160] *Société Technique Minière* (n 75) at 250.

[161] *Asnef-Equifax* (n 72) [46]–[56].

considered to be a buyers' cartel, and therefore did not qualify as a restriction by object,[162] for it was making 'way for more effective competition'.[163]

In *Pierre Fabre*, the Court held that clauses in a selective distribution agreement that would otherwise be restrictive by object fall outside Article 101(1) TFEU if there is an 'objective justification' for them.[164] If an agreement is aimed at the 'attainment of a legitimate goal capable of improving competition' – in other words if it is capable of having procompetitive effects – then it would obtain this objective justification.[165] In *Cartes Bancaires*, the Court objected to the characterisation of the arrangement as a by object restriction since the contentious clauses could be understood as a proportionate means to tackle a free-rider problem.[166]

In *Budapest Bank*, the ECJ considered that a multi-lateral interchange fee (MIF) agreement, imposing a uniform amount for interchange fees relating to payments made by cards issued by banks belonging to the card payment system offered by Visa or MasterCard, did not qualify as a restriction by object for the following reasons: the examination of the content and the provisions of agreement did not demonstrate a sufficient degree of harm; the objective of the agreement was to maintain a balance between issuing and acquiring activities within payment systems; there was not sufficient 'solid and reliable' and 'general and consistent' experience that the agreement was harmful to the proper functioning of competition; and, in the absence of the agreement, interchange fees would have been higher.[167] Given that the agreement had a procompetitive explanation (ie sought to tackle a collective action and a free-rider problem) an effects analysis was required to assess the impact of the agreement on competition. Hence, *Budapest Banks* suggests that it is necessary to consider the procompetitive effects of an agreement, before concluding that the agreement restricts competition by object. Thus, 'any time an agreement appears to have ambivalent effects on the market, an effects analysis is required'.[168] If there are 'a priori, strong indications capable

[162] Guidelines on horizontal co-operation agreements (n 64) [200] (noting that joint purchasing can be a cartel-like arrangement if it serves as a tool to engage in price fixing, output limitation or market allocation).

[163] ibid [32] (noting that 'in a market where product prices vary according to the volume of orders, the activities of cooperative purchasing associations may, depending on the size of their membership, constitute a significant counterweight to the contractual power of large producers and make way for more effective competition').

[164] ibid [39].

[165] ibid [40].

[166] ibid [74]. As already noted, though in the end the agreement was found unlawful in virtue of its anticompetitive effects (see n 91).

[167] *Budapest Bank* (n 46) [82]–[83] ('In addition, if there were to be strong indications that, if the MIF Agreement had not been concluded, upwards pressure on interchange fees would have ensued, so that it cannot be argued that that agreement constituted a restriction "by object" of competition on the acquiring market in Hungary, an in-depth examination of the effects of that agreement should be carried out, as part of which, in accordance with the case law recalled in paragraph 55 of the present judgment, it would be necessary to examine competition had that agreement not existed in order to assess the impact of the agreement on the parameters of competition and thereby to determine whether it actually entailed restrictive effects on competition').

[168] Opinion of Advocate General Bobek in *Budapest Bank* (n 46) [81].

of demonstrating' that the agreements are procompetitive or even ambivalent, the restriction by object characterisation is not warranted.[169]

In all these judgments, the ECJ started its analysis by identifying the procompetitive effects that the agreements might have. Such elements are taken into consideration under the by object analysis as elements of the context of the agreement, 'in so far as they are capable of calling into question the overall assessment of whether the concerted practice concerned revealed a sufficient degree of harm to competition'.[170] The fact that the agreements were a plausible source of procompetitive effects was sufficient to conclude that they were not restrictive by object. Consequently, the procompetitive effects of an agreement or a practice can propel against its characterisation as presumptively unlawful, and necessitate an effects analysis for finding an infringement.

It should also be noted that the Court in *Generics* set a precise standard for proving procompetitive effects and repudiating a finding of by object restriction. Following AG Kokott, the Court noted that procompetitive effects should be demonstrated, relevant, specifically related to the agreement concerned and sufficiently significant 'to justify a reasonable doubt as to whether the settlement agreement concerned caused a sufficient degree of harm to competition, and, therefore, as to its anticompetitive object'.[171] The mere existence of procompetitive effects cannot as such preclude a 'restriction by object' characterisation.[172] If such effects are minimal or uncertain they would not pass the test.[173] Therefore, after *Generics* it is clear what is the requisite legal standard for the defendant to make out their case.

The role of procompetitive effects as counterindicators under Article 101(1) TFEU does not end in the by object analysis; it extends further to the by effect inquiry. The purpose of the effects analysis is to demonstrate whether a practice or agreement that has not been found to restrict competition by object has a negative actual or potential effect on competition.[174] This analysis consists of three main steps. First, the plaintiff would have to show that the agreement is capable of restricting competition (eg rivalry) that would have otherwise existed by comparing the conditions in the market with and without the agreement (the so-called counterfactual test).[175] In other words, if the defendant shows either that the conditions of competition would have been the same with and without

[169] Opinion of AG Trstenjak (n 58) [53].

[170] *Generics* (n 47) [103]–[104] ('where the parties to that agreement rely on its pro-competitive effects, those effects must, as elements of the context of that agreement, be duly taken into account for the purpose of its characterization as a "restriction by object"... in so far as they are capable of calling into question the overall assessment of whether the concerted practice concerned revealed a sufficient degree of harm to competition'. Such effects are relevant because they are indicative of 'the objective seriousness of the practice concerned').

[171] *Generics* (n 47) [105]–[107].

[172] ibid [106].

[173] ibid [108], [110].

[174] *Delimitis* (n 109) [13]–[25].

[175] *Pronuptia* (n 75) [16]–[17].

the agreement because, for instance, of the risks and/or the level of the investments involved in a project,[176] the agreement will not be considered as restricting competition.[177]

Second, if an overall procompetitive agreement contains certain suspicious clauses, then the relevant question becomes whether this agreement would have been concluded in the absence of such clauses. If the suspicious clauses are found to be objectively necessary for the procompetitive agreement to exist, then the clauses in question cannot be said to restrict competition (the so-called 'ancillarity doctrine').[178] If, for instance, a clause is necessary for a franchise agreement[179] or to bring a novel product in the market,[180] then such a clause would not be found as restricting competition in virtue of the procompetitive features of the overall arrangement. For example, in *Pronuptia*, the Court after discussing the economics of franchise agreements,[181] considered that certain ostensibly restrictive clauses aimed at preserving the know-how of the franchisor and the uniformity and reputation of their formula were necessary for the overall agreement to take place. On this basis, the Court found that there was no violation of Article 101(1) TFEU (at the time Article 85(1)).[182] Hence, if the clauses in question are strictly necessary for concluding an overall procompetitive agreement, no restriction of competition would be established.

Third, in case the clauses at stake are found not to be objectively necessary to attain a legitimate or procompetitive aim, the plaintiff's job is not done yet. To demonstrate the existence of a restriction by effect they would have to conduct a full-blown effects analysis which essentially involves defining the market, identifying the relevant competitive constraints and ascertaining a mechanism through which anticompetitive effects could be incurred. Such a mechanism can

[176] For example, two pharmaceutical companies seek a medicine that none of them would have been willing to produce alone because of the risks involved. Another example could be an agreement which is necessary for an undertaking to penetrate a new market or an agreement that allows the parties to combine skills and capabilities and develop a product that would not have been able to developed otherwise.

[177] The impact of a practice on competition is to be assessed in the 'actual context' in which it is implemented. *Société Technique Minière* (n 75) at 249, 250; *John Deere* (n 53) [76]; *Asnef-Equifax* (n 72) [49]; *Generics* (n 47) [116].

[178] Case 42/84, *Remia BV and others v Commission* EU:C:1985:327 [19] (suggesting that a noncompete obligation may be necessary for the buyer to agree to the acquisition of a business to the extent that it is, it would not restrict competition, whether by object or effect).

[179] Franchise agreements have been found in general as procompetitive for various reasons. For instance, because they allow an undertaking penetrate a new market. See *Société Technique Minière* (n 75) at 250; *Pronuptia* (n 75) 15–17.

[180] Guidelines on Vertical Restraints (n 77) [172], [185], [191], [202], [207].

[181] *Pronuptia* (n 75) [15]–[17]. The Court noted that such agreements grant (i) to independent traders, for a fee, the right to establish themselves in other markets using their business name (ie a way for an undertaking to derive financial benefit from its expertise without investing its own capital) and (ii) to traders, who do not have the necessary experience, access to methods which they could have learned with considerable effort, and allows them to benefit from the reputation of the franchisor.

[182] ibid [16]–[17] (noting that for such a to work it is necessary (i) to protect the know-how of the franchisor via non-compete obligations and prior-approval for transfers, and (ii) to protect the uniformity and the reputation of the franchise).

take two forms: anticompetitive effects could be incurred either via collusion (ie absorption of a source of competitive pressure or reduction in the incentives to compete) or via exclusion (ie removal of a source of competitive pressure or inhibiting a competitor's ability to compete). In the first scenario rivals' incentive to compete are diminished, whereas in the second what is lessened is their ability to compete. On both occasions a negative effect to the parameters of competition (ie price, output, choice, quality, innovation) to the detriment of consumers is to be expected.[183] Hence, the purpose of this analysis is to show that the agreement is unlikely to have any procompetitive virtues and likely to bear anticompetitive effects before declaring it null and void.

B. Procompetitive Effects as Counterindicators under Article 102 TFEU

When it comes to Article 102 TFEU the role of procompetitive effects as counterindicators is similar to the role they play under 101(1) TFEU. They can either deny a finding of a by object abuse or show no harm to competition. Arguably a similar distinction between by object and by effect abuses (or types of analysis) exists under Article 102 TFEU.[184] Naked restrictions, exclusive dealing,[185] tying,[186] loyalty rebates,[187] and predatory pricing (ie pricing below average variable cost)[188] could qualify as by object abuses, whereas selective price cuts,[189] standardised rebates,[190] refusal to deal[191] and margin squeeze[192] could be categorised as by effect abuses.

[183] *Delimitis* (n 109) [24]–[27], [30]–[32]; P Ibañez Colomo, 'Anticompetitive Effects in EU Competition Law' (2020) 17 *Journal of Competition Law & Economics* 337–42.

[184] Whish and Bailey (n 5) 206.

[185] *Hoffmann-La Roche* (n 34) [89]–[90]; *Intel* (n 9) [138]–[139].

[186] Guidance (n 114) [48] (tying refers the commercial practice according to which customers that purchase one product (the tying product) are required also to purchase another product from the dominant undertaking (the tied product); *Hilti* (n 112) [99]–[101], [115]–[119]. Even though in *Microsoft* the Commission examined closely the actual effects and sought for a foreclosure effect. Case T-201/04, *Microsoft Corp. v Commission of the European Communities (Microsoft)* ECLI:EU:T:2007:289 [43]–[45], [842], [846]–[859].

[187] Case C-549/10 P, *Tomra Systems and Others* v *Commission* EU:C:2012:221 [70], [71] (noting that 'in that regard, it is necessary to consider all the circumstances, particularly the criteria and rules governing the grant of the rebate, and to investigate whether, in providing an advantage not based on any economic service justifying it, the rebates tend to remove or restrict the buyer's freedom to choose his sources of supply, to bar competitors from access to the market, or to strengthen the dominant position by distorting competition').

[188] *AKZO* (n 124) [71], [72].

[189] *Post Danmark I* (n 36) [20]–[28].

[190] *Post Danmark II* (n 131) [7], [20], [32], [37].

[191] *Magil* (n 127) [49]–[55]; *Oscar Bronner* (n 125) [27]–[47].

[192] Case C-280/08 P, *Deutsche Telekom AG v European Commission* ECLI:EU:C:2010:603 [148], [155]–[185], [199], [234]–[236], [253]–[259]; Case C-52/09, *Konkurrensverket v TeliaSonera Sverige AB (TeliaSonera)* EU:C:2011:83 [60]–[77].

While it is true that if a 'naked restriction' is established, it cannot be countered based on efficiency claims or on the absence of actual anticompetitive effects,[193] it would not be accurate to say that procompetitive effects do not function as counterindicators on this occasion. The existence of procompetitive effects, as defined in section III.A-D, would suggest that there is no naked restriction in the first place. In other words, the practices that are recognised as naked restrictions under Article 102 TFEU are deprived of any procompetitive rationale. If the practice has a procompetitive explanation, it will not qualify as a naked restriction. Hence, the defendant can raise procompetitive claims even at the initial stage of the analysis to block a finding that their practice is a naked restriction. For example, in *Intel*, Intel's payments to customers who agreed to delay or cancel the marketing of competitor's products were described as 'naked restrictions' of competition.[194] Other examples of naked restrictions are Irish Sugar's purchases of a competitor's sugar from customers in order to replace it with its own sugar;[195] AstraZeneca's misuse of regulatory procedures;[196] and Lithuanian Railways' dismantling of a section of rail track to prevent a customer from using a competitor's services.[197] The common denominator of all these practices is that they are not a plausible source of any procompetitive effects as these are understood here. If such procompetitive effects existed they would indicate the absence of a naked restriction.

Exclusivity rebates could be considered another type of by object abuse according to *Hoffmann Laroche*.[198] Yet, if a prima facie exclusionary rebate scheme is shown to be incapable of excluding an as-efficient competitor, it would not qualify as an abuse since it would be considered as a credible source of procompetitive gains.[199] Thus, it is clear post-*Intel* that rebates that may have a loyalty-inducing effect would not be considered abusive if they are incapable of having a market foreclosure effect to an undertaking as efficient as the dominant undertaking (the AEC test).[200]

With regards to predation the ECJ has repeatedly said that there is no recoupment requirement.[201] This inability to justify predation by proving the lack of a

[193] *ENEL* (n 9) [53]–[56].

[194] Commission Decision of relating to a proceeding under Article 82 of the EC Treaty and Article 54 of the EEA Agreement (COMP/C-3 /37.990 – Intel) [1641]–[1681], upheld on appeal Case T-286/09 *Intel v Commission* EU:T: 2014:547 [198]–[220] (this practice was not discussed on further appeal to the Court of Justice).

[195] Case T-228/97, *Irish Sugar plc v Commission* EU:T:1999:246 [226]–[235].

[196] Case T-321/05, *AstraZeneca AB v Commission* EU:T:2010:266 [352]–[613]; Case C-457/10 P, *AstraZeneca AB and AstraZeneca plc v European Commission* EU:C:2012:770 [36]–[52], [55]–[60], [74]–[100], [105]–[113], [129]–[141], [147]–[156].

[197] Case T-814/17, *Lietuvos geležinkeliai AB v Commission* EU:T:2020:545 [76]–[283].

[198] *Hoffmann-La Roche* (n 34) [89]–[91].

[199] *Intel* (n 9) [136]–[144].

[200] *Post Danmark I* (n 36) [29].

[201] *France Télécom v Commission* (n 124) [110] ('it does not follow from the case law of the Court that proof of the possibility of recoupment of losses suffered by the applicant, by an undertaking in a dominant position, of prices lower than a certain level of costs constitutes a necessary precondition to establishing that such a pricing policy is abusive').

dangerous probability of recoupment may signal that when it comes to predation, procompetitive effects could not function as counterindicators. Yet, this would not be accurate. The Court adopted this position pertaining to recoupment because it considered that pricing below average variable cost cannot be a credible source of procompetitive gains. Such a pricing strategy is highly likely to generate anticompetitive effects as it does not make economic sense except as a monopolisation strategy.[202] Hence, procompetitive effects were already incorporated in the crafting of the test.[203] Would the addition of a recoupment requirement for establishing predation bring additional coherence to the abuse of dominance law in virtue of *Intel*[204] ? In other words, should the existing law on predation be considered as an outlier, implying that a 'clarification' is due to allow the defendant to claim procompetitive effects on the basis of low likelihood or impossibility of recoupment? Arguably, such a development would be problematic since it would give more than appropriate weight to claims of procompetitive effects at the initial stage of the analysis.[205]

Another type of abuse that could lead to an objection to the proposition that procompetitive effects function as counterindicators also under Article 102 TFEU is tying. As things currently stand, the plaintiff has to only show that an undertaking is dominant in the tying market; the tying and tied products are distinct products; and the tying practice is likely to lead to anticompetitive foreclosure.[206] Accordingly, this test could be viewed as entailing that procompetitive effects are to be used only to justify a prima facie anticompetitive tying, and not to counter its finding in the first place.[207] Yet, the dominance prong[208] requires that the

[202] *France Télécom v Commission* (n 124) [112] ('lack of any possibility of recoupment of losses is not sufficient to prevent the undertaking concerned reinforcing its dominant position so that the degree of competition existing on the market, already weakened precisely because of the presence of the undertaking concerned, is further reduced and customers suffer loss').

[203] In line with Intel the existing test suggests that pricing below AVC is incapable of foreclosing an equally efficient competitor and should be presumed procompetitive. See *Intel* (n 9) [138], [139].

[204] ibid [138]–[147].

[205] Pricing below AVC is unlikely to be a plausible source of procompetitive effects. Furthermore, if the authority intervenes only when recoupment is probable it will not be able to prevent predatory strategies aimed at (i) preventing the competitor from competing vigorously instead of eliminating them, (ii) preventing or delaying a decline in prices that would have otherwise occurred. Guidance Paper (n 114) paras 69 and 71; H Hovenkamp, 'Predatory Pricing under the Areeda-Turner Test' (2015) *Faculty Scholarship at Penn Law* 1, 3–11 (arguing that such a test would suffer from a serious problem of underdeterrence).

[206] Guidance Paper (n 114) [47]–[62]. Although a common commercial practice, tying may violate TFEU, Art 102 where. The requirement of foreclosure effects was added in *Microsoft* (n 186) [842], [859]–[862], [867]–[869].

[207] Guidance Paper (n 114) [62] (suggesting that type-(ii) or (iv) procompetitive effects can be raised only as a defence). In *Hilti* and *Tetra Pak II* the Commission and the Court presumed anticompetitive effects and were strict on procompetitive claims. *Hilti* (n 112) [99]–[101], [115]–[119]; *Tetra Pak II* (n 112) [82]–[85], [134]–[141]. In *Microsoft* and *Google Shopping*, the two undertakings claimed that there tie-ins were procompetitive. Their claims where assessed by the Court mainly as possible justifications of a prima facie abusive conduct. See *Microsoft* (n 186) [1091]–[1101]; Case T-612/17, *Google LLC, formerly Google Inc. and Alphabet, Inc v European Commission (Google Shopping)* ECLI:EU:T:2021:763 [140], [251], [513], [544], [545], [557], [558], [560], [615].

[208] As already noted in section III.E, the dominance requirement functions as a general-applicatior filter of pro- and anticompetitive effects.

defendant can argue that their practice does not consist in anticompetitive tying for it is not able to act 'to an appreciable extent … independently of its competitors, customers and ultimately of its consumers'.[209] In addition, the distinct product requirement allows the defendant to claim that the tying and tied products in fact are not distinct – eg no substantial number of consumers would buy the tied product – and show thereby that the tie-in generates procompetitive gains because it brings to the market a product which would not have been produced otherwise, as its stand-alone production would not be profitable.[210] Hence, the legal test for tying allows the defendant to use procompetitive effects as counterindicators of an abuse.[211] In addition, after *Intel* and *ENEL* it can be argued that the dominant undertaking can rebut a finding of anticompetitive tying by showing that its practice is not capable of producing foreclosure effects.[212]

According to ECJ case law, if it is not the object of a dominant firm's conduct to harm competition, a finding of abuse is warranted only if actual or potential anticompetitive effects are demonstrated.[213] Actual or potential consumer harm is not required to establish such restrictive or distorting effects; harm to the structure of competition will suffice to infer consumer harm and find a breach of Article 102 TFEU.[214] As noted in *ENEL*, a competition authority is not required to show that a practice has the capacity to harm consumers; it will satisfy its burden of proof by demonstrating that a practice is likely to undermine competition, by using resources or means other than those governing an effective competitive structure.[215]

Consequently, to establish a by effect abuse, the plaintiff must show that the practice pursued by the dominant undertaking is capable of having actual or potential anticompetitive effects. Yet, the plaintiff is not required to establish actual effects; it suffices to show that the conduct in question is capable of restricting

[209] *United Brands* (n 37) [65].

[210] The distinct product test can be understood as a filter to screen out procompetitive tying. If both products are not distinct, ie are in general demanded and offered as a tie by the industry regardless of market power of firms, it is safe to assume that the tie-in or bundle is efficient. D Evans, J Padilla and C Ahlborn, 'The Antitrust Economics of Tying: A Farewell to Per Se Illegality' (2003) available at ssrn.com/abstract=381940; K-U Kuhn, Stillman, R Stillman and C Caffarra, 'Economic Theories of Bundling and Their Policy Implications in Abuse Cases: An Assessment in Light of the Microsoft Case' (2004), available at ssrn.com/abstract=618589; *Microsoft* (n 186) [917]–[922].

[211] The question whether this or any other Art 102 TFEU legal test gives *sufficient weight* to procompetitive effects as counterindicators remains and is separate from the question whether procompetitive effects play this role in general. In other words, one might argue that the existing test on tying is overly strict and likely to generate false positives because it makes it excessively hard for the defendant to use procompetitive effects as counterindicators. This may or may not be the case; but the point made here is only that procompetitive effects also function as counterindicators in the abuse of dominance case law. The question of 'sufficient weight' (ie whether procompetitive effects play this role *satisfactorily* with regards to a particular abuse) requires a normative inquiry that goes beyond the scope of this study.

[212] Guidance Paper (n 114) [52]–[58].

[213] *TeliaSonera* (n 192) [64]; *Post Danmark I* (n 36) [26]; *Post Danmark II* (n 131) [29]; In several cases the Commission sought to produce anticompetitive effects. *Microsoft* (n 186) [1031]–[1090]; *Google Shopping* (n 207) [368]–[395], [401]–[442], [432]–[459].

[214] *ENEL* (n 9) [44].

[215] ibid [47], [53].

competition and/or to demonstrate potential effects depending on the category of abuse.[216] In this context, it could be argued that when it comes to by effects abuses (ie categories of practices that are in principle considered as plausible sources of procompetitive effects), procompetitive effects could be used to deny the existence of anticompetitive effects. Therefore, with regard to a by effect abuse the defendant can either show a lack of anticompetitive effects[217] or demonstrate that the effects deriving from the practice are essentially procompetitive, to indicate that there is no prima facie abuse.

For example, selective price cuts will be found abusive only if, without objective justification, they produce an actual or likely exclusionary effect on as-efficient competitors.[218] Such price cuts would be detrimental for competition and reduce consumer welfare. Otherwise, price discrimination would be considered procompetitive and lawful as the exclusion of less efficient rivals is likely to generate efficiencies, intensify rivalry and benefit consumers. Standardised or quantity rebates will also be found unlawful if the plaintiff demonstrates actual or potential anticompetitive effects.[219] This test presumes that such rebates are a plausible source of procompetitive effects and allows the defendant to cast doubt on a finding of anticompetitive effects. The defendant may claim that the features of the rebate scheme (eg granting criteria, reference period, market coverage, economic justification) and the market context suggest that the scheme in question is, for instance, likely to generate efficiencies without softening rivalry.[220]

Another example of a by effect abuse is refusal to deal, which is notoriously hard to establish as the plaintiff has to show indispensability, the absence of objective justification and the elimination of all effective competition.[221] The indispensability requirement is an avenue by which the defendant can claim that there is no

[216] ibid [50], [53].

[217] As already noted, the dominant undertaking cannot escape liability only by showing the absence of concrete anticompetitive effects; it has to show in addition that this absence is not attributable to external factors (ibid [56]). Yet, the categorisation of a practice as abusive cannot be altered simply by the fact that it ultimately did not achieve the desired result. See *Google Shopping* (n 207) [442]; *TeliaSonera* (n 192) [64], [65].

[218] *Post Danmark I* (n 36) [22], [25].

[219] *Post Danmark II* (n 131) [23], [28]–[42].

[220] ibid [31] ('it first has to be determined whether those rebates can produce an exclusionary effect, that is to say whether they are capable, first, of making market entry very difficult or impossible for competitors of the undertaking in a dominant position and, secondly, of making it more difficult or impossible for the co-contractors of that undertaking to choose between various sources of supply or commercial partners. It then has to be examined whether there is an objective economic justification for the discounts granted'). If competition on the market is very limited (eg high barriers to entry, existence of significant economies of scale, structural advantages enjoyed by the dominant undertaking, a must stock item) a rebate scheme can make it more difficult for dominant undertaking's customers to obtain supplies from competing undertakings, and thus it can produce an anti-competitive exclusionary effect). See also *Tomra* (n 187) [72].

[221] *Magil* (n 127) [52]; *Oscar Bronner* (n 125) [46] ('For such access *to be capable of being regarded as indispensable*, it would be necessary at the very least to establish, as the Advocate General has pointed out at point 68 of his Opinion, that it is not economically viable to create a second home-delivery scheme for the distribution of daily newspapers with a circulation comparable to that of the daily newspapers distributed by the existing scheme').

abuse since: (i) access to their input or facility is not necessary for intensifying competition or for producing new or better products or services; and (ii) a duty to deal would undermine their R&D investments and innovation efforts.[222] In this sense, the indispensability requirement[223] operates as a limiting principle precluding overenforcement. This requirement makes procompetitive effects cognisable at the stage of establishing a refusal to supply as the defendant can highlight the procompetitive aspects or effects of their conduct (and the absence of competition harm) when debating this point of law. For instance, they can argue that access to the input is not necessary for rivals to compete upstream or downstream or that a refusal to supply does not preclude an equally efficient competitor from providing the target product.

In margin-squeeze cases the legal test is twofold. First, it should be examined whether given the wholesale and retail price charged by the dominant undertaking an equally efficient rival could not profitably offer their products (or would have to sell at a loss); and second, whether the margin squeeze is likely to exclude equally efficient competitors.[224] Yet, in the absence of any effect on the competitive situation of competitors, the Court said, such a pricing practice cannot be classified as an exclusionary practice.[225] Hence, to find an abuse, the authority or the court would have to examine if the pricing practice at stake hinders 'the ability of competitors at least as efficient as the dominant undertaking to trade on the downstream market'.[226] Therefore, there is scope for the defendant to oppose a finding of abuse by demonstrating the procompetitive effects of the practice (eg by showing that the practice did not create any barriers to the growth of the retail market).[227]

Generally, to ascertain a prima facie abuse under Article 102 TFEU the nature of the practice, and its potential to harm competition and consumers, should be established.[228] If the conduct is not a plausible source of procompetitive effects (ie if it does not satisfy any of the four identification criteria presented above), it would be presumptively unlawful irrespective of its impact on competition (ie naked restriction).[229] If the conduct is presumed to be capable of having procompetitive effects (eg if it can intensify competition by excluding a less efficient rival,

[222] AG Jacobs in *Oscar Bronner* (n 125) [57]–[58].

[223] It could be argued that the indispensability requirement is a manifestation of the as-efficient competitor principle discussed in section III.E as it requires showing that the input cannot be replicated in an economically viable manner by a firm that is equally efficient as the dominant one.

[224] *Deutsche Telekom* (n 192) [177]–[183]; *TeliaSonera* (n 192) [31]–[34], [61]–[77]. The cost and prices of the dominant undertaking are the relevant benchmark (only exceptionally those of competitors [46]. Demonstrating concrete or actual effects is not necessary, but at least a potential effect affecting as efficient competitors needs to be established [64], [66], [72].

[225] *TeliaSonera* (n 192) [66]; *Deutsche Telekom* (n 192) [254].

[226] *TeliaSonera* (n 192) [54]–[55], [67].

[227] ibid [62].

[228] Ibañez Colomo, 'What is an Abuse of a Dominant Position?' (2022) 3.

[229] *Hoffmann-La Roche* (n 34) [89]–[91]; Case T-286/09, *RENV Intel Corporation Inc v European Commission* ECLI:EU:T:2022:19 [27], [32], [45], [86]–[96]; Ibañez Colomo (n 39) 17. Conduct may be said to be inherently abusive where it can be safely presumed to have anticompetitive effects irrespective of the context of which it is a part

generate efficiencies or net consumer benefits without fully eliminating effective competition), it will be deemed a valid expression of competition on the merits, and thereby it will be considered prima facie lawful.[230] In this case only if actual or potential anticompetitive effects are shown (eg anticompetitive foreclosure) will such a practice be considered abusive. On such an occasion the dominant undertaking can deny the existence of anticompetitive effects or claim procompetitive effects – as understood in section III.A-D – to cast doubt to the existence of competition harm. To be sure, the absence of actual anticompetitive effects is not sufficient, in itself, to preclude the application of Article 102 TFEU,[231] but it can be an indication that the conduct in question was not capable of restricting competition.[232]

It is not entirely clear what the threshold is for proving procompetitive effects as counterindicators under Article 102 TFEU. No similar statement to the one found in *Generics* exists with regard to by object or by effect abuses. The ECJ has not expressed any overarching principle in this regard, and as a result the standard of proof of procompetitive effects has raised controversies in numerous cases. Yet, this absence of an overarching principle for establishing procompetitive effects should not come as a surprise. Competition assessments under Article 101 TFEU consist in a by object and a by effect inquiry, whereas the Article 102 TFEU analysis is structured around legal tests associated with particular categories of abusive conduct. Hence, the threshold of procompetitive effects could be assumed to vary with the category of abuse and symmetrically to the threshold of anticompetitive effects. The more likely the anticompetitive effects of a specific type of abuse are assumed to be, the higher the threshold for establishing procompetitive effects must be. The less likely the anticompetitive effects are assumed to be, the lower the threshold must be for establishing procompetitive effects.

For instance, in the case of naked restrictions, ie practices assumed to be deprived of any procompetitive virtues, establishing actual or potential anticompetitive effects is not necessary since such effects can safely assumed to be likely. Thus, it would be reasonable to expect from the defendant to prove with certainty or quasi-certainty the relevant procompetitive effects to repudiate a 'naked restriction' characterisation. For predation the threshold for demonstrating procompetitive effects could be a tad lower (eg high likelihood), but still relatively high. This would be reasonable since if an authority or plaintiff has managed to provide evidence of pricing below average variable cost, anticompetitive effects could be safely assumed.[233] Therefore, the defendant would have to make a

[230] Ibañez Colomo (n 39) 5, 8, 25.

[231] *ENEL* (n 9) [55], [54] (noting that even when a conduct has been in place for a sufficiently long time, the fact that it did not produce concrete anticompetitive effects does not automatically mean that such conduct did not have such capacity).

[232] ibid [56] (noting that it is up to the dominant undertaking to supplement this prima facie evidence with evidence showing that the lack of concrete effects was indeed the consequence of the inability of the conduct to have such effects and [54] noting that such a lack of effects could result from other causes such as changes in the relevant market or dominant firm's inability of the dominant undertaking to carry out the anticompetitive strategy'.

[233] Intel (n 9) [139].

compelling case of procompetitive effects to justify (but not counter) a finding of abuse. For exclusivity rebates, tying, and bundling, the threshold appears to (or should) be even lower since these practices are considered generally capable of procompetitive effects, and likely to produce anticompetitive effects only under specific conditions.[234] The threshold for proving procompetitive effects could be assumed to be even lower for margin squeeze and refusal to deal as such practices are less likely to bear anticompetitive effects.[235] For this reason margin squeeze and refusals to deal are subject to different, but relatively strict conditions.[236]

Accordingly, as a matter of principle it could be said that the more likely the competition harm, the higher the threshold of procompetitive effects should be, and the more remote or unlikely the anticompetitive effects, the easier it should be to establish procompetitive effects.[237] Nonetheless, no such overarching principle can be discerned in the abuse of dominance case law at the moment.

C. Procompetitive Effects as Justifications of Anticompetitive Conduct

The previous analysis shows that procompetitive effects can function as counterindicators, (i) debunking a presumption of unlawfulness when it comes to agreements or practices that are deemed prima facie unlawful irrespective of their actual or potential anticompetitive effects; or (ii) casting doubt to the existence of actual or potential anticompetitive effects when an effects analysis is carried out. However, the role of procompetitive effects in competition analysis does not stop there. The procompetitive aspects or effects of an agreement or practice can excuse it, despite its anticompetitive object or effects. For example, if an agreement is found to be restrictive by object or by effect under Article 101(1) TFEU, it can still be saved if it satisfies the cumulative conditions of Article 101(3) TFEU, as already noted above. Hence, Article 101(3) TFEU exists to ensure that an agreement that has an anticompetitive object or actual or potential anticompetitive effects could still be lawful as long as its positive effects to competition and consumers outweigh its negative ones.

In this regard, one might argue that Article 101(3) TFEU serves no purpose since the procompetitive effects of an agreement are already considered under Article 101(1) TFEU. Nonetheless, such an argument would be misguided. First, Article 101(3) TFEU involves a balancing exercise whereby anticompetitive effects

[234] ibid.

[235] *TeliaSonera* (n 192) [31]–[34], [61]–[77]; *Oscar Bronner* (n 125) [37]–[47]; *Magil* (n 127) [49]–[56].

[236] Opinion of AG Jacobs in *Oscar Bronner* (n 125) [57]; *TeliaSonera* (n 192) [41]–[48], [69]–[74] (clarifying that clarified that the *Oscar Bronner* requirements do not need to be satisfied in order to establish margin squeeze liability. Hence refusal to supply and margin squeeze are treated by the ECJ as two distinct infringements, with the latter requiring a less demanding test. The potentially exclusionary effect of negative margin squeeze suffices to be 'probable' to establish an abuse, while in the case of a positive margin it must be demonstrated that that the conduct is 'likely to have the consequence that it would be at least more difficult for the operators concerned to trade on the market concerned').

[237] Ibañez Colomo, 'Anticompetitive Effects' (2020) 343–48.

are measured against procompetitive ones, whereas Article 101(1) mainly involves a screening exercise aimed at identifying the anticompetitive object of effects of an agreement.[238] Such screening exercise can be more superficial (ie by object analysis) where there is already established knowledge or experience suggesting that an agreement of that kind is obviously inimical to competition or more in-depth (ie by effect analysis) when the agreement has ambivalent effects and a more cautious analysis is required to identify actual or potential negative effects.

Consequently, in the context of Article 101(1) TFEU, the procompetitive aspects of an agreement are indispensable to discern either the object of the agreement in question (ie what it can objectively achieve, irrespective of the subjective intent of the parties) or whether the agreement is likely to have anticompetitive effects (eg lead to collusion or market foreclosure). In this respect, procompetitive effects are indicia that could be used to either deny a finding of a restriction by object or to cast doubt on the existence of harm to competition under an effects analysis.[239] On the other hand, in the context of Article 101(3) TFEU, the role of procompetitive effects is to substantiate a justification of a (by object or by effect) restrictive agreement. The analysis of procompetitive effects is more intense at this stage. Under Article 101(1) TFEU, the question is whether the agreement is a plausible source of procompetitive gains (ie by object analysis) or likely to have actual or potential anticompetitive effects (ie by effect analysis). A cursory analysis suffices, and no quantification is needed.[240] The analysis is much deeper under Article 101(3) TFEU. If the authority establishes an anticompetitive object or effect, the burden of proof shifts, and it is for the defendant to show that the procompetitive gains generated by the agreement are likely to outweigh its anticompetitive object or effect. Such burden-shifting is reasonable since it relies on a proximity principle,[241] and takes place when it is established that the agreement, despite the relevant counterindications, is restrictive by object or by effect.

In voluminous case law the ECJ has reiterated that it is open to a dominant undertaking to provide justification for behaviour liable to be caught by the prohibition under Article 102 TFEU.[242] To make out such a justification the dominant undertaking has two options: either to demonstrate that its conduct is objectively necessary;[243] or that its conduct produces or is likely to produce efficiencies that are sufficient to guarantee that no net harm to consumers is likely to arise.[244]

[238] *O2 (Germany)* (n 93) [69]–[73].

[239] The analysis of the pro-competitive aspects of an agreement is relatively superficial under the first paragraph as indicated by *Asnef-Equifax* (n 72) [46]–[63], *Pierre Fabre* (n 84) [32]–[47]; *Cartes Bancaires* (n 2) [48]–[94]; *Pronuptia* (n 75) [9]–[27]; *Delimitis* (n 110) [10]–[12].

[240] Case T-111/08, *MasterCard, Inc. and Others v European Commission*, ECLI:EU:T:2012:260 [80].

[241] The actors who have cheaper access to the relevant evidence are asked to provide them.

[242] *United Brands* (n 37) [184]; Joined Cases C-241/91 P and C-242/91 P *RTE and ITP* v *Commission* [1995] ECR I-743 [54], [55]; and *TeliaSonera* (n 192) [31], [75].

[243] Case C-311/84, *Centre belge d'études de marché – Télémarketing (CBEM) v SA Compagnie luxembourgeoise de télédiffusion (CLT) and Information publicité Benelux (IPB)* ECLI:EU:C:1985:394 [27].

[244] *British Airways v Commission* (n 11) [86]; *TeliaSonera* (n 192) [76].

To successfully plead the latter, the dominant undertaking has to show that there are efficiency gains likely to result from the conduct under consideration; that such gains counteract or outweigh any likely negative effects on competition and consumer welfare in the affected markets; that the conduct in question is indispensable for the realisation of the said efficiencies (no less anticompetitive alternative); and that it does not eliminate effective competition, by removing all or most existing sources of actual or potential competition.[245] Therefore, as in the case of Article 101 TFEU, procompetitive effects could be used in the context of Article 102 TFEU to make out a justification for anticompetitive conduct, even though such a justification is difficult to succeed.[246]

Procompetitive effects also play a similar role in merger control. It is well recognised that mergers can bring about efficiencies.[247] Therefore, in order to assess whether a merger would significantly impede effective competition,[248] the Commission needs to perform an overall competitive appraisal which involves analysing the likelihood of non-coordinated[249] or coordinated effects[250] against any merger-specific and verifiable efficiencies that benefit the consumers.[251] These three conditions are cumulative and exist to ensure that the efficiencies generated by a merger would likely enhance the ability and incentive of the merged entity to compete fiercely for the benefit of consumers.[252] In other words, the raison d'être of these three conditions is to ensure that the procompetitive aspects or effects of the proposed concentration would counteract or outweigh the adverse effects on competition which it might otherwise have. Therefore, also under merger control procompetitive effects function as a justification of an otherwise anticompetitive practice.[253]

V. Conclusion: The Changing Role of Procompetitive Effects and the Bounds of EU Competition Law

Procompetitive effects have always played an important role in the analysis of the key provisions of EU competition law. Yet, as the law evolves we can observe that

[245] *Post Danmark I* (n 36) [42].

[246] It is not sufficient for the dominant undertaking to put forward 'vague, general and theoretical arguments' in support of an objective justification. *Microsoft* (n 6) [698]; Guidance Paper (n 114) [31]. Whish and Bailey (n 5) 222 (noting that they are not aware of any case where an efficiency defence has succeeded under Art 102).

[247] EUMR, Recital 4 (noting that mergers are capable of increasing dynamic competition and the competitiveness of industry, thereby improving the conditions of growth and raising the standard of living in the Community).

[248] EUMR, Art 2(2) and (3).

[249] HMG (n 12) [24]–[38]; NHMG (n 12) [29]–[78].

[250] HMG (n 12) [39]–[57]; NHMG (n 12) [79]–[90].

[251] HMG (n 12) [76]–[88]. NHMG (n 12) [53].

[252] HMG (n 12) [77].

[253] As in the case of TFEU, Art 102, this author is not aware of any case where an efficiency defence was successful.

the concept has acquired a more concrete meaning.[254] When the EU courts or the Commission seek to identify whether a practice or an agreement is capable of having procompetitive effects, they examine whether it alleviates a market failure in a non-anticompetitive manner; whether it intensifies a dimension or parameter of competition while softening another; whether it makes possible a welfare-enhancing arrangement or increases the value of a product or a service without eliminating or overly restricting rivalry; or whether it leads to net consumer welfare gains without fully eliminating effective competition. There could be overlaps between these identification criteria, and a particular finding of procompetitive effects may satisfy more than one of these criteria. Yet, it is argued here that under the existing case law it is sufficient to satisfy one of these criteria to establish procompetitive effects. Against this background, it could be also said that the fundamental economic concepts of market failure, efficiency and consumer welfare, and the less concrete, yet still economically informed, notion of rivalry operate as the main sources of inspiration for procompetitive effects.

Furthermore, this study showed that not only the meaning but also the legal role of procompetitive effects is similar in all three main areas of EU competition law: they function as either counterindicators or justifications. Two clarifications are due in this regard. First, it should be noted that the legal techniques through which procompetitive effect may be inferred differs depending on the relevant provision.[255] This is hardly surprising given that competition analysis under Article 101 TFEU consists in a by object and a by effect inquiry; under Article 102 TFEU is structured around legal tests attached to particular categories of abuse; and under EUMR involves a two-step exercise under which the authority examines, first, if a concentration is likely to generate non-coordinated or coordinated effects and, second, if these effects are outweighed by merger-specific and verifiable efficiencies that benefit the consumers.

The second clarification pertains to the relationship between the four identification criteria and the two legal roles that procompetitive effects play. Arguably, procompetitive effects type (i)-(iii) function as counterindicators, while type (iv) are usually invoked as justifications of a prima facie unlawful practice or agreement. Type (iv) procompetitive effects are mainly used as justifications because at this later stage of analysis competition harm has already been established, and procompetitive effects need to be clear-cut and highly probable to excuse the practice. Undoubtedly, type (iv) procompetitive effects are the most clear-cut case of effects beneficial to competition. However, the fact that type (iv) procompetitive effects usually serve as justification, does not imply that they cannot also function as a counterindicators. For instance, when an agreement or practice is highly likely to generate type (iv) procompetitive effects, it will be considered prima facie

[254] Arguably, the more economic approach and the effects-based approach have contributed to this evolution. See AC Witt, *The More Economic Approach to EU Antitrust Law* (Hart Publishing, 2016) 110–58.

[255] See for instance the discussion on tying in section IV.A.

lawful or easily escape the by object characterisation and be subjected to an effects analysis. Under the latter, the same type of procompetitive effects could be also used to deny the existence of competition harm.

Another crucial point is that the concept of procompetitive effects remains relatively open. The category of procompetitive effects is not exhaustive and it could be maintained that new economic[256] insights can reveal new types of procompetitive effects. In this sense, the bounds of EU competition law, even though relatively stable, are simultaneously sufficiently flexible to allow for contextualised application and adaptation to epistemic change. As observed by Amato, the border of antitrust law shifts in light of new economic knowledge, market developments, broader policy considerations and value judgments.[257]

In this regard, a particular trend is observable: the EU courts are frontloading procompetitive effects at the first stage of the analysis of all key regimes rather than leaving them to the assessment of Article 101(3) TFEU, Article's 102 TFEU and merger control's efficiency defence. Take, for instance, *BIDS*. In her Opinion, AG Trstenjak considered that to find whether the agreements at issue constitute a restriction by object the reviewing court should examine whether 'the restrictive elements are necessary in order to achieve a procompetitive object'.[258] Having not found an unobjectionable procompetitive object of the BIDS agreements, the AG considered that the agreement will have, as a necessary consequence, a restriction of competition.[259] The Court arrived at a similar conclusion without however referring to procompetitive effects. The Court considered that this type of arrangement 'conflicts patently with the concept inherent in the EC Treaty provisions relating to competition, according to which each economic operator must determine independently the policy which it intends to adopt on the common market' as it deliberately substitutes practical cooperation between undertakings for the risks of competition.[260] Therefore, *BIDS* suggests that a restraint can qualify as a restriction by object if it can be safely presumed to have anticompetitive effects.[261]

Gradually the role of procompetitive effects as counterindicators became more prominent. After *Cartes Bancaires*, *Budapest Bank*, and *Generics*, it would be safe to say that a restriction by object is not an arrangement that is obviously

[256] Here economics are understood in the broadest sense possible as including not only microeconomics but also behavioural economics, feminist economics and environmental economics.

[257] Amato (n 16) 96.

[258] Opinion of AG Trstenjak in *BIDS* (n 41) [60].

[259] ibid [94], [100]. It was clear in the eyes of the AG Trstenjak that even if an agreement pursues a legitimate objective or a sector experiences a cyclical or structural crisis, the agreement can still count as a restriction by object except if it 'pursues either a pro-competitive object or an object which is neutral from a competition point of view'.

[260] *BIDS* (n 41) [34]–[38] (in the absence of the BIDS agreements, the Court noted, the involved undertakings would have no means of improving their profitability other than by intensifying their commercial rivalry or resorting to concentrations).

[261] Guidelines on the application of Article 81(3) (n 3) [21]; Jones, Sufrin and Dunne *EU Competition Law* (2019) 203; R Whish, 'Object Restrictions', New Frontiers of Antitrust Conference (10 February 2012), available at www.concurrences.com.

anticompetitive as per *BIDS*, but one that is deprived of any plausible procompetitive explanation.[262] Similarly, in the abuse of dominance area, *Post Danmark I*, *Intel*, and the recent *ENEL* make it clear that a unilateral practice that is not capable of having foreclosure effects cannot but be procompetitive, and therefore not qualify as abusive, unless actual or potential anticompetitive effects are shown.[263]

A similar trend could be discerned in merger control. *CK Telecoms* is the first case where a theory of non-collusive oligopoly is assessed by the GC as a stand-alone theory of harm.[264] The purpose of such a theory of harm is to capture the mergers that, although they do not lead to the creation or strengthening of a dominant position, eliminate an important competitive constraint and reduce the competitive pressure exercised by the remaining competitors. In doing so, according to this theory of harm, a merger could significantly impede effective competition on the market.[265] According to the Commission, the acquisition of Hutchison 3G UK Ltd ('Three') by O2 was likely to have significant non-coordinated effects on the retail market, because Three was an important competitive force and exerted an important competitive constraint. Therefore, the proposed transaction could eliminate an important competitive constraint, reduce the intensity of competition in the market, exercise an upward price pressure in prices for mobile telephony services in UK, and restrict consumers' choice.[266] However, the GC was not convinced by the Commission's analysis and annulled its decision in its entirety.[267] One of the Commission's mistakes – according to the GC – was that in its quantitative analysis of price effects failed to consider standard efficiencies which would be the direct consequence of the transaction resulting from the rationalisation and integration of production.[268] Hence, *CK Telecoms* introduced with the efficiency credit and the concept of standard efficiencies an additional filter to screen out

[262] Ibañez Colomo, 'Market Failures' (2012) 549 (anticipating this development).

[263] *Post Danmark I* (n 36) [25], [38], *Intel* (n 9) [138], *ENEL* (n 9) [50] (noting that the abusive nature of exclusionary conduct presupposes that such conduct has the capacity to restrict competition, and in particular, produce the alleged exclusionary effect).

[264] Case T-399/16, *CK Telecoms UK Investments Ltd v European Commission (CK Telecoms)* ECLI:EU:T:2020:217.

[265] HMG (n 12) 25; EUMR, Recital 25.

[266] Commission Decision of 11.5.2016 declaring a concentration to be incompatible with the internal market (Case M.7612 Hutchison 3G UK / Telefonica UK) C(2016) 2796 final.

[267] According to the GC the Commission mistakenly confused the two criteria focusing on reduction of competitive pressure without demonstrating sufficiently well that an important competitive constraint would be eliminated *CK Telecoms v Commission* (n 264) [175] (noting that the Commission mistakenly confused the two criteria and focused on the reduction of competitive pressure without demonstrating sufficiently well that an important competitive constraint would be eliminated), [172] (holding that the Commission wrongly considered that 'the mere decline in the competitive pressure which would result, in particular, from the loss of an undertaking having more of an influence on competition than its market share would be sufficient, in itself, to prove a SIEC'); [175] (holding that the Commission disregarded the fact that an 'important competitive force' needs to stand out from its competitors to qualify as such) and [247] (holding that the Commission did not establish that the merging entities were 'particularly close mobile network operators' only that they were 'relatively close competitors').

[268] ibid [277] (noting that 'any concentration will lead to efficiencies, the extent of which will also depend on external competitive pressure').

procompetitive mergers[269] at the characterisation stage where the authority is supposed to examine the existence of non-coordinated or coordinated effects. In this sense *CK Telecoms* enlarged the scope of procompetitive effects as counterindicators and seems to follow the logic of frontloading discerned in *Cartes Bancaires*, *Budapest Bank*, *Generics*, *Intel* and *Enel*.

Thus, we can observe that procompetitive effects as counterindicators of a restriction of competition play an increasingly prominent role than as justifications of an established restriction. The causes of this phenomenon could be various. Perhaps the courts are aware of the actual difficulties of a case-by-case balancing, and therefore use proxies, heuristic devices and shortcuts[270] to decipher the nature and the potential implications of an agreement or a practice instead of requesting an actual balancing of anticompetitive and procompetitive effects. Another reason might have to do with the increasing use of economics in competition assessments: the abundance of procompetitive effects indicates that efficiency and consumer welfare have come to occupy an ever more prominent role in analysing and rationalising commercial conduct. The more economic approach, the effects-based approach, and the increasing use of economics could be the catalysts for such a development.[271] As Amato observed, the use of economics cannot but transform the way competition law is understood and interpreted, and move its shifting boundary.[272]

Another possible explanation of the aforementioned development could relate to due process considerations, the right to be heard, and the principles of good administration and full justification of administrative decisions: the frontloading of procompetitive effects might be intended to achieve a more equitable balance between plaintiffs and defendants.[273] Decision theory considerations; assumptions of the likelihood and magnitude of false positives and false negatives;[274] and

[269] ibid [278], [279] (noting that 'efficiencies within the meaning of the Guidelines must be taken into account in the overall competitive appraisal of the concentration, in order to ascertain whether they are likely to counteract the restrictive effects of the concentration. However, the category of efficiencies at issue in the present case is merely a component of a quantitative model designed to establish whether a concentration is capable of producing such restrictive effects. It is therefore an evidential matter relating to the existence of restrictive effects which arises prior to the overall competitive appraisal as provided for in paragraph 76 of the Guidelines').

[270] Kalintiri (n 6) 424–26; Easterbrook (n 7) 14–17.

[271] Witt, *EU Antitrust Law* (2016) 7–76.

[272] Amato (n 16) 20–38, 95, 115.

[273] H Dindjer, What Makes an Administrative Decision Unreasonable? Modern Law Review (2021) 84 *MLR* 265. P Daly, 'Updating the Procedural Law of Judicial Review of Administrative Action' (2018) 25 *University of Cambridge Faculty of Law Research Paper*, available at ssrn.com/abstract=3145268. See *Intel* (n 9) [138]–[140]; *ENEL* (n 9) [51]–[52] (noting that 'where a dominant undertaking submits, during the administrative procedure, on the basis of supporting evidence, that its conduct did not have the capacity to restrict competition, the competition authority concerned must examine whether, in the circumstances of the case, the conduct in question did have such capacity').

[274] A false positive occurs where an authority incorrectly prohibits procompetitive behaviour (overenforcement problem), while a false negative when an anticompetitive practice is permitted (underenforcement problem). Given the inherent difficulty of determining which practices are anticompetitive and which are procompetitive, it is inevitable that courts and authorities will sometimes

postulations about the institutional strengths and weakness of the current public enforcement institutional apparatus may have also played a role in this trend. Be that as it may, this change in the sequencing of procompetitive effects is indicative of the moving boundaries of EU competition law.[275] This development may make competition analysis less formulaic and more accurate, increase the evidentiary burden for the plaintiffs and decrease the risk of overenforcement. Yet, it can raise administrative and enforcement costs and increase the risk of underenforcement.

At this point it is worth asking how the prominent role of efficiency and consumer welfare in the definition of procompetitive effects, and the Court's front-loading of procompetitive effects at the first stage of competition analysis, affect the shifting boundaries of EU competition law. One could argue that the law has moved away from a Jeffersonian or Ordoliberal ideal of 'equal liberty for all' towards a legal regime predominantly occupied with maximising a version of efficiency.[276] This would be a development that Amato already anticipated when he discussed the history and the evolution of both US and EU antitrust law and observed a tendency of both jurisdictions to focus almost exclusively on efficiency.[277] On this basis, Amato was wondering whether EU competition law will remain faithful to its original inspiration to protect the market as an institution of freedom and competition as a device for taming economic power, or if it will turn into a legal tool exclusively focused on efficiency.[278]

Our analysis of the concept of procompetitive effects suggests that the original inspiration of EU competition law to 'defend the freedom of small producers to stay in the market', to 'fight against economic power' and to protect 'the fight itself'[279] has not been fully abandoned. Even though efficiency and consumer welfare play an increasingly important role in the interpretation and application of the notion of procompetitive effects, concerns pertaining rivalry have not vanished. A key

make errors. Hence when legal tests are designed a key question is to decide which of the two errors is preferable. Whish and Bailey (n 5) 193–94.

[275] Beckner III and Salop, 'Decision Theory' (1999) 42 (arguing that courts should consider low cost and easily available information in the initial stage of antitrust analysis, and not engage in a quantitative evaluation of the magnitude of likely efficiency benefits. According to these authors a more refined analysis of the likelihood of efficiency benefits is warranted when there are probable market power harms. On this basis, they claim that judicial bodies should use sequential information gathering and decision analysis to reduce informational costs).

[276] Amato (n 16) 97–98 (describing the Jeffersonian ideal as 'a society of producers as far as possible equal among themselves and all independent of each other, so as to avoid the inequality of wealth and that disparity of power it entails, not only in civil relationships but in the relationship with political power itself, which may be corrupted both by the abuses of the powerful and by redistributive claims by the mass of dependent workers') and 98 (observing that 'when liberal culture managed to make its way among the meshes of the many varieties of European statalism and began to impose antitrust law (and not the State) as the means to combat that power, the similarities with the original principles of American antitrust law became considerable').

[277] ibid 10–19 (noting that the Sherman Act was inspired by an urge to fight against trust or against economic power in defence of small producers and small traders who risked being crushed by it), 20–36 (presenting the Chicago revolution and its impact), 46–64 (discussing the evolution of case law on restrictive agreements) 65–92 (discussing the evolution of the abuse of dominance law) 95.

[278] ibid 96–97.

[279] ibid 95.

finding of this study was that an analysis of the case law suggests that it would be inaccurate to simply equate procompetitive effects with efficiency gains. The concern to maintain a vigorous competitive process – or to not overly restrict rivalry – features in all four identification criteria. The Court has always combined the notions of efficiency, consumer welfare and rivalry when identifying an agreement or a practice as procompetitive. Thus, it could be argued that Amato's call for caution has been heard by the EU antitrust institutions and EU competition law has not transformed into a branch of microeconomics, single-mindedly focused on efficiency. Far from being monolithically focused on the value of efficiency, the Court has incorporated in its analysis of procompetitive effects concerns associated with rivalry which can be associated with freedom to compete and equality of opportunity.

At the beginning of the *Antitrust and the Bounds of Power*, Amato cautions the reader that the intellectual DNA of antitrust is complex and that technical arguments involve and rely on 'political and philosophical options with which antitrust law still remains bound up'.[280] As he insightfully pointed out, competition law was not invented by the technicians of commercial law, nor by economists, but 'by politicians and scholars attentive to the pillars of the democratic system'.[281] Due to this reason, competition law (on both sides of the Atlantic) seeks to address a crucial problem for democracy: to tame private power so that it does not infringe the economic freedom of other private individuals, nor does it undermine public decision-making.[282] From this perspective, the key mission of competition law is to prevent private power 'from becoming a threat to the freedoms of others'.[283] Such a mission requires bold intervention as well as self-restrain from antitrust institutions. According to Amato, it is of paramount important that courts and enforcers, while pursuing competition law's mission, they do not enlarge their powers 'to the point of destroying the very freedoms [they] ought to protect'.[284] The careful way the EU Courts and the Commission approach the issue of procompetitive effects echoes these concerns.

In an era where there is growing discontent about the predominant consumer welfare paradigm and increasing trepidation about the economic power of digital giants in virtue of the special characteristics of digital markets,[285] Amato's framing of the nature and key dilemmas of competition law is more topical than ever.

[280] ibid 2.

[281] ibid 2–3.

[282] ibid 2–3 (noting that 'power in liberal democratic societies is, in the public sphere, recognised only in those who hold it legitimately on the basis of law, while in the private sphere, it does not go beyond the limited prerogatives allotted within the firm to its owner').

[283] ibid 3.

[284] ibid 95–100.

[285] I Lianos, 'Competition law for the digital era: a compex systems; perspective' (2019) 6 *CLES Research Paper Series* 1; E Deutscher, 'Reshaping Digital Competition: The New Platform Regulations and the Future of Modern Antitrust' (2022) 67 *Antitrust Bulletin* 302; O Andriychuck, 'Shaping the New Modality of the Digital Markets: The Impact of the DSA/DMA Proposals on Inter-platform Competition' (2021) 44 *World Competition: Law and Economics Review* 261; F Jenny, Changing the way we think: competition, platforms and ecosystems (2021) 9 *Journal of Antitrust Enforcement* 1.

Against this backdrop, we could argue that the notion of procompetitive effects suggests that the boundaries of EU competition law are indeed shifting and that technical arguments are indeed interwoven with value-laden judgments. The purpose of this contribution was to flesh out the meaning and the role of procompetitive effects in EU competition. Whether the meaning and weight given to these effects and the key legal mechanisms through which they currently are cognisable allow EU competition law to effectively set boundaries to power is a matter of further examination. Amato's *Antitrust and the Bounds of Power*, with its rigorously descriptive analysis and solid theoretical underpinnings offers a solid vantage for such a normative inquiry. This fact alone is a testament of the timeless value of a book published 25 years ago.

PART III

The Concept of Power

8

Preserving the Bounds of Power

The Narrow Path to a Future-Proof Competition Policy

GINEVRA BRUZZONE

I. Introduction

In 1997, when Giuliano Amato published his book, *Antitrust and the Bounds of Power: The Dilemma of Liberal Democracy in the History of the Market*, the focus of the debate within the EU competition community was on how to make a proper use of economic analysis in antitrust enforcement. Since competition is an economic process, an economic view necessarily underpins the design of competition rules and their application. In the 1990s, the challenge was to make this view more explicit, with reference to the impact of competition law on the market. In parallel, at the international level the main efforts were being devoted to finding common languages and methodologies across jurisdictions to address restrictions of competition by undertakings and by public authorities.

At that time, pointing out the political relevance of antitrust, as a policy whose specific goal entails setting boundaries on both private and public power, could be perceived as merely an enlightening intellectual perspective, with no direct relevance for the concrete policy issues which had to be faced in day-to-day antitrust enforcement or when updating regulations and guidelines.

After the first decade, however, things started to change. Several developments contributed to emphasising the political dimension of the market process and of the rules aimed to ensure its proper operation. The financial and economic crisis of 2008/09, although its direct causes cannot be attributed to competition, led to social tensions and uneasiness in many sectors. Increasingly, the globalisation of markets resulted in strong competitive challenges leading to requests of protection or, at least, of an enhanced level playing field to be reached by means of some combination of industrial and trade policy.

In addition, it soon became clear that the digital transformation, which was leading to the emergence on the market of unprecedently powerful players, required specific policy responses. More generally, trends leading to an increasing concentration of supply in many sectors, in parallel to a growing inequality in wealth, raised the issue of whether the traditional approach to competition policy is inadequate to the needs of society or, worse, responsible of an undesirable economic evolution. Similar considerations hold for the climate and environmental challenge.

Today, on the one hand, the common perception is that antitrust policy was unable to restrain the growth of private power, and on the other, a more direct involvement of public power in the management of markets is often called for. As a result, pressures to revise substantive antitrust enforcement criteria push in opposite directions: we face demand for a broader scope of prohibitions and stricter enforcement of existing rules, as well as requests of a softening of competition rules so as to pursue broader public goals.

A new language in international debates on the future of competition law testifies to raising concerns ('Competition under fire';[1] 'Competition policy: time for a reset?';[2] 'Horizontal agreements in a world of fire'[3]). Also the topics addressed in recent books ('Competition overdose';[4] 'Populism and antitrust'[5]) are different from the ones we were used to in the second half of the twentieth century.

On both sides of the Atlantic the issue of how to make sure that competition policy is fit for new challenges is hotly discussed. In the EU, the European Commission holds that it is carrying out a review of its competition policy tools 'with unprecedented scope and ambition' and, in parallel, is seeking to equip itself with new instruments aimed at tackling emerging challenges in the Single Market, such as digital gatekeepers or the distortive effects of foreign subsidies.[6]

In this context, the claim that in order to preserve a liberal democracy we need to set proper boundaries for both private and public power is at the heart of the debate on the choices to be made for a future-proof competition policy.

Taking this claim seriously, we need to answer three different questions. First, how can we avoid that taking into account broader policy goals leads to a structural weakening of competition and to new forms of centralisation of power? Second, what should we do, within competition policy or by means of complementary tools, to ensure that private economic power, especially but not only, in the digital environment, does not trespass the boundaries which are needed to preserve a liberal democracy? Finally, how should we proceed to ensure that new tools aimed at restraining private powers remain rooted in the Rule of Law and are bound by clear limiting principles? In this chapter I will discuss these challenges with specific reference to EU competition policy.

[1] Global Forum on Competition (2019).

[2] Global Forum on Competition (2020).

[3] ICN Annual Conference, 2020.

[4] M Stucke and A Ezrachi, *Competition overdose: how free market mythology transformed us from citizen kings to market servants* (Harper Business, 2020).

[5] M Bernatt, *Populism and Antitrust. The Illiberal Influence of Populist Governments on the Competition Law System* (CUP, 2022).

[6] European Commission, 'A competition policy fit for new challenges' COM (2021) 713 final, 3–4.

II. Coordinating Antitrust with Other Public Policies

A. The Reasons for a Strong Protection of Competition

Recent criticisms of competition law are often based on the misconception that the fact that competition is not sufficient to achieve other public policy objectives outside the competition area should be seen as a fault. It is clear, from both a theoretical and a practical perspective, that competition and competition policy tools alone cannot reach all the objectives of the current policy agenda: they need to be accompanied by complementary policy tools. Nevertheless, we have no substitute for a vigorous protection of competition to preserve a dynamic market economy and an open decentralised society.

From an economic viewpoint, competition is a formidable mechanism which leads firms, in a context of imperfect information, to look for efficiency and better products, through innovation and imitation, and to contain prices. Unlike most public policy measures, the process works on a continuous basis. During the process, undertakings may make mistakes: they may invest too much, or not enough, or in fruitless directions; they may propose unsuccessful products; or they may set prices at the wrong level. However, the mechanisms for the correction of such mistakes (decreasing market shares and profits; exit from the market) are embedded in the system. If we wish to maintain dynamic incentives to improvements of products and processes to the ultimate interest of consumers, there is no effective alternative to the competitive market process.

Moreover, especially in times of populist calls for new forms of centralisation of power, it is worth recalling the broader view of the Freiburg school whereby a competitive economic order, as opposed to a centralised political economy, is also a precondition for a society which protects human dignity and personal freedom, and provides opportunities for participation to all its members.

For these reasons, whenever possible, broader public policy strategies should aim to pursue the various public policy objectives with no undue distortion of the competitive process.

These remarks are directly relevant to the current policy debate on antitrust in Europe since, especially after the Commission's decision to prohibit the *Siemens-Alstom* merger,[7] some Member States and stakeholders, as well as the European Parliament, have been asking for a stronger coordination of competition policy with other EU policies (industrial policy, environmental policy, trade policy). The choice of how to proceed is crucial: depending on how the attempts to combine the protection of competition with other objectives are carried out, we may be able to preserve the values of a competitive order or, instead, pave the way for a framework more prone to an unbounded expansion of private and public powers.

[7] Case M.8677, *Siemens Alstom*, decision of February 6, 2019, C(2019) 921 final.

B. Multitask Competition Policy and Public Interest Approaches

The shift to a more multitask model, charging competition law with further missions beyond protecting undistorted competition, may seem an appealing way to make competition policy fit for the new challenges. Indeed, an obvious possibility to accommodate calls for a closer coordination of antitrust and other public policies would be to soften competition law enforcement in the application of Article 101 and merger control by widening admissible justifications to give room to industrial or other public policy concerns.

However, multitask competition policy is a slippery slope, entailing risks similar to those associated with competition law models in force in several European countries in the first part of the twentieth century. Such models were typically based on a public interest standard whereby restrictions of competition could be declared unlawful when their costs exceeded their benefits for society, on the basis of a case-by-case assessment with broad administrative discretion. Their features made them susceptible to the pressure of vested interests and ideological onslaughts: with no significant support, competition was easily set apart and remained at the margin of economic policy.[8] Similarly, today a shift to a more multitask application of competition rules may lead to a less transparent and more politicised enforcement of competition rules and broader administrative discretion, which would weaken the ability to effectively constrain private power much beyond what is needed to pursue legitimate public goals.

C. The Ordoliberal Features of EU Competition Rules and their Relevance Today

Competition rules in the Treaty of Rome were not based on a public interest model but on a different approach which, according to the suggestions of the Ordoliberal school and similarly to the German competition law of 1957, entailed a stronger institutional framework for the protection of competition.[9] The substantive rules, which have remained unchanged since their adoption, contain the prohibition of anticompetitive agreements and abuse of dominance, and the possibility of justifications/exemptions is narrowly designed. Similarly, for mergers entailing a significant impediment to effective competition, justifications/defences are admitted only under narrow conditions. The structure of the rules leaves little room for balancing the protection of competition with other public policy goals in the application of EU competition law.

[8] For an overview, see D Gerber, *Law and Competition in Twentieth Century Europe – Protecting Prometheus* (OUP, 1998), esp chs 3-6.

[9] For an in-depth analysis of the roots of EU competition law, see KK Patel and H Schweitzer (2013), *The Historical Foundations of EU Competition Law* (OUP, 2013).

Article 101(3) is the only provision which apparently departs from this strict approach. Article 101(3) clearly contemplates the possibility of balancing the protection of competition with other goals, since restrictive agreements improving the production or distribution of goods or promoting technical or economic progress can be deemed compatible with the Treaty. However, the exemption is subject to three further cumulative constraints: not only should the restriction be necessary to obtain the efficiency-enhancing effects, but also consumers, ie the ultimate beneficiaries of the competitive process, should receive a fair share of the resulting benefits, thus impeding restrictions which, for instance, merely avoid cost duplications in the interest of producers. The fourth condition requires effective competition not to be eliminated for a substantial part of the products in question, at least for some parameters. The underlying assumption is that Article 101(3) does not allow eliminating effective competition, ie a significant rivalry for a substantial part of the products involved, just because the restriction may lead to some efficiency-enhancing effects.

Under Council Regulation 17/1962, when the Commission had the exclusive power to apply Article 101(3), in some cases it was able to use this power to carry out some balancing of interests, entailing a significant degree of administrative discretion.[10] Things have changed with the adoption of Regulation 1/2003, since with the modernisation of EU competition rules, the exception contained in Article 101(3) became directly applicable, also before national courts. The direct applicability of Article 101(3) requires that the interpretation of its four conditions should be based on predominantly pure legal arguments. In this respect, one of the consequences of the modernisation was a decrease in the Commission's discretionary powers in the application of Article 101(3), shifting the system closer to an Ordoliberal model.

Tellingly, only after the adoption of Regulation 1/2003 did the Court of Justice accept, by way of interpretation, that it is also possible in the application of Article 102, under narrow conditions, to take into account efficiency considerations, provided that a number of strict requirements, modelled on those contained in Article 101(3) are met.[11] Certainly the Court did not intend to open the door to administrative discretion and to a discretionary balancing of different policy goals in this area.

Similarly, as anticipated, for EU merger control both the rules and the case law indicate that efficiency justifications, as well as failing firm defences, do not call into question the approach aimed at preventing anticompetitive mergers: pursuant to the EU Merger Regulation, concentrations entailing significant impediments to effective competition should be prohibited unless effective remedies remove competition concerns.

[10] G Amato, *Antitrust and the Bounds of Power: The Dilemma of Liberal Democracy in the History of the Market* (Hart Publishing, 1997) 54–64.

[11] Case C-209/10, *Post Danmark I* EU:C:2012:172 [40]–[43]; Case C-413/14 P, *Intel* [140].

It is within this legal framework, which is clearly designed as an alternative to a public interest model, that today the Commission is trying to ensure a stronger coordination of competition law and the broader EU strategy for sustainable growth.

D. The Revision of the Horizontal Cooperation Guidelines as an Example

This effort is clear, for instance, in the ongoing revision of the Commission's guidelines on the application of Article 101 TFEU to horizontal cooperation agreements.[12] For the first time, the draft Guidelines on the application of Article 101 TFEU expressly refer to broader EU public policy documents on industrial and environmental policy.[13] In the Commission's view, the revised Guidelines 'aim to provide legal certainty by assisting undertakings in the assessment of their horizontal cooperation agreements' while ensuring an effective protection of competition, and also 'to make it easier for undertakings to cooperate in ways which are economically desirable and thereby, for example, contribute to the green and digital transitions and to fostering the resilience of the internal market'.[14]

Since the reduction of legal uncertainty, provided it is not too resource-intensive, does not entail any weakening in the protection of competition, the Commission may also be willing to provide targeted individual guidance in cases of genuine uncertainty on the application of Article 101 by means of opinions, comfort letters or positive decisions pursuant to Article 10 of Regulation 1/2003.[15] Some steps in this direction have already been made for cooperation projects aimed at addressing a shortage of supply of essential products and services during the COVID-19 outbreak as well as in the revised Notice on informal guidance in antitrust cases published on 3 October 2022 (C(2022) 6925 final).

Importantly, the draft horizontal Guidelines indicate how far the Commission, holding the other EU public policy objectives in mind, is disposed to go in the interpretation of the four requirements of Article 101(3).

The wording of the first condition (improving production or distribution or promoting technical or economic progress) is broad enough to allow the Commission to include many examples in the category of efficiency-enhancing effects (eg the use of cleaner production or distribution technologies, less pollution, more resilient infrastructure or supply chains, increased rapidity in bringing

[12] See Communication from the Commission, Approval of the content of a draft for a communication from the Commission 'Guidelines on the applicability of Article 101 of the Treaty on the Functioning of the European Union to horizontal co-operation agreements', 1 March 2022 C(2022) 1159 final.

[13] The Guidelines mention both the communication 'Updating the 2020 New Industrial Strategy: Building a Stronger Single Market for Europe's Recovery' of 5 May 2021, COM(2021) 350 final, and the communication 'The European Green Deal' COM (2019) 640 final.

[14] ibid, para 1.

[15] Commission (n 6) 11.

sustainable products to the market, helping consumer choice by facilitating the comparison of products).[16]

As to the fourth condition (no elimination of competition), the Commission confirms that it can be interpreted so as to include agreements involving all companies in a market, provided that there remains competition on other key parameters.[17]

The third condition (necessity of the restrictive agreement) remains crucial to resist requests of a weakening of the protection of competition in name of public policy goals. For instance, with respect to sustainability-enhancing agreements, in several markets there may not be a problem of first-mover disadvantage because there is a sufficient number of customers (consumers/companies/public administrations) willing to pay for more sustainable products, or because regulation already takes care of negative externalities. In these situations, the Commission is unwilling to justify a restrictive sustainability agreement as necessary, unless the agreement turns out to be indispensable for reaching the sustainability goal in a more cost-efficient way, always subject to a careful assessment of whether restrictions do not go beyond what is necessary to achieve the aim of the agreement.

The second condition, whereby the restrictive agreement should allow consumers a fair share of the resulting benefits, is the most controversial, especially in the context of the debate on how to integrate environmental protection into the definition and implementation of EU competition law, as prescribed by Article 11 TFEU. The Commission, on the one hand, adopts a broad view of the benefits which should be considered when assessing whether consumers have received a fair share of the efficiency-enhancing effects,[18] but maintains the approach whereby the consumers negatively affected by the agreement in the relevant market should be compensated.

Therefore, the draft Guidelines do not go as far as to interpret the second requirement of Article 101(3) as a tool allowing to compensate the anticompetitive harm of the agreement with its total benefits for society. Indeed, although there exist methodologies for attributing a price to the polluting impact of the purchasing act,[19] in cases of clear trade-off between lower prices and better environmental conditions, the legitimacy of competition authorities to substitute a welfare-enhancing choice to express consumer preferences may remain contentious. It is worth recalling that, while for environmental protection EU law provides several alternative instruments, for the protection of less wealthy consumers from

[16] ibid, para 578.

[17] ibid, paras 610–14.

[18] Not only traditional benefits from individual use (eg price, quality, efficiency etc), but also individual benefits non-associated to the use of the product (eg willingness to pay for more sustainable products and processes) as well as objective collective benefits for a group of people which includes consumers in the relevant market.

[19] See, for instance, M Dolmans, 'Sustainable Competition Policy' (2020) 5 and 6 *Competition Law and Policy Debate*.

restrictions of competition the application of competition rules is the only available tool (apart from ex-post social support measures).

Thus, the policy position emerging from the draft Horizontal Guidelines is that whenever a restrictive agreement creates a significant anticompetitive impact which remains uncorrected/uncompensated, the Commission or any other competition authority cannot reach welfare-enhancing goals simply by means of the application of competition rules.

Nevertheless, the possibility for companies to discuss with the Commission or competition authorities whether cooperative solutions are compatible with Article 101 TFEU may also turn out to be useful in those cases in which a market failure cannot be properly dealt with by means of Article 101(3) for the reasons outlined above. In such situations, competition authorities may proactively promote other ways to correct the market failure. In particular, the Commission may take the initiative to propose mandatory requirements, either following the so-called 'New Approach' to technical harmonisation (with the related standardisation initiatives) by means of traditional regulatory measures. Compared to an agreement, such solutions may be less rapid but would ensure democratic legitimacy for choices adopted in the general interest which may entail an appreciable worsening of conditions for some consumers. A further advantage of regulatory initiatives, compared to agreements, is that they would be binding on all companies. The Commission has already followed this approach, for instance, within the EU Strategy for Plastics in the Circular Economy, where, inspired by the activities of the Circular Plastics Alliance, it proposed mandatory requirements for recycled content and waste reduction measures for a number of key products such as packaging and construction materials.

E. A Procompetitive Strategy for Sustainable Growth

Summing up, even when trying to incorporate industrial policy concerns and the green deal objectives into the definition and application of EU competition policy, the European Commission tries to maintain an approach which preserves a strong protection of competition, stressing the role of the competitive process for the Union's economic prosperity and ability to promote a strong and resilient Single Market. The current strategy aimed at making competition policy fit for new challenges is meant to support other EU public policies, so as to provide responses to the broader demands of society, without accepting a structural weakening of the protection of competition which would easily lead to new forms of centralisation of power. The design of EU competition rules, with little room for administrative balancing of different interests in the application of competition rules, is helpful in this respect.

At the same time, although the policy debate often focuses on how to adapt competition law and make it more flexible, competition authorities can usefully point out that the current policy challenges can also be addressed from a slightly different viewpoint, outlining a procompetitive strategy for sustainable growth which makes the most of the benefits of the competitive process in pursuing other policy goals.

When evaluating policy initiatives, a systematic use of competition impact assessment, supported by competition advocacy by national authorities as well as by the Competition Commissioner within the European Commission, can play an important role in promoting the more procompetitive solutions and more generally a regulatory framework capable of supporting decentralised competitive initiatives.

An equally important role in setting procompetitive boundaries to public intervention is played by the control of State aid, which limits selective support of specific undertakings by means of public resources. Clearly, compared to the application of antitrust rules, in the control of State aid there is a closer and more systematic relationship between the protection of competition and the pursuit of other policy goals, since Article 107 TFEU enables the Commission to declare State aid measures compatible with the Treaty whenever they are necessary and proportionate to pursue other public policy objectives falling within one of the broad categories listed in Article 107 TFEU.

At the same time, however, State aid control ensures that competition is not unduly distorted and that selective public support does not merely crowd out private investment. The policy principles for the application of Article 107, which have been gradually spelled out by the Commission in the last 15 years, initially in the framework of State aid modernisation and more recently looking at the challenges of Next Generation EU, can be viewed as the principles of a procompetitive industrial policy aimed at pursuing public goals while at the same time minimising market distortions and ensuring an efficient use of scarce public resources. In this respect, State aid control is an important part of the broader commitment to competitive neutrality, which has also recently been advocated by the OECD as crucial to maintain proper bounds for public and private power in a competitive environment.[20]

III. Achievements and Challenges in the Application of EU Competition Rules

A. Policy Reasons for the Impact-Based Approach

The second and third questions addressed in this chapter consider how to constrain private economic power while keeping public power within proper boundaries.

[20] OECD, 'Recommendation of the Council on Competitive Neutrality' OECD/LEGAL/0462, May 2021. The main objective of the Recommendation is 'to ensure a level-playing field both between state-owned and privately-owned enterprises, and between different privately-owned enterprises' (3).

Starting with traditional competition rules, and having already discussed how EU competition law leaves little room for compensating restrictions of competition with other policy goals, I will focus on whether a more impact-based approach makes competition policy less effective vis à vis economic power.

Undoubtedly, in the light of the case law of the Court of Justice, the direct objective of EU competition rules is the protection of a system of undistorted competition and not the maximisation of consumer surplus, nor a broader notion of economic efficiency.[21] However, there was already in 1997 a widespread awareness that making the protection of 'competition as such' operational entailed several challenges.

Especially for vertical agreements, a heated debate had been ongoing since the early 1990s on whether the approach of the European Commission on the assessment of vertical restraints should be revised. At the time, in most instances the application of Article 101(1) merely looked at whether the agreement entailed a restriction of the freedom of action of the parties: the focus on bilateral relations entailed a broad scope of application of the prohibition of Article 101(1) and shifted the assessment of compatibility with the TFEU to the application of Article 101(3), with a straightjacket effect on harmless agreements.

The discussion was, at least in part, influenced by the debate in international fora such as the OECD aimed at promoting a mutual understanding and possibly convergence between the approaches to competition law enforcement in the different jurisdictions and by the increased role of economists within the Directorate General for Competition, which followed the adoption of the first Merger Regulation in 1989.

As a result of the revision, at the end of the 1990s the Commission adopted a new type of block exemption regulation for vertical agreements and accompanying guidelines, which clearly endorsed an impact-based approach. Since then, a similar approach has been followed by the Commission in all subsequent block exemption regulations and guidelines on the application of Article 101 – not only for vertical agreements, but also for horizontal and technology transfer agreements.

The main takeaway of the reform of the late 1990s is the Commission's acknowledgement that in order to assess whether an agreement is restrictive of competition within the meaning of Article 101(1) the focus should not be on restrictions of the parties' freedom of action, but rather on the external actual or potential impact of the agreement on the market, namely on the parameters which are typically affected by the competitive process, ie price, quality, choice and innovation. Since competition law is meant to support the competitive operation of the market, a mere focus on whether a bilateral relation is unreasonably unbalanced, accompanied by the application of Article 101(3), did not seem to be an adequate approach, whereas a focus on bilateral relationships may remain appropriate in other fields of law, such as the national rules prohibiting the abuse of economic dependence.

[21] For an in-depth discussion of the case law, see Komninos, ch 5 of this volume.

As to Article 102, a similar debate on how to draw the boundaries of exclusionary abuses took place 10 years later. Although the Court of Justice had already made reference in *Hoffmann La Roche* to the objective nature of the notion of abuse and to the link between the prohibition and the impact of the conduct on the market,[22] two main weaknesses were perceived in the case law. First, reference to the purpose of protecting a competitive market structure as such, with no clear criteria on how to distinguish abusive conduct from normal competition or 'competition on the merits' made it intrinsically difficult to distinguish between the protection of competition and the protection of competitors, although the goal of Article 102 is the first, not the second one.[23] Moreover, unexplained differences remained in the assessment of types of conduct with similar effects.

For Article 102, reaching a shared vision within the Commission turned out to be more difficult than for the assessment of agreements. In the 2008 Guidance Paper on the Commission's enforcement priorities, the Commission proposed a distinction between foreclosure as such and anti-competitive foreclosure, that is the conduct of a dominant company which, by foreclosing actual or potential competitors, may have a negative impact on competitive variables (increase in price, worsening of quality or choice, decrease in innovation).[24] Thus, similarly to the approach followed in the application of Article 101, the notion of anticompetitive foreclosure suggests an application of Article 102 to allegedly abusive exclusionary conduct based on a theory of harm that looks at the actual or potential impact on competitive parameters.

For many years some resistance remained, both within the Court of Justice and in some cases also within the Commission, against fully accepting an impact-based approach to setting the boundaries of legitimate conduct in the application of Articles 101 and 102. Let us assume that the discussion is not about the objectives of competition law – ie let us assume that the objective is the protection of the competitive process – the issue is whether it is appropriate/desirable to follow an impact-based paradigm, whereby the assessment of whether an agreement or conduct has a restrictive impact on the competitive process should be grounded on a theory of harm that looks at the actual or potential impact of the agreement or conduct on competitive parameters (price, quality, choice, innovation), in the short and longer term.

There are three main questions which should be addressed in preserving the bounds of power by means of competition law:

- Does the impact-based approach, as described above, substantially weaken the ability to constrain private economic power?

[22] Case C-85/76, *Hoffmann La Roche v. Commission* (1979) EU:C:979:36 [91].

[23] Case C-209/10, *Post Danmark I* (2012) EU:C:2012:172 [21]–[22]; Case C-43/14 P, *Intel Corporation Inc v Commission* (2017) EU:C:2017:632 [133]–[134].

[24] European Commission, Guidance on the Commission's enforcement priorities in applying Article 82 of the EC Treaty to abusive exclusionary conduct by dominant undertakings, OJ C-45/7, 24 February 2009, para 19.

- Is the impact-based approach, although in principle fit for the challenges, too complicated for effective enforcement?
- Is the impact-based approach an obstacle to an in-depth judicial review, thus weakening checks and balances with respect to the fulfilment of public tasks by competition authorities?

These are discussed below.

i. Ability to Constrain Private Power

The risk that a more economic approach may contribute to transforming competition policy in an area of technicalities, meaningful only to specialists and far from its deeper political and philosophic roots, was clearly evoked in *Antitrust and the Bounds of Power*. At the end of the book, however, looking towards the antitrust of the future, Amato argued that there is not necessarily a relationship between an impact-based approach and a weakening of competition policy:

> [W]e should nonetheless stress what by contrast is not inevitable: the limitation of antitrust that some see in the intervening refinement of economic analysis applied to it, which on this interpretation has even detached it from the question of economic power and rooted it in the soil of efficiency alone. This is not so. Antitrust law has in fact become better and stronger by becoming able (thanks to economic analysis) to distinguish restrictions of contractual freedom and restrictions of competition. It becomes unilateral and questionable when, over and above that and irrespective of that, it attributes to objective reasons of economic analysis such retreat in the borders of its own intervention as to ignore the economic power whose formation is allowed. This was and is not at all inevitable.[25]

Twenty-five years later, although both the legal and the economic assessment of cases have become so technical that sometimes it is not easy even for experts to find a soul in the matter, it would be clearly misleading to blame the impact-based approach for weakening antitrust enforcement.

Of course, taking the freedom of action or the number of competitors as the operational objective would easily prohibit a large number of cases, but it is doubtful that such prohibitions would be the most appropriate way to proceed for a strong protection of the competitive process. Linking the prohibitions to the actual or potential negative impact of the agreement or conduct on competitive parameters supports a better targeted enforcement.

Importantly, according to the EU case law, since competition is a multidimensional process, the range of competitive variables which can be considered in the assessment of the impact of agreements, unilateral conduct and mergers is quite broad, since it does not include only price, but also – as anticipated – quality, choice and innovation. Thus, for instance, it remains possible to prohibit a conduct

[25] Amato, *Antitrust and the Bounds of Power* (1997) 125–26.

which does not entail an increase in price because of its expected negative impact on choice or innovation.

This flexibility, and the possibility to consider not only the short term but also the longer term, make it still possible for competition authorities to prohibit those restrictions of the freedom of action or those exclusionary conduct which, by decreasing effective competition, hamper the working of the competitive process.

Thus, although as discussed in section I above, in EU competition law there is not much room for balancing the protection of competition with other policy goals, within the competition box the dynamic and multidimensional nature of competition protection leaves room for some discretionary choices.

Competition law enforcers may have to balance the competitive impact in the short term against the competitive impact in the longer term, with appropriate discount factors. For the sake of transparency, consideration of the impact of the agreement/conduct in the short term and in the longer term should always be clearly spelled out. Although there may be different approaches to the choice of discount factors, to compensate a negative impact in the short term the effect in the longer term should typically be significant and supported by convincing evidence.

As to trade-offs between different competitive parameters, when the impact on choice is considered separately from the impact on other competitive variables, the standard easily become the protection of a plurality of competitors as such, with no limiting principles. Thus, a commitment to consider the impact on choice/variety together with the impact on other competition parameters, ie a comprehensive picture of competitive harm, taking all dimensions into account, may be helpful to ensure fully informed enforcement.

Thus, there is apparently nothing intrinsically weak in a system of competition law based on impact assessment. More than on the variables which are considered when assessing the boundaries of legitimate conduct, the degree of severity of enforcement depends on the required standard of proof. This crucial issue cannot be properly addressed here, but arguably, on the basis of the precautionary principle, the standard should vary depending on how intrinsically harmful is the agreement or conduct.

ii. Impact-Based Approach and Administrability of the Rules

In response to allegations that the impact-based approach is too complicated and requires too lengthy assessments for effective enforcement, it should be recalled that it is possible to combine an effect-based approach with a structured assessment which entails the use of presumptions, quick-look approaches and reallocation of the burden of proof, with no need to change the conceptual framework.

This is the lesson which can be drawn, for both Article 101 and 102, from the case law of the Court of Justice on restrictions by object in the *Cartes Bancaires* judgment of 2014 and on presumptive abuses in the *Intel* judgment of 2017.[26]

[26] Case C-67/13 P, *Groupement Cartes Bancaires c. Commission* (2014) EU:C:2014:2204.

These two judgments can be viewed as symmetric cornerstones of a systematic approach, whereby the boundaries of restrictions of competition are set taking into account the actual or potential impact on competitive parameters.

According to the view of the Court in *Cartes Bancaires*, also for restrictions by object, the impact of the agreement on competition variables is still relevant, in two respects. First, the assessment of whether an agreement is restrictive by object should be based on the experience of the negative impact of this type of coordination on the market. Second, consistently with the case law, in assessing whether the agreement reveals a sufficient degree of harm to justify skipping the impact assessment, regard must be had to the content of its provisions, its objectives and the economic and legal context, including the nature of the products and the real conditions of the structure and operation of the markets in question.

As to Article 102, in its 2017 *Intel* judgment the Court of Justice indicates that exclusivity rebates (and exclusivity clauses), are still to be considered abusive within the meaning of Article 102, consistently with the *Hoffmann-La Roche* case law, but the conclusion may be rebutted if the undertaking shows that the conduct is not capable of restricting competition and, in particular, of producing the alleged foreclosure effects. Thus, for instance, the share of the market covered by the agreement, its duration and the amount of rebates may matter. Clearly, the more serious is the nature of the infringement (eg a hardcore cartel), the less likely it is that consideration of the other aspects will suffice to rebut the presumption.

By admitting the use of presumptions, quick-look assessments and some reallocation of the evidentiary burden of proof for those types of agreements/conduct whose harmful impact clearly emerges from settled experience, the Court usefully reconciles an impact-based approach with the administrability of the rules.

iii. Judicial Review and the Other Features of the Institutional Framework

For review courts, technical complexities notwithstanding, if the theories of harm are clearly spelled out and supported by evidence, an impact-based approach is in principle fully compatible with an in-depth judicial review. It is apparent from the case law of the Court of Justice that, in areas giving rise to complex economic assessments, the EU Courts must not only establish whether the evidence put forward is actually accurate, reliable and consistent, but also determine whether that evidence contains all the relevant data that must be taken into consideration in appraising a complex situation and whether it is capable of substantiating the conclusions drawn from it. Thus, even with the shift to a more impact-based approach, in decisions involving economic matters the review of legality provided for by Article 263 TFEU may still satisfy the requirements of the principle of effective judicial protection contained in Article 6(1) ECHR, which corresponds to Article 47 of the European Charter of Fundamental Rights.[27]

[27] Case C-295/12P, *Telefonica SA v. Commission* EU:C:2014:2062 [53]–[57] and case law cited therein.

B. Exploitative Abuses in the Competition Policy Toolbox

Differently from other jurisdictions, in the EU the traditional competition policy toolbox includes the prohibition of exploitative abuses of a dominant position, which in principle may be used as a substitute for economic regulation of dominant undertakings. In particular, Article 102(a) TFEU expressly refers to the conduct by one or more dominant companies 'directly or indirectly imposing unfair purchase or selling prices or other unfair trading conditions'.

This type of provision, which was already present in the German competition law of 1957, can be seen as a legacy of the Ordoliberal view whereby, when it is not feasible or efficient to prevent market power, dominant companies should behave as if they did not have such power. More broadly, the notion of fairness suggests that a dominant company should exercise some self-restraint in the exploitation of their economic power, taking into account the interests of their commercial counterparts (customers, suppliers, etc).

Clearly this tool is more a regulatory instrument than one aimed at promoting a competitive market process. However, it can contribute to some of the objectives which, at least indirectly, are also pursued by more mainstream antitrust tools. Indeed, if properly used, the prohibition of excessive prices and other unfair practices may contribute to allocative efficiency, to the protection of purchasers/suppliers and, more generally, to constraining the economic power of dominant companies.

Of course, an indiscriminate use of the prohibition of exploitative abuses should be avoided, since it may be counterproductive for the competitive process. A broad consensus exists on the fact that direct control of prices or trading conditions should not be the main tasks of competition authorities. Normally, high prices or other 'unfair conditions' attract entry and thus contribute to the dynamic self-correction of the market, with no need for a centralised intervention setting the right price. In the presence of structural obstacles to this process, the best possible intervention is enforcement or advocacy action to eliminate or reduce such obstacles. Moreover, when competition is not sustainable because of the features of the market (eg a natural monopoly on a lasting basis) *ex ante* regulation is more appropriate than antitrust intervention.

For these reasons, traditionally the prohibition of exploitative abuses has been applied sparingly. Competition authorities normally use such tools only under very narrow conditions, ie when the market in which the dominant firm operates is characterised by high and non-transitory barriers to entry, leading to a monopoly or near monopoly, there are no effective ways to eliminate these barriers, no regulatory measure is available to address the problem and innovation is limited. As to the limiting principles for the application of the rules on excessive pricing (which can also be useful for assessing other exploitative conduct), the recent case law of the Court of Justice provides important suggestions for an economic-wise assessment by means of a proper use of benchmarking.[28]

[28] See in particular Case C-177/16, *AKKA/LAA c. Koncurences Padome* EU:C:2017:689 [37]–[42].

Looking at the antitrust toolbox from a political economy perspective, the availability of this 'impure' instrument has turned out to be important for consensus-building, especially in times of crisis.

Consensus-building is also important for antitrust, and represents a specific task for public enforcers (the Commission and national competition authorities), which should be able to apply competition rules on the basis of priorities, entailing a strategic policy view. Since the financial and economic crisis of 2008, the role of a strategic policy view has become increasingly visible in the statements of EU Competition Commissioners, due to the increasing challenges for the economy and society. In this context, there has also been a kind of renewed interest by competition authorities of the European Competition Network (ECN) in cases concerning excessive prices and the unfair exploitation of market power, especially, but not only, in the pharmaceutical sector.[29] In a 2016 speech Commissioner Vestager explained the approach:

> The last thing we should be doing is to set ourselves as a regulator, deciding on the right price .... But, as the recent action by the British and Italian competition authorities shows, there can be times when competition rules need to do their bit to deal with excessive prices.[30]

In the same vein, especially in 2017/18, much of the debate on EU competition policy centred on the role of 'fairness' in the design and application of the rules.[31]

More recently, as shown by the German case against Facebook, the possibility to intervene against an unfair exploitation of market power has turned out to be a potentially useful tool which can be employed by competition authorities to constrain the power of digital platforms.[32]

Of course, the prohibition of exploitative abuses has to be used with caution (also in the digital world) in order to preserve not only the incentives to invest but also the economic incentives to enter the market. According to the conventional

[29] For an overview of cases and approaches in the different jurisdictions, see OECD, 'Excessive Pricing in Pharmaceuticals', OECD Policy Roundtable, 208.

[30] M Vestager, *Protecting Consumers from Exploitation*, Brussels Chillin' Competition Conference, 21 November 2016.

[31] For recent overviews and references to the debate on fairness in the EU, see D Gérard, A Komninos and D Waelbroeck, *Fairness in EU Competition Policy: Significance and Implications*, Global Competition Law Centre Conference Series no 9 (Bruylant, 2020). LA Pera, 'Some Thoughts on Fairness, Competition and Article 102' in EA Raffaelli (ed), *XIV Antitrust Between EU Law and National Law* (Bruylant, 2021) 206–24.

[32] In its 2019 decision in the Facebook case the Bundeskartellamt argued that a violation of consumer protection standards such as the GDPR rules can result in an exploitative abuse. On 23 April the Higher Regional Court of Düsseldorf filed a request for a preliminary ruling to the European Court of Justice focusing on the application of the GDPR (Case C-252/21). In its more recent *bpost* judgment the Court of Justice apparently does not exclude the possibility of a parallel application of data protection and competition law, provided that the application of both rules is properly coordinated, within a systematic approach, predictable and ensures that the global amount of fines is not disproportionate. See Case C-117/20, *bpost SA v Autorité Belge de la Concurrence* ECLI:EU:C:2022:202. Other cases of exploitative abuse in digital markets include the French *Google Ads Rules* case of 2019 and the Dutch *Apple Store* case of 2021.

wisdom, regulating excessive prices (though similar consideration may apply to other exploitative conduct) is not a proper instrument in areas where innovation plays an important role. Still, taking into account that the features of digital markets may contribute to the establishment of entrenched dominant positions and that regulatory initiatives, even when adopted, cannot cover any foreseeable circumstances, the ability of competition authorities to make use of this exceptional tool also with respect to the conduct of digital platforms may be reassuring. Whenever competitive forces on the market are not sufficient to constrain economic power, even the traditional competition rules provide a rich and potentially far-reaching toolbox.

C. Developments in Merger Control

Merger control may be a powerful instrument to prevent increases in economic power reached by different means from competing on the market. Since the challenges currently facing EU competition policies entail pressures going into opposite directions, for merger control we also face different demands. On the one hand, there are calls for a more flexible application of the rules for the sake of competitiveness of national or European firms or to facilitate industry consolidation after the crisis. On the other hand, there are calls for a more severe and extensive control, related to global concerns for increasing concentration of economic power and aimed in particular at more effectively constraining the expansion of digital ecosystems. A more specific concern is the insufficient ability to prevent killer acquisitions, which may hinder innovation especially in digital and pharmaceutical markets, but often fall below the notification thresholds.

Comparing the current situation with that of 1997, it is undeniable that several important initiatives have been undertaken to keep the EU merger control framework fit for the emerging challenges.

Since 2004, the substantive test for the competitive assessment of concentrations pursuant to the EU Merger Regulation has been broadened to cover all concentrations which would entail a significant impediment to effective competition in the common market, even in the absence of the creation or strengthening of a dominant position.[33] The change was meant to increase the ability to control economic power in oligopolistic markets even in the absence of coordinated conduct. It is clear from the EU case law that, even when applying the new test, the Commission has to prove that the operation would have a negative impact on competitive parameters, eg prices and the quality of services, to the requisite legal standard. For this reason, the Commission's decision to block the proposed acquisition of Telefonica UK by H3G UK in the mobile telephone market was annulled

[33] Council Regulation (EC) No 139/2004 of 20 January 2004 on the control of concentrations between undertakings, OJ 2004 L 24, p 1, Art 2(3).

by the General Court in 2020.[34] Nonetheless, from a legislative viewpoint a clear gap in the pre-existing merger legislation has been filled.

Moreover, in recent years there has in some cases been a clear focus on preventing a negative impact of the concentration on innovation, going beyond an approach focused only on the short-term impact on price and quality.[35]

As to potentially anticompetitive acquisitions falling below the notification thresholds, the Commission, showing a remarkable ability to fully exploit already existing tools, set up an enforcement mechanism centred on the application of Article 22 of the Merger Regulation. Pursuant to this provision, Member States can refer to the Commission for its review under the Merger Regulation potentially problematic transactions, even if they do not meet the national notification thresholds. In its new Guidance on the application of Article 22 the Commission encourages Member States to use this tool to refer potentially problematic acquisitions of innovative companies having a competitive potential beyond what their turnover would indicate.[36] This mechanism will be further strengthened by the obligation on digital gatekeepers, addressed in the Digital Markets Act (DMA), to inform the Commission of all their planned acquisitions, regardless of the size of the target company.

The Commission is also updating its Market Definition Notice, which has remained unchanged since 1997. The approach is expected to clarify some aspects but stick to the fundamental principles, which are flexible enough to ensure that, when supported by evidence, some markets may be broader than the EU and even global in size.[37] At the same time the Commission, looking at the industrial policy debate, stresses, by means of examples, that European merger control 'allows companies to grow and gain the necessary scale to compete, subject to sufficient competition and choice remaining in the market to drive continued innovation and investment'.[38] A new emphasis is devoted to the fact that European merger control can contribute to preventing dependencies and increasing the resilience of the EU economy by making sure that supply chains remain diversified.

The main open issue, with respect to the ability of EU competition law to constrain the growth of economic power by means of acquisitions, is whether for the acquisition of potential competitors by entrenched dominant companies the current system of allocation of the burden of proof should be revised, as suggested

[34] Case T-399/16, *CK Telecoms UK Investments v. Commission* EU:T:2020:217.

[35] Case M 7932, *Dow/Du Pont.*

[36] Commission Guidance on the application of the referral mechanism set out in Article 22 of the Merger Regulation to certain categories of cases, 26 March 2021, C(2021) 1959 final. In its *Illumina* judgment, the General Court upheld an interpretation of Art 22 whereby the referral mechanism can be applied to a transaction that did not have to be notified in the state which made the referral but entails the acquisition of an undertaking whose significance for competition is not reflected in its turnover. See Case T-227/21, *Illumina v Commission* EU:T:2022:447.

[37] See Commission Staff Working Document, 'Evaluation of the Notice on the definition of relevant market for the purposes of Community competition law of 9 December 1997' SWD(2021) 199 final.

[38] n 6, 16.

by some authors.[39] The idea would be for a well-defined subset of situations relating to potentially harmful acquisitions by entrenched dominant companies, to shift onto the dominant company the burden of proving that the acquisition has no anticompetitive impact. It remains to be seen whether in the forthcoming years these proposals will find some room in the EU legislative agenda.

IV. The Bounds of Power in the Design of Complementary Tools

The issue of whether competition rules should be accompanied by complementary regulatory tools to effectively constrain the economic power in digital markets is currently hotly debated worldwide.

In the EU, the European Commission and national competition authorities have in recent years made intensive use of their traditional competition tools, especially the prohibition of abuse of dominance, often proactively and experimenting with new approaches.[40] In parallel, in some Member States stricter or more easily applicable national rules such as the prohibition of abuse of dependence have also been used to constrain the economic conduct of big tech.

New regulatory tools have also been adopted or proposed aimed at setting specific *ex ante* obligations or prohibitions on digital platforms so as to prevent some conduct perceived as unfair or as undesirably strengthening their power. The new Section 19a of the German Competition Act against Restraints of Competition (GWB), for instance, gives the Bundeskartellamt the power to prohibit *ex ante* certain types of conduct by companies which, due to their strategic position and their resources, are of paramount significance for competition across markets. In the UK a proposal for a new procompetition regime for digital markets is still pending.[41] In the EU, the DMA establishes that companies declared 'digital gatekeepers' based on a number of criteria will have to comply with several predetermined regulatory constraints, listed in Articles 5 and 6 of the Regulation. The application of the new rules is with no prejudice of the application of competition or other national rules on unilateral conduct.

Comparing the approaches, the main difference is that, while pursuant to the German and UK models regulatory remedies are designed on a case-by-case basis by competition authorities taking into account the specific concerns relating to each big tech company, the DMA contains a broad, predetermined list of

[39] See for instance M Motta and M Peitz, 'Removal of potential competitors: a blind spot on merger policy?' (2020) 6 *Competition Law and Policy Debate* 19, and the authors cited therein.

[40] For an overview of such cases, see European Competition Network, 'Joint Paper of the heads of the national competition authorities of the European Union – How national competition authorities can strengthen the DMA', June 2021.

[41] Competition and Markets Authority (CMA), 'Advice of the Digital Markets Taskfore on a new procompetition regime for digital markets', December 2020.

regulatory requirements which should be applied to all the core platform services of digital gatekeepers. Differently from Article 102 TFEU or even the prohibition of abuse of economic dependence, the DMA obligations are not based on general and abstract notions and are meant to be more directly prescriptive 'dos and don'ts'. There is expected to be room for some regulatory dialogue with the Commission on the way in which each platform will have to comply with the obligations, but in practice the provisions of the DMA leave no room for objective justifications and exceptions.

Clearly, this broadening of the policy toolbox enables public authorities in Europe to more effectively constrain the power of big tech companies. However, there are further dimensions which should be explored, looking in particular at the DMA in light of the continuous search for a system which sets proper bounds on economic power while maintaining proper constraints also on regulatory powers and their enforcement.

When transforming specific rules of conduct emerging from the case law into general rules which constrain the fundamental freedoms of regulated companies, or when introducing completely new rules, EU legislation should comply with its commitment to better regulation and thus respect the necessity and proportionality principles. These principles should be considered, first of all, in the legislative process, ie when adopting the rules, but may be relevant also when the rules will have to be interpreted and applied.

In this respect, it is of the utmost importance that the objectives which are being pursued by means of the DMA are also clearly bounded, so that it is easier to ascertain what is necessary and when it is proportionate to pursue them.

The DMA refers to two different objectives: fairness and contestability. The reference to fairness is not a source of concern because the notion is already used not only in Article 102(a) but in several other pieces of EU legislation.[42] Hence, it does not seem too difficult to find limiting principles.

On the contrary, the reference to contestability, ie the reduction of barriers to entry and exit, is new in EU legislation. It may be interpreted in two different ways with diverging results. If the contestability goal is interpreted as removing specific barriers which hamper effective competition in digital markets, thus linking contestability to the objective of ensuring effective competition, we remain in an area of known objectives and notions. If, instead, contestability is considered a value in its own right, going beyond ensuring effective competition, we enter into an unexplored area, with unclear boundaries.

The experience of competition law shows that a strength of the EU system that has contributed to making it a good model for competition policy worldwide is its

[42] See, for instance, Directive 2005/29/EC of the European Parliament and the Council of 11 May 2005 concerning unfair business-to-consumer commercial practices in the internal market, OJ L 49/22; Directive (EU) 2019/633 of the European Parliament and the Council of 17 April 2019 on unfair trading practices in business to business relationships in the agricultural and food supply chain, OJ L 11/59; Regulation (EU) 2019/1150 of the European Parliament and the Council of 20 June 2019 on promoting fairness and transparency for business users of online intermediation services, OJ L 186/57.

firm roots in the Rule of Law, entailing legitimacy in the perspective of a liberal economy. New public tools aimed at limiting the power of big companies should also be based on transparent goals and be bounded by clear limiting principles, thus ensuring appropriate checks and balances. Otherwise, these new tools may also be copied in other jurisdictions, but it is doubtful that this evolution would contribute to strengthening the values of liberal democracy worldwide.

Hopefully, in the enforcement of the DMA, regulatory dialogue will suffice to ensure compliance with the proportionality principle. Otherwise, we can in the future expect extensive litigation on the application of the new regulatory constraints, and the Court of Justice will be called to play a crucial role in tuning the system.

V. Institutional Design for an Effective Competition Policy

One of the main teachings of the Freiburg school is that, in the absence of strong institutional safeguards, the protection of competition is easily demoted from the priorities of the political agenda under the pressures of private and public interests which may benefit from restrictions of competition. In this section I will focus on the institutional features of public enforcement which, following the Ordoliberal suggestions, should be based on independent authorities whose decisions are subject to judicial review.

The experience of several decades in many jurisdictions, and notably the recent experience of enforcement under populist governments, have provided plenty of examples of the different ways in which a lack of independence, understood as a situation in which the public enforcer is exposed to political or other external interferences in the fulfilment of his/her institutional tasks, may hamper an effective protection of competition. For instance, a competition authority may be reluctant to use its powers to investigate and open proceedings; it may make a weak use of its fining powers for serious infringements, thus jeopardising deterrence; it may use its powers for personal or other public policy objectives different from the protection of competition; it may treat certain undertakings more leniently because of personal relationships, nationality or public ownership; it may adopt a hands-off approach in the application of competition rules in presence of public restrictions; and so on. All these potential distortions may adversely affect not only the application of the rules on agreements and abuse of dominance, but also competition advocacy and merger control.

As clearly shown in a recent volume by Maciej Bernatt, in-depth judicial review of the decisions of competition authorities is necessary, but not sufficient to avoid all these problems.[43] Lack of resources and biased incentives for public enforcers

[43] M Bernatt, *Populism and Antitrust* (CUP, 2022).

(eg expected personal advantages or fear of being removed from the duty before expiry of the term of appointment) may also weaken the ability to strive for an effective protection of competition.

In the EU, a significant development in the construction of an effective institutional framework for public enforcement was the establishment, with Regulation 1/2003, of the ECN: the competition authorities of Member States are linked together in the network and may use their joint forces to strengthen the system and react to perceived weaknesses and gaps. Interestingly, when mounting populist waves in Europe made it evident that the effectiveness of competition enforcement was at risk in some Member States, concerns within the ECN led the Commission to propose a legislative initiative (the ECN+ Directive) aimed at strengthening the institutional safeguards for competition authorities in the Member States.[44] While Article 35 of Regulation 1/2003 simply required Member States to ensure that national competition authorities were capable of effectively applying EU rules, the new Directive goes into greater detail, setting more specific requirements for independence, resources, powers and obligation of mutual assistance.

Given the importance of the institutional framework for an effective public enforcement of competition rules, it is worth pointing out how it can be affected by developments in substantive rules. In particular, the current debate on how to ensure a closer coordination of competition policy and other public policies and whether to make competition policy more 'multitask' should take into account the potential impact of the different solutions on the decision-making process.

Looking at decision-making within the European Commission, if competition rules are not designed in a way which ensures a strong protection of the competitive process, the role of the Competition Commissioner would be weakened and other public policy concerns falling within the specific mandate of other Commissioners would more easily prevail. In the Member States, the broader the power of national enforcers to balance different goals, the less likely it will be that national governments will refrain from applying pressure to national competition authorities in individual decisions.

Clearly, in the broader political system there may be cases of true trade-off in which other public policy goals (eg sustainability) may prevail over the protection of competition as such. However, for a proper operation of this broader system it is wise to preserve the role of specialised competition authorities, acting as independent competition advocates. If such a role is preserved, competition authorities may be able to effectively perform their task with overall benefits for the system. With respect to legislative and administrative measures, they can focus on showing that in most cases it is possible to pursue other policy goals in a non-anticompetitive

[44] Directive (EU) 2019/1 of the European Parliament and the Council of 11 December 2018 to empower the competition authorities of the Member States to be more effective enforcers and to ensure the proper functioning of the internal market, OJ L 11/3.

way; when trade-offs are unavoidable, they may usefully suggest how to minimise distortions of competition.

VI. A Permanent Agenda

In his seminal book of 1997 Giuliano Amato wrote that his aim was to remind both young students and specialists that, beyond technical profiles, competition law has a deep political and philosophical dimension: antitrust is meant to address the fundamental dilemma of the liberal democracy, ie how to set proper boundaries for both private economic power and public power.

In the last quarter of a century, many things have changed, both in the US and in Europe. However, the objective of setting effective boundaries around private and public powers remains at the core of an intellectual and political agenda aimed at preserving a decentralised, free and dynamic economy and society. Recent developments have made the crucial role of this goal increasingly clear. Thus, we can claim that the agenda outlined in Amato's book can be seen as a permanent agenda, which the competition community and policymakers should pursue for years to come.

Looking at the EU in this way, in this chapter I have argued that one of the main current challenges is to find a way to coordinate antitrust with other public policies while preserving a strong role for competition. As to the enforcement of competition rules, in the last 25 years – also in light of the case-law of the European Court of Justice – we have reached a better understanding of how to combine economic and legal tools. Moreover, the multidimensional nature of the competition process, ie the possibility to develop theories of harm looking at the impact of a firm's conduct not only on price, but also on quality, choice and innovation, provides the needed flexibility to address new challenges arising, for instance, from the digital transformation. A key open issue, at the interface of the protection of rights and the effectiveness of competition policy, remains the standard of proof which should be required for findings of infringements of antitrust rules and for merger control.

9

Digital Antitrust and Private Powers: The (Uneasy) Case of Marketplace Platforms

ROBERTO PARDOLESI

I. Digital Nightmares and Competition

Twenty-five years ago, Giuliano Amato portrayed liberal democracy as coping with a structural paradox: the fundamental freedom to trade of individuals, assumed to be the very essence of economic liberalism, can lead, via the creation of market power, to the opposite phenomenon of private power. This event, then, is able not only to trigger infractions of the economic freedom of other individuals, but also to reshape the balance of public decisions. Time has gone by, and even if the overall framework may appear different (or, if you, prefer, 'digital'), the dilemma is still there – only, one might say, with diverse mood and touch.

When Professor Amato was teaching his classes in New York, the antitrust mainstream was busily involved in the attempt to redefine its impact through the lens of economic efficiency. The consumer welfare paradigm – as outlined, with some approximation, by Robert Bork – emerged as a reaction (populist, albeit in academic disguise) to the enthusiasms and excesses of a populism of opposite vein, which from the very beginning sensed the anti-monopoly discipline as a means to counter the economic and political power of the 'robber barons', as such open to further social solicitations – to the point of making the overall picture confused and, at times, contradictory. The 'new learning', with a Chicagoan imprinting, would have derived scientific validation from the rigorous use of microeconomic approach, redesigning the entire framework for US competition enforcement and attracting elsewhere scholarly attention, even though filtered, such as in the case of Giuliano Amato. Be it as it may, something collapsed in recent times: the lone star of allocative efficiency wavers against the growing discomfort of a social fabric in deep crisis. And the demand for justice (including economic fairness) becomes more pressing and vocal.[1] Impatience is the daughter of discomfort.

[1] There is some truth, of course, in the heartfelt appeals of those who denounce the inanity of today's antitrust in the face of social imbalances that are increasingly worsening and point to other very noble

The unease – 'competition betrayed' is the underlying slogan – translated into the widespread call for the return to the 'golden era'. A movement has formed ('neo-Brandeisian' for its followers, 'hipster antitrust' for sceptics), that is eager to return to a structurally oriented conception of competition, which can be receptive of 'other' interests, as well as political considerations.

Such a discomfort is linked, among other things, to the increasing compliance with the monopoly aggregates, which seems to derive from the assignment of a role of technocratic centrality to allocative efficiency (identified by its most resolute critics as a grotesque distortion of the painstakingly outlined objectives in 1890). Criticisms also point to the obviously implicit preference for underenforcement, justified by the theory of error costs: a preference that runs through slogans such as 'protection of competition and not competitors', and which often favours passivity and inaction, and tolerates the paralysis induced by the substitution of easy per se rules with the unsolved difficulties of the rule of reason. The lowest point is the practical divestment of Section 2 of the Sherman Act, prompting critics to complain that monopolisation no longer exists in the US. (Europe, which has a moderate anti-American gradient, tells a different story.)

The result is even more harsh considering that the digital dimension, propitiating an 'extreme return to scale', dramatically amplifying network externalities and creating the 'power of data'[2] from scratch, has indeed triggered new threats that fundamentally differ from those in the past.[3] In the view of traditional antitrust scrutiny, tech giants/titans/behemoths are aliens: they don't raise prices, because

values that would be worth including in the list of purposes to be pursued with resolute determination (*cf*, *ex permultis*, EA Posner and CR Sunstein, 'Antitrust and Inequality (1 February 2022), available at ssrn.com/abstract=4023365 or dx.doi.org/10.2139/ssrn.402336531, suggesting that 'antitrust law could, with little violence, be turned toward advancing consumer welfare (in the sense of utility) rather than consumer surplus'). But it is likely that, in this – decidedly inclusive – way, more is asked of antimonopoly enforcement than it can objectively give, exposing it moreover to the risk of nullifying the heuristic heritage accumulated up to now. Getting hands in such a tangle of vipers is an undertaking into which I have already ventured; and I'll be careful not to repeat the mistake. For those who manage to avoid the morbid coils of the ideological debate, however, the argument of a scholar who has always given proof of calm wisdom (deserved the title of 'dean of American antitrust law') may be provident: see, starting right from his most recent contribution, H Hovenkamp, 'President Biden's Executive Order on Promoting Competition: An Antitrust Analysis' (18 July 2021), available at papers.ssrn.com/sol3/papers.cfm?abstract_id=3887776. Of course, no one has a magic wand, but there are those who show to know how to look further away, without being overwhelmed by the emotionality of the contingent.

[2] 'Power of data' refers both to abusive deployment of personal data, triggered by the vulnerability of data subjects, and to the entirely different problem of data sharing, in the face of the fact that a small number of Big Techs hold most of world's data and determine access opportunities. This latter problem is the very core of the recent European proposal of a regulation 'on harmonised rules on fair access to and use of data (Data Act)', COM(2022) 68 final, 2022/0047 (COD); to be compared to the fanciful alternative sketched by KA Houser and JA Bagby, 'The Data Trust Solution to Data Sharing Problems', forthcoming in *Vanderbilt Journal of Entertainment & Technology Law*, available at papers.ssrn.com/sol3/papers.cfm?abstract_id=4140083.

[3] See, for an overview (among the many, more or less apocalyptic, accumulated in recent times), the 'disruption analysis' by J Crémer, YA De Montjoye and H Schweitzer, 'Competition Law for the Digital Age, Final report' (European Commission, 2019) 19 ff.

very often they provide services for free; they do not reduce the output, which – according to the canonical criterion – should exclude that their activity involves antitrust dangers, though (somebody pretends) it ought to be evident that GAFAM and its surroundings[4] degrade the quality of the product, particularly in terms of privacy; they increase the forms of social surveillance; they operate spectacular shifts of wealth; they reduce confidence in the markets; impose significant diseconomies on third parties, restrictively modulating innovation; they feed widespread moral, social and political concerns; and they show a marked ability to endure.[5]

Of course, the main actors of the new digital economy, with a market capitalisation amounting to a trillion dollars, have scaled the world, achieving in a short time (most of them did not exist 30 years ago) turnovers exceeding the budgets of many industrialised countries. They have also profoundly changed that world, radically reshaping our lives: the most recent novel by Don De Lillo induces us to take note of it, imagining a blackout capable of eliminating technology, leading to a digital apocalypse that recedes humanity to the analogical dimension, condemning it, in practice, to silence.[6] The extraordinary contribution made by new technologies is implicit in all of this: their advent has marked conspicuous progress, on closer inspection, disrupting innovations, though promptly absorbed as indispensable; but it has also laid bare possible inadequacies of the existing discipline. A recent OECD snapshot of the field looks like a *cahier de doléance*:

> [12] The market power of the digital platforms … results partly from the digital markets' distinctive economic features that, when taken together, may lead to a degree of failure of the natural competitive process to deliver competitive outcomes … [14] Together, these features generate a winner-takes-all/winner-takes-most dynamics where markets are prone to tipping and become highly concentrated around a single or a few dominant platforms. If a platform has access to key inputs (such as data or access to essential online infrastructure), capital and a large, stable number of users … it can leverage such market power on other markets. Such strategy can be carried out throughout the acquisition of other companies, for example in order to obtain a crucial data set or to eliminate a potential competitor (so-called 'killer acquisitions'), creating 'moats' around their businesses. Given the significant barriers to entry that make them not easily contestable, large incumbent players appear not to be under threat from new

[4] The magnificent four – Google, Apple, Facebook and Amazon – plus Microsoft, which in itself makes a story because it belongs to the generation prior to the advent of the Internet.

[5] For this vibrant indictment, see already, emblematically, M Stucke, 'Should We Be Concerned About Data-opolies?' (2018) 2 *Georgetown Law Technology Review* 275, which can be counteracted (also in this case *ex permultis*) by the 'technocratic' defence of DD Sokol, 'Antitrust's "Curse of Bigness" Problem', (2020) 118 *Michigan Law Review* 1258, 1280 (review of Tim Wu's book, *The Curse of Bigness: Antitrust in the New Gilded Area* (Columbia Global Reports, 2018): 'Antitrust does well dealing with antitrust problems. To the extent that there are other related problems, the right answer is not to create an antitrust that lacks democratic accountability (because antitrust becomes regulation via the backdoor) and exceeds its mandate of the past forty years. Rather, the better solution is to identify the underlying problem and solve it with more effective tools').

[6] *The Silence* is, in fact, the title of the book, published by Scribner.

> entry and are hard to dislodge while innovative digital firms and start-ups that do not have access to the same competitive advantages (eg, user base, data, presence across different markets) find it difficult to compete with them. [15] The leveraging of market power means that gatekeeper platforms are able to create an ecosystem of services, in which users may become locked-in by high switching costs that may be raised by each new service added to the ecosystem. In some cases, damage to competition may be difficult to reverse'.[7]

To complete the picture, the digital tsunami contributed to a spectacular sublimation of private powers, never so cogent in their previous epiphanies. The dizzying growth and entrenchment of digital giants met scarce resistance in still indefinite markets, and this might be already a chapter for the indictment of classical antitrust:

> [The existing competition rules] are only meant to prevent the creation of market power through means other than internal growth and competition on the merits. They cannot, and are not meant to, prevent an undertaking from becoming dominant because they develop and offer a good product. [At least as currently interpreted, they] are insufficient to protect competition in digital platform markets that are prone to tipping. For one, competition law is only meant to prevent the creation of market power through means other than internal growth resulting from competition on the merits. If it is true that markets, once they have tipped, are subject to such strong barriers to entry that the incumbent becomes impossible to dethrone, then even legally acquired monopolies can result in serious harm to consumer welfare that market forces and competition law cannot address. Merger control and abuse of dominance rules are powerless against these situations, as long as the dominant undertaking does not engage in exclusionary or exploitative conduct.[8]

These feeds increasingly favour diagnoses on irreversibly hegemonised markets (or clusters of markets), all converging on a fatal decline of competition.[9] To be revitalised at any cost, fighting back with initiatives ranging from the demise of the ex-post antimonopoly niceties, such as relevant market and dominance, to

[7] OECD Secretariat, 'Ex ante regulation of digital markets – Background Note', DAF/COMP (1 December 2021) 15, 8-9 (footnotes omitted).

[8] AC Witt, 'Platform regulation in Europe – per se rules to the rescue?' (forthcoming in (2022) 18 *Journal of Competition Law & Economics*), 18 February 2022, available at ssrn.com/abstract=4017504 or dx.doi.org/10.2139/ssrn.4017504a.

[9] 'There are growing concerns that these platforms have unprecedented market power, which if left unchecked could lead to worse economic but also political outcomes for society, thus negatively impacting the benefits of the digital revolution': D Geradin and D Katsifis, 'Selecting the right regulatory design for pro-competitive digital regulation: An analysis of the EU, UK, and US approaches', www.ssrn.com, 19 March 2022, available at ssrn.com/abstract=4025419 or dx.doi.org/10.2139/ssrn.4025419, who at 5 state: 'While a valuable tool and arguably the primary mechanism for preserving competition in a free market economy, it is widely acknowledged that antitrust enforcement suffers from certain limitations which render it insufficient to deal with competition challenges in digital market'. Accordingly, 'There is thus an increasing consensus across the world that ex post antitrust rules should be complemented by ex ante regulation for digital markets, the purpose being to act prophylactically to protect and promote competition to the benefit 'of consumers. The question is not whether but when and how ex ante regulation will be introduced' (33).

some sort of targeted *ex ante* regulation,[10] up to the (un)confessed deconcentrating anxiety of the 'big is bad'.

Approaches of this kind have the undoubted advantage of focusing attention on critical issues of considerable depth,[11] which must be taken seriously, in order, if nothing else, to avoid worsening problems; but their propensity to make a bundle of all grass and to outline the stereotype of the new algorithmic villain, which attracts intransigent reactions (up to the specter of a dystopic crusade), does not help to unravel the problem. Digital platforms do not exhibit unitary physiognomic traits.[12] The so-called aggregators, starting from general search engines, have indigenous features and create 'local' problems, as they are very different from those that characterise transaction platforms, such as Amazon. In particular, those who govern a marketplace, where – in the perspective of a 're-intermediation', which has taken the place of the dream of a network capable of eliminating the need to resort to vertical distribution chains – supply and demand converge, manage relationships with both commercial users (P2B) and final consumers (P2C) and need to implement the reliability of the former to obtain the loyalty of the latter (and thus justify the extraction of their personal data, to be conveyed in the flow of Big Data processing: this is common to all information society services, among which those connected to online intermediation constitute a specific subset); and all this takes place, at both levels of relationships, on the basis of the deployment of contractual clauses unilaterally arranged by the relative platform, which thus expresses its corporate regulatory power. 'Terms and conditions', to be evoked with a click and approved by ticking a check, reproduce – at least in appearance – the logic of standard forms, typical of the industrial era supplanted by the digital revolution. It is, therefore, the version in bytes of a legal technology that emerged with the massification of market operations, so that, on the one hand, we are led to note that not everything that pertains to the protagonists of the internet reifies unexplored dimensions, on the other hand, to opine that solutions workable in the past can be reproduced, with the appropriate adjustments, and perhaps even work.

In fact, this is exactly what the euro-unitary legislator seems to think: as will be seen further, Regulation 2019/1150, Article 3, proposes an approach based on

[10] Plenty of initiatives, as remarked by DD Sokol, 'A framework for digital platform regulation' (2021) 17 *Competition Law International* 95, yet exposed to the danger of ending up 'overly broad and overly sweeping' in terms of the impact on the organisation of the activities of digital platforms, with likely unintended, negative consequences on competition and innovation.

[11] With the consequence, emphasised by W Kerber+, 'Digital Revolution, Institutional Coevolution, and Legal Innovations' (8 December 2021) 5, available at https://papers.ssrn.com/sol3/papers.cfm?abstract_id=3991012, that 'From an economic perspective, it can be expected that such a radical and disruptive technological and economic change as in the digital transformation will also lead to a significant change of the legal and regulatory framework for markets and the economy, *ie* that a technological revolution will and has to be followed by an institutional coevolution'.

[12] For an updated inventory of taxonomic criteria, and of their produce, see E Murati, 'What are digital platforms? An overview of definitions, typologies, economics, and legal challenges arising from the platform economy in EU' (2021) 1 *European Journal of Privacy Law and Technologies* 19, 27ff.

transparency and accessibility of the general (standard) contract terms (GCTs), on the assumption that the availability of adequate information is the best way to restore an authentic (and salvific) competitive relaunch, designed to denervate the arrogance of great private powers. Except that this story has already been told; and it looks too much like wishful thinking imbued with ineffable naivety. The fourth revolution, in the taxonomy of Luciano Floridi, might need a legal upheaval.

From the above, it is possible to derive a series of 'interlocutory morals', all in the vein of reasonable obviousness: that private powers are not an invention of our time; that they are divided into various formats, not all attributable to crude economic power, are sometimes expressed in, so to speak, 'procedural' versions (attention will be given to these in the following pages), and postulate remedies, when necessary, tailored to specific problems and not on the basis of recipes *bonnes à tout faire*; that competition, when it exists, is usually good, but it is far from untying all the knots.

II. At the Roots of Corporate Regulatory Power

Although the GCTs practised by Google and other gatekeepers[13] appear on users' monitors as tick-boxes, they are not ontologically different from those used in the earlier practice of large public utility service providers. From this point of view, it can be agreed that it is, as already mentioned, a phenomenon with origins dating back to – even important, but fragmentary – judicial incursions.[14] Out, therefore, from the radar of the legislator: with the only exception, starting from 1942, of the Italian one, which introduced, in Article 1341 of the Civil Code (later complemented by Article 1342), a visionary discipline (for that era). Visionary, yet doomed to become sterile within a few seasons, for two basic reasons. First: the clauses predetermined by the entrepreneur in view of a generalised application

[13] A term that, shortly thereafter, due to the arrival of the Euro-unit Digital Market Act, will indicate the 'providers of core platform services' that '(i) have a significant impact on the internal market, (ii) operate one or more important gateways to customers and (iii) enjoy or are expected to enjoy an entrenched and durable position in their operations' (as stated in the Explanatory Memorandum accompanying the proposal made public on 15 December 2020), whereas it would perhaps be more appropriate to reserve it for the 'emerging regulatory conscription of large firms' – Big Banks, Big Oil, Big Pharma, etc – playing a role (improper but effective) of 'public regulator': *cf*, for a first review of a scenario full of novelties (and, needless to say, of pitfalls), R Van Loo, 'The New Gatekeepers: Private Firms as Public Enforcers' (2020) 106 *Virginia Law Review* 467.

[14] See R Pardolesi, 'Clausole abusive (nei contratti dei consumatori): verso una direttiva abusata?' (1994) 117 *Il Foro Italiano* 137; R Pardolesi, 'Clausole abusive, pardon vessatorie: verso l'attuazione di una direttiva abusata' (1995) *Rivista critica del diritto privato* 523; also R Pardolesi and A Pacces, 'Clausole vessatorie e analisi economica del diritto: note in margine alla ragioni (e alle incongruenze) della nuova disciplina' *Diritto privato 1996, II, Condizioni generali e clausole vessatorie* (Giuffrè, 1997) 377.

to his commercial relations would be binding if knowable by the counterparty according to a duty of ordinary diligence (a criterion definitely punitive for a consumer inevitably 'distracted'). Second: the clauses deemed to be particularly vexatious would be subject to the obligation of specific written acceptance, featuring the sort of danger signal expected to provoke the conscious reaction of the counterparty (an optimistic expectation, given that most consumers fail to read the small print).

However, rather than following a well-trodden trajectory, it is probably better to take a shortcut, that of economic analysis of law (EAL), which, in a deliberately eccentric perspective, promises to grasp links otherwise destined to remain in the shadows. Even at the cost of moving from its asphyxiated original position, conditioned by the perception that GCTs, on the one hand, involve a drastic reduction in transaction costs, without which the 'mass contracts', in particular those that Gino Gorla labeled 'quick-hand transactions',[15] would simply be unworkable and, on the other hand, reify a systematic deviation from the dispositive/default rules of code extraction, it follows that, as a rule, it signals the 'bad quality' of the pretermitted disciplinary index (better to say, its inability to manage interests of the majority of the associates, but which, in the specific case, must be taken with a pinch of salt, given that the deviation is not the result of an instinctive convergence of the contracting parties on a shared programme, but of the unilateral predisposition by those who adopt modules, forms and so on).

From this view, the GCTs appear to be a necessary evil: evil represented, according to common sense, by their 'one-sidedness', that is, by the fact that they are programmatically bent in the sense of privileging the position of the predisposing – at the limit, unaware of the jugulatory character of the imposed discipline and even inclined to disapply it, when it ascertains its excesses, freeing it from the burden of risks that are regularly charged to the counterparty. Considering for a moment (but without conceding) that this narrative corresponds to the truth[16] and doing summary justice of a series of clarifications that would also contribute to a more realistic recognition, 'a question spontaneously arises': why is all this not remedied? This question can be reframed by asking why the GCTs are so monotonically oriented. And, in this regard, the EAL provides a valuable contribution, removing from the circle some replies mistakenly accredited as common sense.

A. Market Power?

First, it should be made clear that the entrepreneur's 'hubris', in the face of a counterpart unable to object to the vexatiousness of the clauses imposed on her, is not

[15] G Gorla, 'Standard Conditions and Form Contracts in Italian Law' (1962) 11 *American Journal of Comparative Law* 1, 7.

[16] On this point (and, indeed, on many other empirical implications of the phenomenon), see TD Rakoff, 'Contracts of Adhesion. An Essay in Reconstruction' (1983) 96 *Harvard Law Review* 1174, 1221.

the product of the market power of the former. The idea that the unequal nature of the adhesion contract derives in a straight line from the monopoly power of the predisposing party, possibly resulting from illicit collusion or enjoyed in the context of the typical oligopolistic indolence, is blatantly denied by the circumstance that the recourse to the CGTs is independent of the connotation, competitive or not, of the reference market: it is used by subjects to whom it would not be possible to attribute the ability to manipulate the general structure. The truth is that the operator endowed with substantial market power has no incentive to offer a product, and therefore a contract, different and worse than the one that would be offered by companies active in a highly competitive sector[17] (provided that conditions are not met in which it is tempting to enter into discrimination among customers), simply because it is easier for them to translate their dominance into profits via a more-than-competitive price. It follows that the monopolistic explanation of 'take it or leave it', dear to Friedrich Kessler[18] and popular in many doctrinal voices of our debate, fails to hold its own, except in very limited circumstances. This is the case, for example, of the German saga of Facebook.

The story,[19] which witnesses (from 2016) the harsh confrontation between the prestigious Bundeskartellamt and the dominant social network over the potential anticompetitive relevance of conduct regarding the processing and analysis of platform users' personal data, recorded the incisive intervention by the Bundesgerichtshof, for which the *punctum dolens* of that arm wrestling is represented by the elimination of the possibility of choice (*fehlende Wahlmöglichkeit*) of users, or by the decision not to offer them a choice when using Facebook services: hence, from the *vulnus* inflicted to what once was magnified as 'consumer sovereignty'; the abuse *sub specie* of compromised decision-making autonomy of users, in association with the infringement of their constitutionally guaranteed right to informative self-determination, perpetrated by denying the choice of those who want to use Facebook but do not wish to share personal data with third parties. In other words, the Bundeskartellamt expresses the belief that the protection of personal data is a province of its own, but can also be scrutinised as a violation of the general clause that prohibits the dominant company from imposing unfair contractual conditions; the Bundesgerichtshof, for its part, detects in those same

[17] See already A Schwartz, 'A Reexamination of Nonsubstantive Unconscionability' (1977) 63 *Virginia Law Review* 1053.

[18] See especially F Kessler, 'Contracts of Adhesion – Some Thoughts about Freedom of Contract' (1943) 43 *Columbus Law Review* 629.

[19] Waiting for the next episode, which involves the Kirchberg judges, see, in summary, R Pardolesi, R Van den Bergh and F Weber, 'Facebook e i peccati da *Konditionenmissbrauch*' (2020) *Mercato concorrenza regole* 507. But there is also an Italian 'version': Cons State, section VI, 29 March 2021, n 2631, (2021) 146 *Il Foro italiano*, III part, 325, with a note by A Davola and R Pardolesi, 'Protezione dei dati personali, tutela della concorrenza e del consumatore (alle prese con i "dark pattern"): parallele convergenti?'.

contractual conditions, which are harmful to privacy, a directly anticompetitive behaviour. The former instance, therefore, endorses the idea that the two disciplines are separate, the latter enhances their integration; both, in every case, presuppose their convergence, in the sign of complementarity. *Prosit.* What is interesting here, however, is that the abuse of a dominant position referred to in §19 GWB, is implemented through the CGTs that, becoming a sinister instrument of governance in the hands of the digital platform, 'trap' the user in a structure that she would surely have discarded if given the opportunity. It goes without saying that the plausibility of this reconstruction is destined to collapse at the very moment at which the monopolistic configuration of the reference market ceases.

B. Contractual Overpower?

It should also be ruled out that the contractual 'imbalance of power', expressed in terms of the mystique of the weaker contracting party, lies at the origin of the inequality stemming from the vexatious CGTs. The confrontation between entrepreneur and consumer within the single operation is intended to be marked by the insuperable fragility of the latter, engaged in a superficial routine, in the face of the professional commitment of the former, even when the economic consistency of the subjects tells, in absolute terms, a contrary story (with the consumer able to buy the company that extorted him). But in this way, one pretends to ignore that the single economic operation is just a piece of an enlarged mosaic, which radically changes the evaluation framework. The consumer dissatisfied with the discipline set up by the other party could simply withdraw the offer and look for better assets elsewhere. Here, then, the alleged overpower of business becomes evanescent. In a competitive market it can be considered close to zero.

In even more general terms, it should be discounted that the allocation of risks in the negotiation phase tends to be inspired by the cheapest-cost-avoider principle, that is, their attribution to the person who is able to avoid them or, where they cannot be eliminated, to better manage them by self-insurance or by purchasing a policy on the market.[20] If the elimination / management of risk is better for the producer, good economic theory wants him to accept it, equating it to one of the living costs of production, and then pass it on in the final sale price of the good or service. If, on the other hand, the person best positioned with respect to the risk is a counterparty, she will assume it herself, without this having to be reflected directly in the contractual price. But the burden resulting from the absorption of the risk will result in a compression of the willingness to pay (because, in order to

[20] For an analytical presentation of the topic, see HB Schäfer and PC Leyens, 'Judicial Control of Standard Terms and European Private Law' in P Larouche and F Chirico (eds), *Economic Analysis of the DCFR. The Work of the Economic Impact Group within the CoPECL Network of Excellence* (Sellier, 2010) 99.

acquire the good or service, the consumer must not only pay the consideration, but also bear the burden of assuming the risk) and, consequently, in a contraction in demand. In theory, this means that the best price (resulting, where appropriate, from the migration of risks to the customer) does not attract consumers who are aware that the apparent convenience of the offer is largely eroded by the possible materialisation of risks which, for reasons of efficiency, should have remained with the manufacturer.

C. Failures Provoked by Information Asymmetry

Therefore, it is not the disparity in contractual power between the parties involved in the relationship and/or the power exhibited on the market that we need to look at to understand why the terms arranged by the predisposing party are so unbalanced. Market failure has deeper roots, that should be sought in the pitfalls of information asymmetry.

In a nutshell, the necessary premise relies on the observation that – usually, although not necessarily – the consumer does not know; moreover, it is good that she does not know.[21] It is already difficult for her to fully appreciate the meaning of a complex contractual clause; in any case, the cost associated with examining and comparing the contractual terms prepared by the various manufacturers is discouraging. Placing the duty to read on the consumer has the sole effect of exacerbating the 'no-reading problem' of texts which often bears the stigmata of programmatic illegibility.[22] In any case, whenever the advantage derived from the acquisition of the necessary information is lower than the burdens to be borne to obtain it, the natural response is 'to close your eyes and hope for the best', trusting the logic of herd behaviour. This response will be almost inevitable when the value of the deal, as often happens in the consumer sector, is low; and, more significantly,

[21] Be careful, however, not to indulge in an overly optimistic version of this line of argument, such as that articulated by GM Cole, 'Rational Consumer Ignorance: When and Why Consumers Should Agree to Form Contracts Without Even Reading Them' (2015) 11 *Journal of Law, Economics & Policy* 413.

[22] See generally (but corrosively) U Benoliel and SH Becher, 'The Duty to Read the Unreadable' (2019) 60 *Boston College Law Review* 2235. The only remedy, in the US context, is 'unconscionability', breached from the right, for its indefinable vagueness, and from the left, for the scarce incisiveness of its applicative scope (even if the summary judgments of those who give it for extinct should, perhaps, be downsized, as JH Russel invites to do: 'Unconscionability's Greatly Exaggerated Death' (2019) 53 *UC Davis Law Review* 965). The fact is that its breathing has been, and continues to be, somewhat reduced. It is no coincidence, to give an example animating very 'hectic' debates, that the tool has proved useless to neutralise the clauses of the 'boilerplate' which require (consumers, workers) arbitration and preclude recourse to class action (see, for some significant testimony, RB Kar and MJ Radin, 'Pseudo-Contracts and Shared Meaning Analysis' (2019) 132 *Harvard Law Review* 1135, 1203 ff., and TD Rakoff and JS Rakoff, 'Arbitration, "Pseudo Contracts", and Objective Theory' (2019) 133 *Harvard Law Review Forum* 13). Nor is it surprising, then, that somebody inclined to activate much less orthodox techniques (evidently grateful to X-T Nguyen, 'Disrupting Adhesion Contracts with #MeToo Innovators' (2019) 24 *Virginia Journal of Social Policy & Law* 165.

any in-depth analysis will be skipped because no request for consideration is made, according to the business model adopted by the platforms such as Google or FB, which is intended to hide the consideration represented by the 'capture' of the user's attention, to be sold profitably to advertisers, or by the transfer of one's personal data, or by both together, without any indication of the consequences.[23]

Given these assumptions, it can be expected that the market will not be capable of expressing redeeming qualities: because consumers, when aware but optimistic (in the sense of presuming that only risks for which they qualify as subjects best positioned to absorb or insure them will be borne), are exposed to the danger of also having to bear risks that should not compete with them; while producers are encouraged to unbalance the contractual setting as much as possible, to the detriment of customers unable to react, so as to be ahead of their rivals. The resulting balance, concerning price and quantity, is doomed to taste like Akerlof's lemons:[24] it will not reflect the overload of risks for consumers, who, therefore, will pay more and suffer an unexpected decrease in terms of welfare, where the profit of the entrepreneurial party, filed by competitive tension, remains unchanged, for want of the signalling practices of producers (who, moreover, have no interest in correcting their customers' optimism) or consumer screening aimed at avoidance of degeneration. Similar results are expected for consumers who, conversely, expect – because they are educated by the media, specialised intermediaries, and online information, etc – to be subjected to unbalanced contractual regulation. Their reluctance will lead to a reduction in supply and suboptimal market outcomes, since the producer willing to offer better contractual conditions will not be given the opportunity to overcome the mistrust of the counterparty.

It is worth noting, incidentally, that this approach removes from the scenario the defence strategy against the failures of the unilateral forging of standardised contracts based on the recovery of contractual parity through the removal of the information asymmetry: this was, after all, the intuition underlying the Italian code discipline of the CGTs,[25] not too different from more modern techniques of

[23] On the 'privacy paradox', ie the net gap, in the sign of the consumer's rational apathy, between declared preferences and those 'revealed' in fact, see, as a first approximation, S Barth and MDT De Jong, 'The privacy paradox – Investigating discrepancies between expressed privacy concerns and actual online behavior – A systematic literature review' (2017) 34 *Telematics and Informatics* 1038. A far more sceptical view, despite the empirical findings according to which 'the most common feeling is that consumers do not like being targeted with advertisements, but they would not want to pay for any of these services, either', is offered by P Akman, 'A Web of Paradoxes: Empirical Evidence on Online Platforms Users and Implications for Competition and Regulation in Digital Markets' (2022) 16 *Virginia Law and Business Review* 217, esp 22ff and 35ff. At the root of the confrontation there is a thorny question: how much is privacy worth? A tentative (and quite surprising) answer, on the basis of empirical findings, is offered by J Price and RS. Wallstein, 'Empirical Evidence of the Value of Privacy' (2021) 12 *Journal of European Competition Law & Practice* 648.

[24] The adverse selection due to information asymmetry, which condemns the market to qualitative degradation, earned GA Akerlof, 'The Market for Lemons: Quality Uncertainty and the Market Mechanism' (1970) 84 *Quarterly Journal of Economics* 488, the Nobel Prize (2001).

[25] The Italian legislator assumed that, warned of the pitfall, the weak contracting party would have regained control of the situation and made her own choices with good reason. But the highlighting

highlighting truly unexpected rules, according to an ingenious proposal by Ayres and Schwartz[26] and, on balance, in accordance – in spirit – with the discipline introduced by the already recalled EU Regulation 2019/1150 (requiring, however, an ad hoc analysis, which we will get to in a moment).

Returning to the information asymmetry, it is difficult to remove to the point of envisaging a real (albeit partial) failure of the market. The effect of speeding up and rationalising commercial operations, promoted by the deployment of CGTs, is substantially distorted by the 'race to the bottom' resulting from competition for those who adopt the most disadvantageous clauses for consumers. (What is the sense, after all, of setting up 'clear pacts' – as Fiat did in 1993, adding to the list of failed attempts to relaunch the virtues of 'right' commercial practices – if the recipient of the most balanced GCTs offer is unable to assess the better quality rather than engaging in the desperate adventure of explaining the advantages of a consumer-friendly contractual text? Is it not easier to abandon the project and propose a more aggressive price, in the knowledge that attention will certainly be paid to that parameter?)

The result is an overall loss of efficiency, for both parties, which market forces are unable to overcome by means of learning economies (which, in our case, are produced only for the small group of subjects who have had the fortune to test its operation).

This explains the (apparently surprising) fact that vexatious clauses never die. The French Commission of Unfair Terms, in Recommendation no 21-01 filed on 10 March 2021,[27] recorded 45 contractual terms, typical of the forms relating to the *contrats de crédit à la consommation*, marked by the stigma of abusiveness, when not resolutely illicit because they are in contrast with the mandatory sector regulations: such clauses should disappear as 'unwritten', yet, as documented by the said Commission, they re-emerge at every foot pushed, if only because (in the absence of authentic deterrence, with adequately sanctionatory implications) it is still worth another attempt to deploy them.

In summary, within business-to-consumer (B2C) relations there are compelling reasons for a corrective intervention of a regulatory nature. Not because the consumer is necessarily inexperienced and defenceless (the opposite is possible; consequently, it is correct for the negotiated clause to be removed from their control), but because it is legitimate to expect that she will act that way in most cases. Bluntly speaking: no restoration of authentic competitive tension would

promoted by Arts 1341 and 1342 of the civil code had the sole effect of propitiating the practice of contracts without an agreement, and of multiple and idle subscriptions.

[26] I Ayres and A Schwartz, 'The no-reading problem in consumer contract law' (2014) 66 *Stanford Law Review* 545.

[27] For a first overview, *cf* G Poissonnier, 'Lutte contre les clauses abusives or illicites dans les contrats de crédit aà la consommation en progès mais beaucup reste à faire (2021) *Recueil Dalloz* 1636. It is hardly necessary to add that, sometimes, the contested clauses survive because the indictment against them is unfounded. But this is definitely another story.

be able to oppose the unfolding of corporate regulatory power as a paradigmatic expression of private power.

III. From B2C (in the P2C variant) to P2B

The theoretical framework that has been rapidly canvassed appears to be very solid. But this is not a good reason to lazily repropose its applicability to B2B relationships, except with regard to marginal entities or minor activities that remain on the periphery of this professional realm: in situations, that is, where it is possible to assume an information asymmetry like that experienced by the consumer (and no less difficult to bypass), according to a logic that, in Italy, has already found expression in the micro-enterprises referred to in Article 19, 1st paragraph, of the consumer code (as amended by Article 7, 2nd paragraph, Law Decree 24 January 2012, no 1, converted into Law 24 March 2002, no 27).

The aforementioned EU Regulation 2019/1150[28] seems to be inspired by a completely different and substantially opposite rationale, intended to 'promote equity and transparency for commercial users of online intermediation services'. In the introduction of the full-bodied *consideranda* accompanying the regulatory text, we read that the marketplace platforms are 'key enablers of entrepreneurship and new business models, trade and innovation', as they 'offer access to new markets and commercial opportunities', while allowing 'consumers in the Union to exploit [the benefits of an increased] choice of goods and services' at competitive prices.[29] Hence the importance of ensuring that

> undertakings can trust online intermediation services with which they enter into commercial relationships. This is important mainly because the growing intermediation of transactions through online intermediation services, fuelled by strong data-driven indirect network effects, leads to increased dependence of such business users, particularly micro, small and medium-sized enterprises (SMEs), on those services in order for them to reach consumers.

As a result of this increased dependence,

> the providers of those services often have superior bargaining power, which enables them to, in effect, behave unilaterally in a way that can be unfair and that can be harmful to the legitimate interests of their businesses users and, indirectly, also of consumers in the Union.[30]

An almost lapidary prescription corresponds to this diagnosis: the need to guarantee adequate transparency,[31] an indication that translates into the obligation for

[28] For a detailed overview of the regulation, see A Palmieri, *Profili giuridici delle piattaforme digitali. La tutela degli utenti commerciali e dei titolari di siti web aziendali* (Giappichelli, 2019), esp 51ff.

[29] Para 1.

[30] Para 2.

[31] Para 7.

the platforms to draw up their CGTs in simple and precise language[32] and to make them 'easily available at all levels of the commercial relationship, including potential commercial users in the pre-contractual phase'.[33]

These ideas bounce smoothly into Article 3 of the Regulation (titled 'Terms and conditions', which rather clumsily stands for GCTs).

The underlying expectation is that imposing the formal and substantial ostensibility of the clauses would suffice to restore the virtuous circuit of the responsible contract: the commercial user is not afflicted by irredeemable ignorance – she is obviously sensitive to the allocation of risks – so that the simple expedient of facilitating the assessment of the discipline intended to regulate the relationship will allow, in a passably competitive environment (where, that is, it is possible to reject offers deemed unattractive, because alternative options are available), to avoid traps and benefit from of a balanced regulation of negotiation.

It is to be believed, however, that the expectation on which the regulatory intervention in question is based, on the one hand, underestimates the aforementioned critical issues which the platform manager must govern to ensure its palatable agility.[34] (In this perspective, the uproar caused by the class action recently brought by a handful of Chinese companies against Amazon, which had closed the accounts of the plaintiffs because of a deliberate violation of the ban on obtaining false positive reviews,[35] should appear less than surprising, given that such techniques involve obvious market distortions. If anything, the really controversial question is whether, on this premise, the self-defence of retaining the funds accrued in favour of the plaintiffs after the termination of the relationship can be considered a reasonable remedy.) On the other hand – and more significantly – they discount an underlying naivete, which condemns them to impotence. This is similar to what happened to our civil code discipline, all hinged on the expedient of signalling possible pitfalls. This strategy should have dispelled shadows and torpor, revamping conscious bilateral negotiation with the stimuli to achieve the most appropriate setting: an ingenuous illusion, as previously observed, which faded in the late 1970s, when it was clear, from a comparative point of view, that the regulatory drift was moving towards other dimensions – ie, the *Inaltskontrolle* – on the assumption that the unfolding of private autonomy in a competitive context was no longer apt to neutralise the failures triggered by private power. From this point of view, indeed, the regulation marks a retreat from continental developments which, in relatively contemporary times, have conspicuously accelerated the

[32] Para 15.

[33] Para 18.

[34] 'The regulatory-technological power enjoyed by the company-platform is not a factor to be stigmatized. It is precisely the ability of the latter to exercise control functions on the market and its participants (in terms of access, exit, content quality, security standards, data flow and information) that generates credibility and trust among third parties': MW Monterossi, 'La tutela dell'utente commerciale nei mercati digitali' (2021) 3 *Contratto e impresa* 920, 948-49 (author's translation).

[35] *cf Shenzen Shileziyou Technologies et al v Amazon*, Class action complaint, Case 5:21-cv-07083-VKD, filed on 13 September 2021, US District Court, ND, Cal.

sector discipline, in a manner certainly at odds with that cultivated at the Euro-unitary level.

It is not possible here to give an analytical account of the reported evolution. The landscape is, in fact, varied; it brings together solicitations of a different tenor, which make it difficult to decipher. Starting from the new French approach,[36] which leaves the GCTs in the sphere of the unspoken, while attention is focused on the imbalance of rights and obligations that occurs in an adhesion contract, characterised by the presence of a group of non-negotiable clauses. Such a choice simplifies some implications, but contributes to the amplification of other doubts, relating to the same paradigm – non-negotiability – which should function as the cornerstone of the entire building. The fact is that the hexagonal byproduct of the reform (in 2018) of the reform (of 2016) crosses the German approach, which, in the version endorsed – at the beginning of the millennium – by the BGB, continues to focus on the formal and substantive control of the standard terms˙. Moreover, the Dutch statutory discipline is inspired by the latter model – albeit with a hint of originality[37] – while the Belgian approach[38] appears to be marked by hybridisations of various kinds: the result of a troublesome parliamentary coup that bore fruit on 27 May 2020 (effective in August 2020), it opts for the sum of separate regulations – one reserved for consumer contracts and the other concentrated on B2B – but then strives for the latter, in order to pursue an ideal conception of 'fair' contract, which passes, on balance, through a large duplication of the lists prepared for the former. As a result, the option, teutonic in inspiration, turns out to be shaped after a two-speed regulation – the province of consumer contracts, on the one hand; the side of business relations, on the other.

It can be argued that these trajectories are in many ways separate.[39] Yet it is possible to record a (quasi-)univocal convergence. Principled resistances to

[36] See, in particular, Art 1171 code civil, as resulting from the changes introduced by loi no 2018-287 of 20 April 2018 (Art 7).

[37] Art 6.233 of the Burgerlijk Wetbock, according to which the judge – on the basis of a concrete confirmation of the nature / content of the contract and the modalities that led to its conformation, of the interest of each party as evident for the other, and any other relevant circumstance – can suppress standardised provisions that are unreasonably burdensome for the non-predisposing party. The rule, as specified in Art 6.235(1)(b), applies to (consumers, as well as) SMEs, identified by the fact that they do not have more than 50 employees.

[38] Art VI 913 code of economic law states, in §1, that 'Pour application du présent titre, toute clause d'un contrat conclu entre entreprises est abusive lorsque, à elle seule ou combinée avec une ou plusieurs autres clauses, elle crée un déséquilibre manifeste entre les droits et obligations des parties', specifying, at § 2, that 'le caractère abusif d'une clause contractuelle est apprécié en tenant compte de la nature des produits qui font l'objet du contrat et en se référant, au moment de la conclusion du contrat, à toutes les circonstances qui entourent sa conclusion, à l'économie générale du contrat, aux usages commerciaux qui s'appliquent, de même qu'à toutes les autres clauses du contrat, ou d'un autre contrat dont il dépend'. The picture is completed by the invitation to take into account the clarity and comprehensibility of the text (as prescribed by the first paragraph of Art VI.91/2) and by the notice of the only legal nature of the abusiveness check, with the exclusion of any appreciation of the economic adequacy of the agreement. Additional basic information in J Blocx, 'Belgian Prohibition of Abuse of Economic Dependence Enters into Force' (2021) *Journal of European Competition Law and Practice* 321.

[39] For some further information, see R Pardolesi, 'Clausole abusive e terzo contratto' (2020) 145 *Il Foro Italiano* V part, 197.

content control of the standard clauses applied in contracts between companies have been overwhelmed. The comparison is no longer on whether there should be a content control or not, but on the latitude of its unfolding. To clarify: the diversity of assumptions (and the consequent divergence of relational philosophies) reveals the fragility of the idea that the extension of content control to the B2B universe (including P2B) can consist of the revival of a regulatory framework propelled by the pro-consumer vocation. Even apart from the obvious observation that information asymmetry cannot be spoken of in the presence of companies engaged in a 'battle of the forms' (with general conditions of sale for one and of purchase for the other) and when the size of the deal is of such a dimension as to postulate careful consideration, on both sides, of the legal implications, it is reasonable to assume a marked sensitivity, on the business side, to the costs underlying the contractual options, even where the strategic choice to accept unfamiliar conditions prevails. To concede everything, the discourse inevitably takes on a very different turn.

IV. An Interim Conclusion: To Each His Own

It is therefore possible to resume some of the interlocutory morals articulated at the beginning: that the pervasiveness of the 'fourth revolution', that of computational power,[40] does not authorise the flattening of phenomena which, although connected by the digital connotation, exhibit autochthonous characters.[41] The platforms, in their various articulations, provoke several problems, which cannot be easily traced back to a unitary matrix only for the identity of certain 'somatic' traits. As a blatant example, self-preferencing, the new catch-all provision covering, under the same umbrella, several practices belonging to the general category of offensive/defensive leveraging, turns out to exhibit different features if referred

[40] In the taxonomy of L Floridi, *La quarta rivoluzione. Come l'infosfera sta trasformando il mondo* (Cortina, 2017), the fourth revolution turns out to be, in all likelihood, the most radical (and potentially devastating), because it removes the centrality of the human being even with respect to his own decision-making process: no longer the outcome of reason but the produce of dynamic impulse forces, to be read from a mechanistic point of view, stripping him of the prerogative of the only 'logical' decision-maker following the developments in technology and the emergence of automatic complexes which, consistently with the requirements of the Turing test, are able to mimic human behaviour, making it impossible to make any significant distinctions. The previous upheavals had recorded the decline of man as a central figure in the divine project and in the unfolding of cosmological phenomena – following the Copernican revolution – the passage to an idea of the human being as the result of an evolutionary process similar to that of other forms of life, determined mainly by the gene / environment interaction typical of Darwin's reflection, up to the removal of the ego, imposed by Freudian thought, from the 'center of itself'. For an overview of these epochal shifts see, in summary, M Durante, *Potere computazionale. L'impatto delle ICT su diritto, società, sapere* (Moltemi, 2019).

[41] In this regard, see the useful inventory prepared by H Schweitzer and F Gutmann, 'Unilateral Practices by Digital Platforms: Facts and Myths about the Reach and Effectiveness of Competition Law' (1 June 2021), available at papers.ssrn.com/sol3/papers.cfm?abstract_id=3857751.

to an aggregator, like Google, or to platforms that, in addition to providing intermediation services, also sell their own products and might have an incentive to favour their own products, by giving them a preferential ranking on the platform over third-party competing products.[42] This reminds us that P2B is an autonomous province with respect to P2C and should be analysed separately.

Along this path, scenarios open up – all still largely to be explored – that here can only be observed from a distance. But it is plausible to hypothesise that, in the proposed dimension, the role of lone star might be up to some declination of the abuse of economic dependence – the 'new emperor's clause'[43] – vocationally oriented, under (almost) every sky of civil law (not so much to restore the salvific virtues of an appreciable competitive structure, but) to intensify the fight against contractual imbalances (well within, therefore, the perimeter of the inter-individual relation). In which case, the scope of P2B could prove to be particularly provident, given that the imprinting of the relationships reveals a marked criticality level (if not so much with regard to access, usually facilitated by the will of the platform manager to enrich the range of offers to the maximum[44]) at the termination level: as commonly noted by sector experts, nesting in the platform is, for the commercial user, a strategy, vital to propitiate success (or, at least, survival) on the digital market. This is what really matters, because, if a commercial operator does not manage to land there by taking root in a consistent, high-ranking way, it is as though he/she does not exist: the more so since the exit from the contract can involve very high costs – even the evaporation of the firm, featuring the realistic traits of an economic dependence that may erode, if not paralyse, the usual bargaining defences.

[42] 'Self-preferencing' – according to P Bougette, O Budzinski and F Marty, 'Self-Preferencing and Competitive Damages: A Focus on Exploitative Abuse', GREDEG Working Paper No 2022-01, available at ideas.repec.org/p/gre/wpaper/2022-01.html – 'can be an instrument of anti-competitive leveraging, as it may come from the online search market to the price comparison market or from mobile operating systems to smartphone applications … Self-preferencing may take forms other than leveraging, such as indirect predatory strategies and exploitative abuses. The Italian Amazon case illustrates the first strategies. Outsourcing their logistics to Amazon pushes independent sellers to opt for single homing and Amazon's growing market share in logistics reduces the competitiveness of other logistics providers …. A second consequence involves exploitative abuses … The manipulation of algorithms by the platform forces its partners to enter into contracts to improve their visibility or to subscribe to ancillary services for the same purpose. This results in wealth transfers to the platform. Consequently, self-preferencing can lead to vertical and horizontal exclusionary abuses, encourage exploitation abuses, and generate economic dependence abuses'.

[43] 'In essence', according to HW Friedeiszick and S Reinhold, 'The economics of dependence: a theory of relativity', ESMT Working Paper, No 21-02 (2021), 'economic dependence is not so much related to the structure of the market — as would typically be the case for abuses of dominance — but instead to the bargaining power of two (or more) contractual partners'.

[44] Unless a situation arises in which the platform, vertically integrated in a secondary market, has an interest in cutting out, or in any case discriminating, the downstream rival: see, in detail, E Hovenkamp, 'The Antitrust Duty to Deal in the Age of Big Tech' (22 July 2021), available at www.competitionpolicy-international.com/the-antitrust-duty-to-deal-in-the-age-of-big-tech.

10

Revisiting the Concept of Power in the Digital Era

ANNA GERBRANDY[1]

I. Introduction

Writing a contribution to celebrate the 25th anniversary of Professor Amato's *Antitrust and the Bounds of Power: The Dilemma of Liberal Democracy in the History of the Market* reminds me of my own discovery of this gem of a book. Law students in the Netherlands in the early 1990s would not necessarily have received even an introduction into European competition law. It certainly was not (yet) a separate subject, though I gained some familiarity with the topic through courses on European Economic Law. Furthermore, the Netherlands did not (yet) have a serious regime of competition law, nor anything like a blossoming enforcement practice. By working in law practice – first at a law firm and then in the court system – with the then newly minted Dutch Competition Law Act coming into force, I deepened my knowledge, both as to substance and as to procedures. It was an exciting time to work in Dutch competition law practice, not only because the new Dutch act gave rise to novel questions, both great and small, but also because around this time the more economic framework for looking at competition law enforcement gained real traction. It was perhaps similar to today's rapidly changing regulatory frameworks, but with the significant difference that 'the Internet' – with up-to-date information on new rules and regulations, all commentaries and learned contemplations at one's fingertips – had not *quite* yet reached the masses. But it was only when I returned to academia and embarked

[1] Anna Gerbrandy is professor of European Competition Law at Utrecht University, School of Law. This chapter builds upon the work of the European Research Council-funded Modern Bigness project team (grant agreement No 852005): Dr Pauline Phoa, assistant professor of European Law; and PhD candidates Viktorija Morozovaite LLM, Laura Lalikova LLM, Lisanne Hummel LLM, Carla Farinhas LLM (all at Utrecht University School of Law) and Jan Polanski LLM (who is also senior policy advisor at the Polish Competition Authority). Their presence in my academic life enriches my understanding and argumentation. Clearly, though, all (logical or other) errors in this contribution are mine.

upon the adventure of dissertation-writing that I not just found the time, but also the sense of necessity, to contemplate the following: I thought I knew the rules quite intimately. I was certainly familiar and up to date with almost all the relevant case law, even beyond competition law (I have now given up on this Herculean task). But that knowledge and familiarity turned out not to be sufficient to really grasp the meaning of the system of competition law.

Then I read Amato's book.

It was eye-opening. It made explicit – and in such succinct prose, too! – the political nature of competition law. This was a point that I had not seen made so clearly before. Amato demonstrates that inherent in any system and application of competition rules is the need to examine the line between public power and private power. And, slightly more implicitly, that where one draws the balance between them is dependent on sociocultural and political contexts; that where one draws that line is ultimately also a personal, normative, preference. This demarcation and balance of power has been a recurring theme in much of my academic teaching and writing since, not just when it comes to competition law *strictu sensu*, but also in the demarcation of the spheres of 'the market' and of 'the state', specifically in relation to public interests. It is also relevant for understanding politics, and the interplay between political philosophy, the Rule of Law basis of liberal democracies and competition law. Though here it is not just Amato that helped shape my thinking; there is a clear link even to the general notion that too much power, held too long, without any checks and balances, ought to be distrusted indiscriminately: true both in the world at large, and within the microcosms of institutions such as universities.

The concept of power is currently also at the core of a research project I am leading, which questions the role of European competition law vis-à-vis the power of big tech companies, which have mostly built an ecosystem around and upon one or more platforms. The *ex ante* question of the research project relates to power itself – what is this power, and how can we grasp it, conceptually? – followed, quite logically, by the question: which bits of that power, should it be possible to separate them, are or ought to be relevant to European competition law?

This is also the topic of my contribution in this volume, set up in a straightforward manner, asking questions which are also posed by Amato himself in more recent writings. After providing some context in section II, I will delve into our conceptualisation of power, referred to here as 'Modern Bigness' (section III), which closely follows a recent publication.[2] In section IV, I will sketch how to answer the question of relevance and implications for competition law, which (obviously) depends on where the line is drawn between public power and private power. Section V concludes.

[2] A Gerbrandy and P Phoa, 'The Power of Big Tech Corporations as Modern Bigness and a Vocabulary for Shaping Competition Law as Counter-power' in R Claassen (ed), *Wealth and Power* (Routledge, forthcoming 2022).

In line with Amato's writing style – which I wish I could emulate! – I have limited references and have focused on the flow of the argument. However, in contrast to Amato's book, which is still standing firm after 25 years, there is no finality to the line of argumentation; in a sense it is a snapshot-in-time of a conceptualisation effort to grasp complexity.

II. The Context of this Contribution: The Digitalisation of Society

Though society is always changing, the shift to a digital society and economy is surely a fundamental one. It has been labeled a transition, a paradigm shift, a new era. Though we can be sceptical about sweeping statements, it is obvious that the impact of digitalisation and datafication must be taken seriously. For the competition law community, the focus logically is on what is happening in the market(s). The relevant lemmas, also in this chapter, are, first, that digitalisation has given us many innovations and provided economic growth (and, perhaps less certainly, that it is expected to continue doing so). Second, that it has also, over time, created several very large and valuable platform companies, such Amazon, Google, Facebook/Meta, Microsoft and Apple, which have branched out into the digital economy in myriad ways. Third, and lest we overlook more recent trends, digitalisation towards integrated platformisation is underway in other segments of the economy too: for example in agriculture, healthcare and transport. Fourth, the classic platform companies – yes, they are still very young, but let us call them 'classic' nonetheless – are built around a core of digital services (or hardware for a digital age) and have branched out towards the more physical economy, which is being swept up into the platform ecosystem. (This is somewhat in contrast to sectors like agriculture and transport which are moving *towards* digitalisation, datafication and platformisation).[3]

Certainly, these classic platforms companies are 'powerful' in the common usage of that word. These platform corporations – a grouping that may include other companies than the five mentioned above – in this chapter are labelled jointly and separately as big tech companies. These big tech companies have impact not only on the market(s), but more generally on how citizens, consumers, employees and business owners work and live, how we interact and play, and how we obtain and perceive information. All this is, in its essence, not really contested. However, it is much more difficult to grasp whether these companies are also 'powerful' in a competition law sense. This is the question of section III. It is, perhaps even more difficult to then ascertain whether their impact is a good or a bad thing – both on

[3] The platformisation and the concomitant rise of platform power in the agri-food sector is the focus of research of Pauline Phoa, postdoc in the ERC project team.

balance, but also zooming in on specific behaviours – and whether this specific bad (or good) thing is relevant for competition law. Or whether it *should* be relevant for competition law. Those are questions for section IV.

III. Corporate Power of Big Tech Companies as 'Modern Bigness'

In my research team's work, presented to the competition law scholarly community, and the more recent contribution to an interdisciplinary edited volume on 'Power and Wealth',[4] we have posited that the competition law conceptualisation of and vocabulary for defining and describing 'power' falls short in recognising fully the extent and intricacies of the corporate power of big tech companies. A more developed conceptualisation is needed, which will also invite better answers to questions on competition law relevance. To enable a better grasp of this corporate power we propose a richer conceptualisation, beyond the competition law notion of 'market power'. We distinguish between the *foundations* of power, the *dimensions* of power and the *domains* across which the power can manifest.

A. Foundations of Power

The foundations of corporate power of big tech companies lie, firstly, in market power. Competition law is intimately familiar with this notion, so I will skip over most of it. However, it is relevant to note that the 'threshold' (not in the merger regulation sense of thresholds, but in a more substantive sense) of market power as leading to a dominant position – which implies the ability to behave to an appreciable extent independently of competitors and consumers, and in economic terms to the possibility of extracting monopolistic prices and excluding competitors – does not necessarily have to be met for market power to be a relevant part of the power-concept we are developing here. Integrated in the notion of market power is, in the platform economy, the understanding of the workings of network effects of multisided platforms (and lock-in and fence-off strategies). These lead to winners that capture a large share of the market and to the emergence of 'super-platforms'.

Secondly, as is also well established, the platform companies of today's digital economy function on the basis of *data*. More specifically, they function on the basis of the gathering of data, the combining of data streams, and the capabilities to infer *information* from the data. There is a continuous feedback loop within each company's systems and services, in which the information gained is fed back into the provision of services, gathering more data. Though there are relevant

[4] Gerbrandy and Phoa, 'The Power of Big Tech Corporations' (forthcoming 2022).

differences between them, for the big tech companies generally the purpose of the loop is focused on strengthening their business model, profit-making and corporate power (and not, just as an example, necessarily improving consumer satisfaction, let alone enhancing democratic institutions; and yes, strengthening democratic institutions is not normally seen as having relevance for a market-based, profit-seeking company, and I am not implying that it should hold relevance for all companies generally; more on this below). This feedback loop is especially important for business models that rely on advertising, such as the Facebook/Meta and Google ecosystems. In order to better understand corporate power of big tech companies, we suggest that having data and being able to gather data – let us call that 'data power' for now – strengthens the market power foundation of big tech companies. It is, however, the capability to do something useful with vast and growing sets of data that moves their power of beyond mere market power. It becomes informational power too.

Thirdly, a further foundation of corporate power lies in enormous, accumulated wealth, which makes it possible to invest in innovation efforts within the company's ecosystem, acquire start-ups or competing businesses, grow in size and branch out into whatever takes their fancy. In a co-tangled course of 'how these things have turned out' it is clearly very often also in the interest of start-ups themselves to be acquired; it is their raison d'être. Thus, innovation within the corporate conglomerate of the big tech companies themselves is flanked by acquiring innovation and enveloping adjacent markets.

B. Dimensions of Corporate Power

The work of Doris Fuchs provides a stepping stone in our understanding of what the combination of these foundations of corporate power of big tech companies means for having power that can be effectuated.[5] Her research focuses on the understanding of political influence by corporations. Fuchs distinguishes three dimensions of corporate power: instrumental; structural; and discursive. Whereas the instrumental dimension of power relates to the direct influencing by an actor of another actor, the structural dimension is about influencing what is placed on the agenda of a (political) process and creating the structures in which that process takes place. The discursive dimension relates to the power to shape norms, ideas and the discourse itself, that create (or limit) the availability of space for communicative practices. We build upon this work to consider that these three dimensions of corporate power of big tech companies (and probably of many other companies too), does not only relate to how power engages in the political domain, but also in other domains.

[5] D Fuchs, *Business Power in Global Governance* (Lynnen Rienner Publishers, 2007).

C. Cross-Domain Manifestations of Power

From just a cursory look at the activities (in the broad sense of that word; see also below) of the big tech companies, it is clear that their corporate power is felt not merely in the political domain, but also in the economic, the social and the personal domains. We distinguish these domains to better understand how the corporate power of big tech companies may manifest in society. Thus, the political domain, for the purpose of this chapter, relates to power structures and decision-making by governments; it is the domain of citizens and governments. This is also the domain in which, formally, but context-specifically, the precise demarcation between (and acceptance of) power between private parties and the government is shaped. It is the public domain, and when Amato speaks of 'public power', this is the domain in which it rests. But this is also the domain where the political decision on where the balance of power is drawn (between private and public power) is, in principle, made (or at least: this is what we mean when we call that a political issue). The political domain is conceptually separate from the economic domain and is not generally thought as being the domain towards which competition law is aimed and towards which it is enforced.

The economic domain, of course, is the domain of competition law. Or, more precisely, the domain of the market for goods and services within the wider economic domain is the main focus of competition law; the economic domain at very least also includes the economic factors of labour and capital, establishment and industry. Here, in the market domain, the interactions are shaped by the market mechanism. While the market and its institutions are of course also shaped by the political domain of legislation and regulation, this is the domain in which 'power' as it is used in competition law terms, and 'private power' as used by Amato, is generally understood. The social domain relates to the sphere of human interactions, within and between groups and networks, where interactions are shaped by social norms and where concepts like 'social capital' play a role in understanding how these interactions form. Finally, the personal domain is the domain of individuals, the domain which relates to or affects a particular person. We include that which is intended to be (and remain) private in this domain too. Thus, in our conceptualisation, corporate power in the personal domain does not relate to the power of individual leaders within the big tech world, but the power over the personal domain of others: users and non-users, predominantly citizens and consumers, but also sometimes workers and others.

How power occurs, and which checks and balances are in place, is both conceptualised and organised – if it can be said to be formally organised – differently for each of these domains. Power (or the prevention of power occurring) is perhaps more implicitly governed in the social and the personal domain, in comparison to the economic and political domain. It is, for example, understood that the more social capital – which is, though, not the same as power in the social domain – is present in a society, the better the shared values, norms and understandings, which means the networks of relationships, allow individuals to work together to achieve a common purpose to function effectively.[6] In relation to the topic at hand, it seems clear that a dominant social structure, in the form of a network, with common norms and purpose, can lead to social exclusion and inequalities, both in the digital sphere and in real life. More familiar to a competition law audience is that in the economic domain, market power is held in check predominantly by the market mechanism itself, by way of competitive pressures. And political power is disciplined, at least in democracies, by political processes of election, representation and legislation, and in many jurisdictions, by the specific safeguards of the Rule of Law.

D. The Corporate Power of Big Tech Companies

It is useful to draw these threads together at this stage to make clear the relationship between the three dimensions of power and the four domains. Focusing first on the instrumental dimension of corporate power, which is effectuated in the political domain, we stay close to Fuchs' findings: here campaign financing and lobbying activities come into view, both those of big tech companies and other large corporations. Also in the political domain, the structural dimension of corporate power is wielded in shaping legislative processes or creating self-regulation, possibly pre-empting democratically legitimised legislation. Discursive power, in this domain, is wielded in political campaigning and directly or indirectly shaping political agenda-setting: what is being talked about (and what is not on the table) is as important as how it is talked about.

Beyond the political domain we find the *instrumental power dimension* in the social domain clearly tied to digital economy, for example in shaping online interactions into groupings. It plays out in the economic domain by excluding competitors; and in the personal domain, for example, by individually tailored steering of users. Possible examples of how the *structural dimension of power* comes to light in the social domain lie in the way platform work is shaped and understandings of platform work are normalised. In the economic domain the structural dimension of power relates, for example, to the structures in which notions of 'property' – including of data – or 'employment' – including for platform work – are shaped. Also here the setting and defining of the structures for interaction between consumers and companies, including the developers of apps using the structures of the platform companies to reach consumers, are elements of the structural dimension of power in the economic domain; as is the cutting off of innovation by (the possibility) of acquiring and discontinuing competitive

[6] R Putnam, *Making democracy work: civic traditions in Modern Italy* (Princeton University Press, 2013).

threats. In the personal domain, examples of the structural dimension of corporate power relate to, for example, the normalisation of tracking devices, and the arrival of digital assistants, smart glasses and other devices into our homes.

The *discursive dimension* of power, when it comes to big tech companies, is perhaps the most elusive, even though it might be what first comes to mind when we talk about the power of big tech companies. This dimension encompasses both the direct impact on discourse(s), and discourse-forming, stemming from the big tech companies themselves; for example by their direct communications and presentations, and their presence on stages during innovation and technology conferences, but also by shaping the discursive space of perception of technology and innovation, or by agenda-setting in, for example, think tanks. But this dimension also encompasses their pivotal role in the news and information system; here the information itself does not necessarily stem from these corporations themselves, but is made, shaped and provided by users (who can in this sense be political parties, individuals, NGOs, dictatorships, etc). Platforms – some more than others – thus play several *roles* when it comes to the discursive dimension. This discursive power reaches in all four domains: big tech companies are shapers of the discourse surrounding themselves, and exercise discursive power through the services offered on their platforms.

E. Modern Bigness

So far the corporate power of big tech companies has been broken down into the components of the foundations of power, dimensions of having power, and the domains in which this power may be manifest. Each of these manifestations – of which only some examples have been mentioned – can, potentially, lead to effects that might be labelled 'positive' or 'negative'. Though a 'standard' of negative effects – which is the focus of our competition law-infused thinking tools – needs to be developed, as would the notion of providing evidence to a required standard of proof, for now 'negative' is still fairly vague, because the conceptualisation so far has not made the explicit jump towards a normative assessment. I will address that more normative point in section IV.

Although looking at the individual dimensions and domains brings into view their potential negative (and positive) effects, looking at them as a coherent whole highlights the formidable power of the big tech companies: the elements are not separate, but strengthen each other in a flywheel effect, leading to positions of, what we have labelled, Modern Bigness. As an aside: whether one understands the notion of 'bigness', which has run through the US discourse on antitrust law for more than a century, as inherently pejorative, is as much tied to the socio-political and normative contexts as the position in the balance between private and public power that is the topic of Amato's book. The currently, seemingly very partisan, antitrust debate in the US is not necessarily the lived context for EU-based competition scholars. At any rate, in this coherence, which is tied to the pervasiveness, scope, and precision and invasiveness of corporate power, the novelty of big tech corporate power (vis-à-vis 'old' corporate power) becomes clear.

Its *pervasiveness* is tied to the foundation in the digitalisation and datafication of society and the economy: much of the current economic and societal shift seems tied to an even further digitalisation and further entwinement of the physical social reality with its digital counterpart. As to *scope*, again the direction of movement is a continual branching out of activities, including an incursion of market-offered services into previously public-run domains (at least: public in many EU countries), in which the services are being now provided by, or make use of, the platforms and technologies of the big tech companies: healthcare, education and identification services are examples. Infrastructural services, such as access to the Internet or cloud computing, are offered mostly by big tech companies, and governments are as dependent on these services as are citizens and consumers. The balance between public services and market services has shifted, and while some of these services are akin to public utilities, the accompanying universal service guarantees are not present. As to the *precision and invasiveness* of corporate power of big tech companies, again the direction seems to be towards the use of data, including private and personal data, becoming more all-encompassing (also as a result of the pervasiveness and scope of power of the big tech companies). Even if one were to reject the notion of 'surveillance capitalism',[7] as too harsh, or too pejorative, the power of big tech companies is formidable, and is set to remain formidable, with digital services being ubiquitous. It is built upon datafication and personalisation, making both precision of tailored services (and advertisements) and a further invasiveness into the private sphere possible.

The flywheel effect comes about in the interconnection between growing pervasiveness, growing scope, and growing precision and invasiveness, and is made even clearer when considering how the corporate power of Modern Bigness spans the four domains. Consider that from the perspective of a user, whether they are a citizen, a consumer, a friend, or a patient, these domains are delineated (at least somewhat, at least conceptually), but that from the perspective of the platform these roles and domains are, in fact, mostly irrelevant. Whether she is engaging in a lively online discussion with friends, reading news to stay updated or to decide upon how to cast her vote, or looking to book a holiday, the user produces and shares data (relevant to both the platform and other parties tracking her online). She moves seamlessly from one activity to another, making it possible for platforms to reach her, and many others, quite personally, across all four domains too. This is an all-encompassing power, based on digitalisation and datafication, which shapes current and future lives, markets and democracies.

[7] S Zuboff, *The Age of Surveillance Capitalism* (Profile Books, 2019).

IV. Too Much Power, or Business as Usual for Competition Law?

The Modern Bigness corporate power of big tech companies is, therefore, quite impossible to overstate. But, let me reiterate the point that though this is a bold statement, it does not necessarily imply that this is a 'bad thing'. To come to a conclusion on whether the power of big tech platforms is, say, too great and problematic and needs to be bound, or not to be worried about too much, several analytical steps need to be taken even before we come to the question of relevance for competition law.

A. The Road Not (Yet) Travelled

The first steps on this analytic path are not explicitly normative, but factual. I will address them fairly quickly, though I note their importance. First, there is an incompleteness to the conceptual analysis presented above, in that 'power' is not localised precisely. Does it rest in each of the big tech companies or is it a conceptualisation of corporate power of these companies taken together? My position here is that it is possibly both, but where one focuses the gaze depends on the question asked (see also below). Second, though the previous section provided a conceptual framework to understand and speak about the different dimensions and manifestations of corporate power of big tech companies across domains, and some examples of how that power might play out are mentioned, we have not yet undertaken the more factual fine-grained analyses of actual manifestations of power, in actions, behaviours or effects. Mapping the activities of big tech companies is necessary to understand our conceptualisation, and why such a richer conceptualisation is useful, but it is also necessary to grasp fully how corporate power of big tech companies actually plays out.

B. A Framework for Analysis: European Competition Law's Possible Response

Our conceptualisation of the Modern Bigness corporate power of big tech companies up to this point leads to the view that it is almost impossible to overstate the power, concentrated within and between a handful of corporate conglomerates, acting centre-stage within digital societies. It is a power that reaches beyond the economic domain and the domain of market transactions, and reaches into the social, the personal and the political domains. So, how can, and how should, European competition law respond?

Amato reminds us that the question of whether, and how, competition law draws the boundaries on corporate power, like a subset of the more general question of the role of law within a society, is ultimately of political nature.

Possible responses of European competition law may take different forms. Amato also reminds us that the provisions of competition law are *flexible* as to their interpretation and can adapt to changing economical and societal circumstances (that, when I started in competition law, the economisation movement, had not yet put down strong roots is a first-hand testimony to this flexibility). At any rate, the response of European competition law might take the form of a renewal of normative underpinnings, new or improved procedural interventions, introducing new(ish) concepts, or take the shape of thinking of new remedies within competition law or within related (novel) regulatory frameworks. It might also move beyond competition law proper and focus on strengthening alternative, perhaps public, infrastructures.

The possible and possibly relevant, response seems to depend on the level of analysis. Whether it can be covered by the inherent flexibility of competition law provisions and procedures, or whether something *new* is required is also tied to the level of analysis. A fairly precise case-tailored level of analysis is presented in a focus on a specific action, an instance of behaviour by an individual corporation which is directly based on business model of the user–platform/service interaction. Such a precise case-tailored level of analysis also occurs by focusing on a specific behaviour which is, however, not directly based on user-platform interaction. Less in relation to specific instances of behaviour, a different level of analysis focuses more on the direction of developments pertaining to size and innovation paths. And finally, we could focus on the power-as-such: on the coherency of what big tech's corporate power entails and how competition law can, or ought to, respond.

Each of these levels of analysis is discussed in turn with a view to the relevance of different types of responses within (and beyond) European competition law.

C. A Focus on Specific Instances of Behaviour, with Effects in the Market Domain and Beyond

Specific instances of behaviour (which we do not need to define precisely for the purposes of this analysis), stemming directly from the business model of the platform-corporation, provide a case-specific focus, with the (ultimately) profit-making business-logic of interaction between platform company and the users (on different sides of the platform) at its core. Such behaviour might manifest within the economic domain, and more precisely to the market. Examples are plentiful. This is where generally accepted competition law applies (though in the platform economy the focus is not so much on price as a parameter, but on consumer choice or degradation of quality): self-preferencing, consumer-targeting, excluding competitors from access, or leveraging practices are examples. If flexibility in the interpretation of competition law provisions is needed, it is not (conceptually) difficult to provide.

However, specific instances of behaviour stemming directly from the business model might also manifest in one of the other three domains introduced above, the social, political or personal domain. For example, shaping a newsfeed or engaging in political microtargeting, and the non-consensual (at least not in a meaningful way) gathering of personal and private data. The difference of the domain in which effects are felt is relevant for competition law purposes, because behaviour which has effects within the other domains is much less easily covered, at least not in the current interpretation of European competition law, by its provisions. More than mere flexibility of interpretation might, if one wishes to extend its application, be needed here.

Focusing on a case-level analysis of specific behaviour also brings into view behaviour which is not directly tied to the business-model logic of extracting value from users and thus not directly in the realm of user-platform interaction. Similar to the business-model-based behaviour, again these actions can have effects in the economic domain or in the other domains. Examples in the economic domain might relate to the establishment of headquarters, with concomitant investments in infrastructure and jobs. Think also of the impact of the Silicon Valley model of corporate culture. Or the way platform work, especially on the precarious side of the spectrum of possible platform work, is being shaped. Outside the economic domain behaviour might relate to campaign financing and lobbying or – relevant for academia too – the financing of chairs, research, research centres and think tanks. Though some of these behaviours can stem from all (large) corporations, other examples (such as platform work) are directly linked to the platform economy. Here, the role of European competition law is, in a current or more flexible interpretation, not immediately clear.

D. Size, Innovation and Power

Zooming out, the focus is on effects of growth (of size, including through innovation paths). Admittedly, this is more vague than the more concrete behaviours mentioned so far, but in considering how competition law might respond to the power of big tech it seems relevant to distinguish 'growing size and innovation paths' from (the resulting) 'power'. Focusing on growing size and innovation paths brings into view – in the economic domain – the competition law-relevant activities of mergers and acquisitions and also endogenous innovations, such as the big-tech-led investment in quantum computing and the (promise of) the metaverse. In the non-economic domains the 'geographical' impact comes into focus: presence in the physical world through various infrastructures (with concomitant relevance for employment); and presence in the geographical political world, in global geopolitics.

Finally, the focus on power-as-such is relevant too. Our conceptualisation of the corporate power of big tech platform companies as Modern Bigness focuses on this level. Power as market power, in the economic domain, being the focal point of competition law, needs no further introduction here. For instance, the potential issues of control over access and control over (dominant) essential facilities are clearly salient; as are those of public utilities and universal service obligations when it comes to the non-economic domains.

E. European Competition Law's Response

It is important to note that, as follows from the above, European competition law – in its mostly uncontested core – *can* and does already cover negative competitive impacts (on price, if that is a relevant parameter, or on consumer choice or degradation of quality), stemming from dominant economic positions in a market. Equally, European competition law *can* already scrutinise mergers and acquisitions for such potential negative impact within the remit of the existing merger regulation. There are also some conceptual frameworks in place relating to services of general economic interest. The EU's Digital Market Act (DMA) adds a regulatory response in relation to the platforms of the big tech companies, for example, adding interoperability requirements, prohibiting self-preferencing, and giving the option to scrutinise or open up possibilities to scrutinise mergers and acquisitions more widely. No *novel* responses are thus needed here, though perhaps a focus on improving the use of existing *procedures* – such as the interim measure procedure at the level of the European Commission – might be sensible.[8] Within the merger control (and the DMA merger scrutiny) regime a struggle can be discerned in relation to the role of innovation in exogenous growth, so that new *concepts* – such as the dominant design theory or complex systems theory – might be useful here.[9] These concepts do not necessarily deviate fundamentally from the accepted logic of how competition law is interpreted and applied. However, these competition law responses are only present when it comes to *economic domain manifestations* of power, and more precisely, where these relate to the market (but not – unless in specific circumstances – when it comes to labour, for example). When focusing on effects that occur in the other domains, competition law's response is generally absent.

So: here the question whether competition law has a role to play (to counter possible negative effects) becomes more political, because these behaviours do not neatly fit into the existing logic of European competition law. But again there are clear differences to be distinguished: compare, for example, the behaviour of political microtargeting and that of lobbying or financing think tanks. For the issue of political microtargeting we can make the argument (and have made this argument elsewhere) that precisely because political microtargeting is, from the perspective of the business model of a platform, *no different* from commercial microtargeting – both are based on obtaining income generated by targeted advertising – it is difficult to grasp why the one could be covered by current competition laws

[8] This is the topic of research in the PhD project of Carla Farinhas, member of the ERC team.
[9] This is part of research in the PhD project of Lisanne Hummel, member of the ERC team.

notions of abusive behaviour, but the other could not. On the level of the reaction by the user, being targeted, the same type of influencing/manipulation takes place, and both targeted commercial advertising and targeted political advertising are based on generated user profiles. The business model, based firmly in the market mechanism, works for both types of targeting and this would be the underlying rationale for extending competition law concepts to also cover political advertising.[10] However, this also means going back to the normative underpinnings of competition law and rethinking competition law purposes as not merely covering negative effects on consumer welfare and consumer choice.

A connection to existing competition law responses is more tenuous, it seems, when it comes to behaviour of big tech companies that results in the shaping of information flows and the shaping of ideas. Though the business model of platforms is probably one of the leading factors in decisions of moderating content, combatting misinformation and removing certain users from a platform connects, on the more aggregate level, or on the conceptual level, to notions of the free flow of information or the market place of ideas. Such a connection could then be used to shape a more concrete theory of harm. But, as also mentioned above, this needs a reconsideration of the normative underpinnings of European competition law more generally, and would go beyond a mere flexibility of the currently dominant interpretation of the competition law provisions.[11]

On the one hand, a connection to the big tech companies' business models is certainly not immediately present when it comes to, say, lobbying or financing think tanks. Neither is it immediately present in relation to geopolitical power. And it might also not be present when it comes to the choice of establishing a new headquarters or campus, or influencing the look and feel of a Silicon Valley startup. But, on the other hand, clearly these are manifestations of corporate power, with potential negative general effects on economic welfare, society, and individuals (across domains). Here the potentially more fruitful level of analysis lies on the level of the concept of power itself: the concept of corporate power as Modern Bigness is much more encompassing than the competition law concept of market power. And while the concept of market power is useful in the economic (market) domain, the wider concept invites the conversation to move beyond that domain and enter into a discussion of where to place the boundaries of power. On this level of analysis of power itself, concepts of innovation as a competitive restraint also need to be reconsidered, as do such concepts of *access*, both for consumers but also for *citizens*, which are implicit in the notions of services of general economic interest and universal service obligations, or within the notion of public utilities more generally but not necessarily applied in this framework of corporate power.[12] We could also broaden our understanding of how competition law could be used to shield collaborative efforts aimed at organising counter-power.

[10] This is part of the research in the PhD project of Viktorija Morozovaite, member of the ERC team.
[11] This is part of the research in the PhD project of Jan Polanski, member of the ERC team.
[12] This is part of the research in the PhD project of Laura Lalikova, member of the ERC team.

On this overarching level it is for me, personally, not difficult to normatively posit that in a democratic society, based on the Rule of Law, too much power needs to be bound. A system of checks and balances is inherent in the concept of a liberal democratic state. The Modern Bigness type of corporate power seems to be too much power (but note the limitations of the research, mentioned above). On the more concrete level of European competition law, this implies that either the corporate power in the form of Modern Bigness needs to be countered, so as to limit its negative effects, and/or all or some of these negative effects directly. As European competition law is one of the legal regimes which is part of the system of checks and balances of the power of corporations, it ought to broaden its conception of power by going back to its normative roots so as to be able to do so. It might mean that European competition law goes beyond the economic (market) domain. This normative position, is, as Amato states, not merely an internal legal position, but also intrinsically linked to sociocultural contexts, and is *political* in nature too. Here, it is based on the legal-historical roots of European competition law, on its place in the EU constitutional set-up, on case law of the Court of Justice, and on the EU's basis in protecting and shaping an open society rooted in the Rule of Law. It is fed by notions of autonomy, equality and sustainable, inclusive welfare, and firmly rooted in the idea that a living democracy needs constant nurturing. Some of these notions are already present, though perhaps somewhat hidden, in the constitutional set-up in which European competition law functions. Thus, on the level of *normative underpinnings* of competition law, such a position would mean a refocusing of competition law on a broader understanding of what it is in service of: not only consumer welfare, but also on these other elements inherent in this richer understanding. This then feeds into how power itself is regarded, including by building upon the notions of joint dominance within interdependent platform ecosystems. Taking the normative position as described here might ultimately also mean considering the introduction of the remedy of breaking up corporate power, not as a remedy against abusive behaviour, but as a remedy against power as such – an instrument which is not present in the EU today and would need a (democratically legitimised) legislative basis.

Importantly, there are responses outside European competition law that seem both (more easily) possible and necessary. To shape these responses the conceptualisation of corporate power as Modern Bigness is also useful. Not only is specific *regulation* – such as the DMA and privacy protection – a counter to (some) manifestations of this power, but other concepts within the system of law (such as ownership of data) can be also conceived. And beyond the realm of legislation and regulation it is also possible to provide more balance in a digitalised society, between private and public power, by *strengthening the public sphere*: this can range from using collaborative open technologies as an alternative (innovation-based) platform to public investment in public-owned infrastructures and digital services, robust democracies and strong, independent media.

V. Conclusion

The conceptualisation of corporate power of Modern Bigness provides a richer understanding of the power of big tech platforms and a vocabulary to be used to shape possible responses. It teases apart the answer to the question 'what power is this?' by distinguishing between foundations of power, dimensions of power and the domains in which this power can potentially manifest. This richer understanding is relevant, too, for the response of European competition law. Taking a normatively informed position on the role of European competition law – as I have done in this chapter – also means taking a position on Amato's line between private and public power. Though it follows from the above that the conceptualisation of corporate power of big tech companies as Modern Bigness implies a greater role for European competition law in combatting its negative effects, sometimes including effects that are felt outside the market domain,[13] this is no argument taking the position that competition law is an instrument to solve all societal woes. But nor is competition law an instrument that should be kept pure, risking detachment from societal developments. As Amato also makes clear, competition law is a formidable instrument of public power, which can be used to legitimately provide checks and balances on private power. It is, again as Amato notes, also a flexible instrument. My conclusion – while acknowledging and making explicit that and how this is a normative position – is that refocusing on the normative underpinnings of European competition law, in relation to a richer understanding of the corporate power of big tech companies, brings a shift in just where flexibility ends and where stepping beyond the current Rule of Law-based bounds of public power starts. This conceptualisation is therefore also an instrument – a vocabulary – to make clear where the demarcation lies between broadening or stretching the scope of the existing competition law concepts, procedures and remedies, and introducing novel concepts, procedures and remedies, either within or beyond competition law. Both the broadening of existing responses and the introduction of novel ones change the overall balance between private power and public power. Making explicit the fact that the question of how that balance is struck, also within European competition law, is an inherently political question, is a lasting legacy of Amato's *Antitrust and the Bounds of Power*.

[13] But note that our analysis is not complete and this chapter is a snapshot of the current position in a bigger research project.

11

Afterword

GIULIANO AMATO

What can an old professor do, when one of his former students, now a professor at Newcastle University Law School, produces a collective volume to celebrate a book he wrote 25 years ago? The first and immediate feeling of the old professor is expressing his deep gratitude to his former student, Oles Andriychuk, and to all the contributors not just for their work, but for the quality of it. As Oles rightly underlines in his Introduction, we don't find here the superlatives of the usual *liber amicorum*. We find debate, arguments and counterarguments; in other words, all the signs of healthy disagreements – as it should be in any lively scientific community, whatever the occasion.

My second reaction is that such disagreements refer to specific issues, not to the generalised and undisputed awareness that reminding all of us that antitrust has to do with power could make sense 25 years ago, with no need to do it today. However, one of the issues upon which there is disagreement, even in this volume, is how far antitrust can go in curbing private power as it manifests itself in our times. And it is mostly to this issue that I will devote my brief comments here.

When I wrote my book in the late 1990s, I was struck by the deep discrepancy between the fundamental issue dealt with by antitrust – the abusive exercise of private power upon others – and the sophisticated technicalities (both legal and economic) of the arguments at the core not only of the cases but also of the debates among the specialists.

There is nothing wrong in being technical when you are not taking part in a political debate and your task is interpreting a legal regulation that embodies the outcome of a legislative procedure in Parliament. To the contrary, technical arguments are essential in appropriately applying rules and clauses, which, as such, are beyond the political opinions and controversies that led to their formulation and approval. However, as Frédéric Jenny rightly writes in his generous Foreword, 'the political intents of the fathers' and the objective aim of the regulation, vis-à-vis the basic issue it refers to, cannot be ignored.

If market power – this was my doubt – is only perceived and treated as the ability to price above marginal costs, can it be understood in all its implications? Nor was I sure that the conflict was adequately appreciated between such private power and the public power necessary to limit and to reduce it. Yet, diverging answers provided at the technical level could implicitly mirror diverging answers vis a vis the great political options that are behind the antitrust architecture: what do we fear more, private or public power? How much private power are we ready to accept in order to avoid an excess of public power? How ready are we to extend public power in order to avoid an undesirable expansion of private power? Like it or not – I wrote at the time – under the different antitrust doctrines and the more or less flexible interpretations of the antitrust rules, these basic options in terms of values are the (frequently) hidden and not declared reasons of our 'technical' choices. At least, let us be aware of them.

Dominant at the time was the consumer welfare doctrine, based more on efficiency than on competition, which had its origins in the Chicago School: a valuable doctrine indeed, well construed and well equipped with a variety of technically undisputable implications. However, under the light of its teaching, much fewer restraints of trade were to be considered illegitimate and much fewer mergers were producing a substantial lessening of competition, at least within the short timeframe that was adopted. Nor were the reasons behind this restrictive interpretation of the antitrust prohibitions completely hidden: the explicit definition of efficiency as the main aim of antitrust was frequent, and equally frequent was the assertion according to which not punishing a false negative is a lesser damage to the market than punishing a false positive.

This doctrine was the mainstream of antitrust enforcement for decades, even if more in the US than in Europe (the difference became a conflict mostly in relation to mergers, as to which Europe remained more demanding in view of their long-term impact on competition). At the same time, neoliberalism also was dominant and played a relevant role in reducing the governance of the globalised economies, while a formidable technological development nurtured the growth of the giants of the Internet. The convergence of these factors brought about an outbreak both of higher inequalities in our societies and of unchecked private powers in our markets that impacted several aspects of our individual and collective lives. Even the specialists most oblivious of the roots of antitrust were forced to acknowledge that antitrust is indeed about power. Had it done enough to prevent what had been happening? Could it do more for the future?

The debate in recent years has centred on these questions. Nor has it been just a doctrinal debate. The enforcement itself of antitrust is being deeply affected with a remarkable U-turn towards a new (and old) direction. It is not at all irrelevant that Lina Khan, who opened the debate with her 2017 article, 'Amazon's Antitrust Paradox',[1] is now heading the US Federal Trade Commission. It is more than a return to origins, as this volume itself demonstrates. However, it is still a return to origins, namely to the Sherman Act for the Americans and to the Treaty of Rome

[1] L Khan, 'Amazon's Antitrust Paradox' (2017) 126 *Yale Law Journal* 710.

for the Europeans. In both legal documents, violations had always gone beyond pricing above marginal costs: dissimilar contractual conditions, supplementary obligations and other unilateral impositions of power were supposed to be under antitrust scrutiny since the beginning.

In this sense – as it has been written – after years of antitrust 'underperformance' in the framework of the preexisting conditions, the reappearance of the 'curse of bigness' (the title of Tim Wu's book of 2018), as well as the renewed attention for the structure of the markets (in Jonathan Baker's *The Antitrust Paradigm*[2]) undeniably are a return; a return that, within limits, is compatible with the methodological approach that became dominant under the Chicago doctrine, namely the effect-based approach. In fact, even by adopting such approach, you can detect market power whenever market power is hidden behind the veil of efficiency. I wrote it 25 years ago, and others are confirming it now, even in this volume. I refer to the chapters by Ginevra Bruzzone and Assimakis Komninos: in Europe consumer welfare has never been identified with short-term prices, due to an enduring attention to an effective competitive structure of the markets. Therefore, through scrutinising the conducts of dominant companies you can identify exploitative abuses. Scrutinising mergers between (not necessarily) dominant companies on the one hand and new, strongly innovative firms on the other, you can detect their impact not just on prices (the reduction of which in the short term does not automatically have to be taken as an evidence of increased efficiency), but on the level of future concentration in relation to the potentialities of innovation in the relevant market. Many steps forward can be made in curbing the market power of our time by using antitrust tools.

However, there is more, much more than that, with the consequence that neither the standards of the consumer welfare doctrine, nor the previous ones (that such doctrine had abandoned) sufficiently reflect what is now emerging. As Eleanor Fox writes in her chapter, the super-profitability of our contemporary big tech companies does not depend on the usual monopolist's behaviours, such as cutting back market output and relying on the consequent increase of prices or directly increasing prices, for no competitors exist who might step in. They happily live upon predatory prices or supplying their customers with services at no price at all and, at the same time, cross-leveraging across distinct markets or across two-sided markets.

There are well-known non-monetary prices that customers pay for being caught up in the 'pervasiveness of a power based on the digitalization and datafication of our societies' (so Anna Gerbrandy writes[3]). Their personal data can be captured and utilised in several ways: either to be directly sold to other companies, which will use them to advertise their products, or to build profiles of each customer

[2] J Baker, *The Antitrust Paradigm: Restoring A Competitive Economy* (Harvard University Press, 2019).

[3] Gerbrandy, ch 10 of this volume.

that will be sold for other more sophisticated purposes. It is an undeniable power which is so exercised upon the customers. Can it be reached and curbed by antitrust means? As we know, in the famous German Facebook case, which has been going on for years and is still pending, in February 2019 the Bundeskartellamt had treated the violation of the privacy rights of customers as an anticompetitive conduct falling under the notion of abuse. Afterwards, in August 2019, the Dusseldorf Oberlandesgericht denied the anticompetitive relevance of such a conduct, while, more recently, in June 2020, the Bundesgerichtshof concluded that there is an abuse, but not for the reasons initially argued by the Bundeskartellamt. In the view of the Bundesgerichtshof, the abuse is not due to the treatment of personal data as such, but to the lack of alternative providers, which puts the costumers in the hands of Facebook.

We are not here to dispute this conclusion. First, because it is not final: it has been reached in a provisional decision and it might be overturned in the decision on the merit. Secondly, for our purposes here it is just an evidence of an existing border we should be aware of: the border of the outreach of antitrust, whose toolbox does not offer all the necessary means to fight contemporary market power in its several manifestations and implications.

It is not a rigid border; a gray area exists around it. Therefore, flexibility is needed, as several contributors to this volume write. Giorgio Monti is very explicit in arguing that restrictions of innovation, harm to market pluralism, even increases in inequality may fall within antitrust prohibitions, as long as the relevant conduct falls within the reading of our legal texts. Furthermore, as Miguel Maduro writes, sometimes the outreach of antitrust prohibitions can be extended to state action itself, whenever such action is pursuing, not perceivable public interests, but private ones that affect the competitive structure of the market.

However, the warning given here by Niamh Dunne should be heeded: procedural rules, fair trial protections, and the presumption of innocence in particular, reflect systemic and not ignorable efforts to uphold the integrity of our legal system, ensuring to the greatest extent possible that decision-making is proper in all senses. Stavros Makris is well aware of all this. He writes that the theory of non-collusive oligopoly aims to capture the mergers that eliminate important competitive constraints and reduce the competitive pressure. But – he adds – it needs proof which may be difficult to obtain.

In conclusion: as Roberto Pardolesi notices, the 'hipster' antitrust of our time, so eager to return to a structurally oriented notion of competition, cannot be rejected because of the 'other' interests and the political considerations, undeniable among its aims. If, in the first place, all this is a return, the first thing that is being restored is the awareness that antitrust essentially means fighting private power. How could I, celebrating the 25th anniversary of my book on antitrust and the bounds of power, reject it? However, as many contributors here note, the core of my reasoning was, and has remained, the dilemma between too much private power and too much public power. Curbing private power is a paramount aim, but the Rule of Law, the fundamental pillar of our liberal democracies, allows public powers to pursue their aims by using the means – and only the means – the law has bestowed upon them. The interpretation might be flexible, the boundaries might not be necessarily rigid, but we can't expect antitrust to solve all our problems when facing the private powers of our time.

To this end, Europe seems better equipped than other parts of the world. In recent years, regulations have repeatedly accompanied antitrust in coping with the abuses of our contemporary digital societies. At the same time, the use of states' taxing power has been promoted to reduce inequalities. The proper use of public power is the first prerequisite for it not to be abused. This also applies to antitrust, which can be neglected, but also abused. This truth is even more true in times when – as Oles Andriychuk writes in his Introduction – authoritarian regimes are taking ground even in countries where we expected liberal democracies to flourish.

In concluding, I still find myself where I was when I wrote my book: antitrust is naturally born to fight private power but, as I wrote, let us always be aware of the limits that any public power, antitrust included, must meet in a liberal democracy. Twenty-five years later, I confirm.

INDEX

abuse:
conduct, exclusionary, 177
dominant undertaking's detection of via procompetitive effects, 119
exploitative, prohibition of, 182–3
power of and antitrust, 29
adhesion contracts, 198
non-negotiable clauses in, 205
Advocate General (AG) Opinions mentioned in consumer welfare, 78–80
AEC test, 103, 104, 149
Amato, Giuliano: ***Antitrust and the Bounds of Power*****, discussion of,** 1–5, 25–6, 87
Amazon, antitrust's call to account, 30
'ancillarity doctrine', 118, 147
anticompetitive:
acquisitions, 184
agreements, centralised notification system for abandoned, 90
foreclosure, 55–6
anticompetitive effects, 151–2
competition and consumers, on, 153–4
procompetitive agreements, in, 148
antitrust:
rules, anti-cartel enforcement for, 90
theory, 3, 7
tools curb market power, 227
violation, establishment of, 100–1
antitrust boundaries, 58–61
competition law, application of, and, 59–60 (case law)
economic welfare and, 58–9
statute requirements, fulfilment of, and, 59
statutory regulation of, 60
antitrust exemptions, 69
economics-based approach to, 63–4
antitrust law:
EU law, effect on, 57
US public enforcement of, 56–7
antitrust principles, 2–3
permeability of, 62–3
AOK **case (2003),** 36–9
Apple, antitrust's call to account, 30
Article 101 (TFEU), 124–6 (case law)
Commission practice under, 54–6, 99–102, 102–7
competition and, 171
consumer welfare cases, 83
procompetitive effects under, 138, 139, 155–6
substantive liability and, 107
Article 102 (TFEU), 105–6 (case law)
Commission practice under, 102–7 (case law)
Commission's approach to, 54–6
consumer welfare cases, 83–5
defence against exception rule, 106–7
dominant undertaking's prohibition under, 156–7
procompetitive effects under, 138, 139
substantive liability under, 107
average variable cost (AVC), 138

balancing and rebalancing, 5, 12, 16, 21, 38, 64, 118, 161
Beef Industry Development and Barry Brothers (BIDS) **case (2008),** 125–6
Bernatt, Maciej, on illiberalism, 28–9
big tech, 27–8
antitrust's control of, 30
conduct question (EU and US), 31
Covid-19's effect on, 28
EU and US control of, 30–1
big tech companies:
competition law's response to, 220–1
corporate power of, 215–16
data gathering is basis of, 212
European competition law's response to, 218–19, 221–3
market power is foundation of, 212
Block Exemption Regulation (1999), 54, 176
bounds of power, presentation of, and competition law, 177–8
Bronner **conditions,** 138
Bruzzone, Ginevra, on competition policy, 17–19
bundling, 155

burden of proof:
cartel cases, in, 101–2
Commission's, 104–5 (case law)
competition, in, 96–7
business-to-consumer relations (B2C), 202–3
P2B, to, 203–6

capital gains tax (CGT), 198, 199, 201–2, 203–4
cartel cases, burden of proof in, 102
***Cartes Bancaires* case,** 83, 120, 131–2, 145, 179
judgment (2014), 100
collective action problems, 126–7 (case law)
commitment:
decisions (EU), 91–2, 109–11 (case law)
procedure, infringement in, 109
companies, state control over, 45–6
company contracts content, control of, 205–6
competition:
anticompetitive effects on, 153–4
Article 101(TFEU) and, 171
assessments, procompetitive effects' role in, 120–1 (case law)
cases, burden of proof in, 96–7
Commission's control and protection of, 88–9, 174
concept and interpretation of, 122
consumer benefits and restriction of competition, 135–6
consumer welfare gains and, 135–6
definition of, 121
elimination of reviewed, 173
freedom of action and, 178–9
harm to, 151
horizontal mergers and, 140
legality principle and, 107–8
mechanism of, 169
mergers and, 64–5
multitask policy, 170
protection of, 187–8, 188–9
public interest approach to, 170
restriction of, 122–3
technical harmonisation, approach to, 174
vertical agreements' impact on, 176
vertical restraints and, 130
violations, presumptions used in, 98–9
competition enforcement, 114
EU-level, 114–15
practice and procedure for, 93–4
competition law:
application of and antitrust boundaries, 59–60 (case law)
big tech companies, response to, 220–1
bounds of power, preservation of, and, 177–8
European, response to big tech companies, 218–19, 221–3
interpretation of, 68–9
legalistic approach to, 94
limits of, 94
power and, 214
procompetitive effects and, 162–3
sickness fund associations in, 37
sustainable growth and, 174–5
competition policy:
Bruzzone on, 17–19
impact-based approach and, 178–9
competition rules:
administrability of and impact-based approach, 179–80 (case law)
consequences of, 91
economic activity's subjection to, 39
EU, 75
freedom of private enterprises and, 92
law and (German), 108, 182, 185, 228
loyal cooperation principle and, 40–4
'modernisation' of and Regulation 1/2003, 171
Ordoliberal, relevance of, 170–2
state action and, debate over, 40
state measures, application to, 45–4 (case law)
concentrations, competitive assessment of, 183–4
consensus-building, 182
'consumer', Commission definition of, 76–7
consumer benefits:
restriction of competition and, 135–6
restrictive agreements, under, 173
consumer welfare, 13–14
AG Opinions, mentioned in, 78–80
doctrine, 226
EU papers and guidelines, in, 75
gains without eliminating competition, 135–6

Guidance Paper on exclusionary abuses (2009), in, 76
Horizontal Merger Guidelines (2004), in, 75–6
introduction, 73–4
consumer welfare case law, 77–82
Article 101 (TFEU), under, 83
Article 102 (TFEU), under, 83–5
CFI, in (2000s), 80–2
Eco Swiss case (1999), 78
1960s–1990s, no references to consumer welfare in, 77–8
consumers, anticompetitive effects on, 153–4
contestability, 186
contracts:
adhesion *see* adhesion contracts
clauses, consumers' understanding of, 200–1
standardised, forging of, 201–2
corporate power:
big tech companies, of, 215–16
dimensions of, 213
modern bigness, as, 222–3
wealth is foundation of, 213
counter indicators, procompetitive effects as, 144–8 (case law), 148–55, 159–60 (case law)
Court of First Instance (CFI), consumer welfare cases (2000s), 80–2
courts:
Commission decisions reviewed by, 97
state measures, control of, 41–2

data gathering is basis of big data companies, 212
decision-making, markets' and states' distinguished, 34
democracy:
illiberal, 28–9
liberal, 1
digital economy, market power of, 193–5
Digital Markets Act 2022 (DMA) (EU), 31, 185–7, 221
Digital Markets Unit (UK), 31
digital platforms, 195
dominance threshold (procompetitive criteria), 137
dominant firms, anticompetitive foreclosure by, 55–6
dominant undertakings:
detection of abuse via precompetitive effects, 119
prohibition against Article 102 (TFEU), 156–7
ECN (European Competition Network), 66, 182, 188
***Eco Swiss* case (1999),** 78
economic:
dependence, 207
efficiency and antitrust, 52–3
power development since 1997, 26–9
undertaking, private enterprise carries out, 36
welfare and antitrust boundaries, 58–9
economic activities:
competition rules, subject to, 39
concept of, 37
ECJ's clarification of, 35–6 (case law)
public and private bodies, carried out by, 38
sickness funds attributed as, 37–8
state pursues, 38–9
economic inequality:
EU antitrust law's effect on, 61–2
merger policy and, 61
economics and antitrust, 57–8 (case law), 68
effect abuses and analysis, 146–7, 148–8
efficiencies and agreements, 134–5
End of History period (antitrust), 2, 7
enforcement:
anti-cartel, antitrust rules for, 90
antitrust, 14–15
competition *see* competition enforcement
exclusionary conduct in, 102–3
priorities (Commission), 103–4 (case law)
private, 113–14
European Commission (Commission):
Article 101 (TFEU) and, 54–6, 99–102, 102–7 (case law)
Article 102 (TFEU), practice under, 102–7 (case law)
burden of proof, 104–5 (case law)
'competition and, 88–9, 174
'consumer', definition of, 76–7
enforcement practice, harm in, 107–9
role in antitrust, 66–7
European Commission decision-making:
courts' review of, 80–2, 97
Regulation 1/2003, under, 90–1
European competition law's response to big tech companies, 218–19, 221–3
European Court of Justice (ECJ):
clarification of economic activity, 35–6 (case law)
consumer welfare considered by, 82–5 (case law)

European Union (EU):
big tech, control of, 30–1
competition rules, 75
internal market, private and public distinction, 8–11
European Union antitrust, 3
single market imperative and, 53
European Union antitrust law:
economic inequality, effect on, 61–2
liberation of, 51–2
procompetitive effects, 16–17
professional, 2
exception rule, 101
defence against under Article 102, 106–7
exclusionary:
abuses, 2009 Guidance Paper, 14
conduct in enforcement, 102–3
exclusivity rebates (effect abuse), 138–9, 149, 155
exploitative abuses, 181
prohibition of, 181, 182–3

Facebook, antitrust's call to account, 30
fair trial and law enforcement, 109
fines, imposition of, 108–9 (case law)
foreclosure and anti-competitive foreclosure distinguished, 177
free market, use of, 33–4
freedom of action and competition, 178–9
'freedom to compete' defined, 107
French Commission of Unfair Terms, Recommendation no 21-01, 202

GAFA (Google, Apple, Facebook, Amazon), 27, 31
general contract terms (GCTs), 196–7, 202, 205
German Facebook case, 198–9, 228
Germany, competition rules and law in, 108, 182, 185, 228
global antitrust, 2
'golden shares', 10–11, 44–8
challenges to, 44–5
definition, 44
Google, antitrust's call to account, 30
Green Paper on vertical restraints (EU) (1996), consumer welfare in, 75
Guidance Paper on exclusionary abuses (2009), consumer welfare in, 76

harm:
competition, to, 151
horizontal mergers and, 141
harm theory, 105 (case law)
Commission enforcement practice, in, 107–9
Herfindahl-Hirschman Index (HHI), 140
horizontal:
cooperation, 65
mergers and competition, 140
horizontal agreements, 65–6, 130–2 (case law)
purchasing, 126–7 (case law)
horizontal cooperation guidelines, efficiency-enhancing effects and revision of, 172–4
Horizontal Merger Guidelines (2004) in consumer welfare, 75–6
hybrid settlement, 112
hybridisation, 7–8

illegality test (antitrust), 68
illiberal:
democracy, 28–9
government power, 28
illiberalism, Bernatt on, 28–9
'imbalance of power', contractual, 199–200
impact-based approach:
administrability of the rules and, 179–80 (case law)
competition policy and, 178–9
indispensability requirement (abuse effect), 152–3
information asymmetries (market failure), 127–8 (case law), 128–9 (case law)
information asymmetry, 201, 202, 203
information sharing agreements, 128 (case law)
infringement:
commitment proceedings, in, 109
decisions, 111–12
rebuttal of, 98–9
***Inhaltskontrolle*,** 204–5
instrumental power dimension, 215
International Competition Network (ICN), 27

judicial review, 180

law enforcement and fair trial, 109
legality principle, 96
competition and, 107–8

liberal democracy, 1
loyal cooperation, 10
principle and competition rules, 40–4
loyalty rebates, 105 (case law)

margin-squeeze cases, 153
Market Definition Notice, 184
market power, 222–3
antitrust tools curb, 227
digital economy, of, 193–5
foundation of big tech companies is, 212
markets:
consequence of failure, 202
decision-making, court's role in, 46–7
decision-making, mode of, 34
failures, avoidance through non-anticompetitive means, 124–9
players, practice of, 122
state intervention in, 42
Member States, consistency or coherence requirement imposed on, 47–8
merger control, 160–1 (case law), 183
procompetitive effects and, 157
Merger Regulation 1989, 57–8, 64, 77, 171, 176, 183–4
mergers, 139–41
analysis of, 58
competition aspects of, 64–5
horizontal, 140–1
non-horizontal *see* non-horizontal mergers
policy and economic inequality, 61
procompetitive, 139–40
vertical, 141
modern bigness, 21, 216–17
corporate power as, 222–3
more economic-based approach to antitrust, 54–6
multi-lateral interchange fee agreement (MIF), 145–6 (case law)

naked restriction (effect abuse), 149, 154
negotiation:
bilateral, 204
regulation of, 204
risk in, 199–200
'new competition tool' (EU), 93
non-anticompetitive means and avoidance of market failures, 124–9
non-horizontal mergers, 141–2
outcomes of, 142
theory of harm and effects of, 142

'object or effect' criterion, 99–100 (case law)
one- and two-handed market models, 9
online intermediation sources, 203–4
Organisation for Economic Co-operation and Development (OECD), 27, 175, 176
***Österreichische Postsparkasse* case (2001),** 80

P2B, B2C to, 203–6
payment systems, interoperability of, 131–2 (case law)
pervasiveness of corporate power, 217
platform-corporation behaviour, 219–20
***Post Danmark I and II* cases (2012 and 2015),** 82–3
power:
competition law and, 214
discursive dimension of, 216
manifestations of, 214–15
social and personal domain, in, 214–15
structural dimensions of, 215–16
precision and invasiveness of corporate power, 217
predation (effect abuse), 149–50, 154–5
presumption:
competition violations, used in, 98
innocence, of, 95–6
private:
autonomy in competitive context, 204–5
bodies, economic activities carried out by, 38
economic power, impact-based approach, 175–8
entities' involvement in legislative process, 42–3
private actions:
public actions and, Court's approach to, 40–2
state action, distinguished from, 44
private enterprise:
economic enterprise carried out by, 36
freedom of and EU competition rules, 92
private power, 225–6
ability to constrain, 178–9
global, control of, 32
individual's, public power's effect on, 92–3
1997 onward, 25–32
Pardolesi on, 20
public power and, 225–6
procompetitive agreements, 128–9
anticompetitive effects in, 148
exclusion in, 148
suspicious clauses, significance of, 147–8 (case law)

procompetitive effects, 118–19, 158
  abuse, detection of by dominant undertakings, 119
  Articles 101 and 102 (TFEU), under, 138, 139, 155–6
  competition assessments, role in, 120–1 (case law)
  competition laws and, 162–3
  counter indicators, as, 144–8, 148–55, 159–60 (case law)
  criteria for and identification of, 135–9, 158–9
  legal interpretation of, 159 (case law)
  legal roles of, 158–9
  merger control and, 157
  rivalry, of, 143–4 (case law)
  sequence of, 161–2
  sources of, 142–4
  standard for, 146
procompetitive practice, criteria for, 118
public:
  bodies, economic activities carried out by, 38
  ownership, state's control over companies through, 45–6
public power:
  individuals' private power, effect on, 92–3
  1997 onward, 25–32
  private power and, 225–6

recoupment (effect abuse), 150
Regulation 1/2003:
  Article 7 decisions, 111
  Article 9 case law, 109–11
  Commission decision-making capacity under, 90–1
  modernised EU competition rules, 171
Regulation 2019/1150, 203
regulatory intervention, 204
restrictive agreements:
  consumers' benefits under reviewed, 173
  necessity of, review of, 173
risk in negotiation, 199–200
rivalry, 129–32
  definition, 129
  procompetitive effects, 143–4 (case law)

sector inquiry work, expansion of, 90
selective:
  distribution agreement clauses, 145 (case law)
  price cuts (abuse effect), 152
self-preferencing, 206–7
sickness funds:
  associations, competition law, in, 37
  economic activity, attribution as, 37–8
  practice of, 36–9 (case law)
single market imperative and EU and US antitrust, 53
***Spanish Glaxo* case (2001),** 80–2
standard-setting agreements, 127
state:
  aid, control of, 175
  alternative decision-making model, as, 34
  companies, privatisation of, 46
  competition rules' application to, 43–4
  control over companies, 45–6
  decision-making, court's role in, 46–7
  economic activity pursued by, 38–9
  intervention in market, 42
  measures, Court's control of, 41–2 (case law)
  power, exercise of, 48–9
state action:
  competition rules and, debate over, 40
  private action, distinguished from, 44
statute requirements, fulfilment of and antitrust boundaries, 59
statutory regulation and antitrust boundaries, 60
substantive liability and Articles 101 and 102 (TFEU), 107

Technology Transfer Guidelines (2004) and agreements, 76, 143, 176
tying practice (effect abuse), 150–1 (case law), 155

undertaking, concept of (TFEU Articles 101-106), 35
United States (US):
  antitrust and single market imperative, 53
  antitrust law, public enforcement of, 56–7
  big tech, control of, 31

vertical agreements, 132–4
  competition and, 176
  VBER and, 132–4
Vertical Block Exemption Regulation (VBER), 119
  vertical agreements and, 132–4
vertical restraints, 54, 129–30, 134 (case law)
  competition and, 130

world competition framework (EU), 26–7
World Trade Organisation, 26–7

www.ingramcontent.com/pod-product-compliance
Ingram Content Group UK Ltd.
Pitfield, Milton Keynes, MK11 3LW, UK
UKHW020806290926
15470UKWH00003B/992